The Shaman Warrior

The Shaman Warrior

By
Gini Graham Scott, Ph.D.

Foreword by Christopher S. Hyatt, Ph.D. & Antero Alli

ASJA Press
New York   Lincoln   Shanghai

The Shaman Warrior
An Investigation of a Group Practicing Shamanism

Copyright © 1988, 2007 by Gini Graham Scott, Ph.D.

ASJA Press
an imprint of iUniverse, Inc.

iUniverse books may be ordered through booksellers or by contacting:

iUniverse
2021 Pine Lake Road, Suite 100
Lincoln, NE 68512
www.iuniverse.com
1-800-Authors (1-800-288-4677)

Originally published by Falcon Press

First Edition 1988

ISBN-13: 978-0-595-43378-0
ISBN-10: 0-595-43378-2

Printed in the United States of America

TABLE OF CONTENTS

FOREWORD

Christopher S. Hyatt, Ph.D. & Antero Alli

The purpose of my portion of this Foreword is to help dispell some of the fear and confusion surrounding Magick and Shamanism. It seems that many individuals have been taught that the Path of Magick and Shamanism is associated with Evil. Of course this form of propaganda is and has been spread by a competing reality model, Religion, which is fundamentally a schismatic outgrowth of Magick.

Simply defined Magick is the art and science of altering realities by Will and Imagination. Assumptive in this definition is the idea that the Universe is an Energy system which man as part can influence by his **actions**. In this sense Magick is more akin to Science than Religion, as it rightly assumes that man has the right and the ability to alter his environment according to his will. Of course this viewpoint assumes that errors in judgment **will be** made.

Somewhere, somehow the New 'Magick--Religion', placed all the power to influence the Planet in the hands of God and his duly ordained priests, who of course were allowed to practice the ancient and powerful magickal arts without being murdered. For the rest of mankind this Male God could be influenced by less powerful forms of magick: appeals, genuflection, and prayer, that is if it pleased Him. The attentive reader will note that the technology of the Model of God is a simple One Up and One Down relationship.

It is this Model of God, which has removed Man from his rightful position as Techno-Magician and placed him in the position of a worthless and helpless slave, gaining what dignity he possesses by his **passive** association with his often dejected, disgruntled and regretful creator.

In passing I should remind the reader that some of the greatest atrocities on this Planet have been committed in the name of this God, and as suggested by Dr. Leary and others, "if God were God(S) this one letter (s) could change the entire course of future history."

If the "Evil" of Magick and Shamanism resides in man's ACTIVE attempt to influence the forces of the Universe to HIS end, then the "Good"of Religion rests in man's PASSIVE attempt to do the same, but only in accordance with the Will of God. In other words the difference between the old Magick and the new is one of a conscious active participating principle and a passive one -- AND -- the centering of Will in Man and the Universe versus the Will of God alone.

I would like the reader to re-read the above paragraph as it points to what will follow. The old Magick is **active**, rebellious and results oriented -- the new is **passive** and more importantly rests on the principle of obedience, resulting in rewards and punishments in an afterlife.

Another more modern objection to Magick often levelled by certain new agers and psychologists is that it is manipulative and Power (**Active**) based, while Mysticism, Psychology and Religion are based on the principle of Love (**Passive**). This argument will be more fully explored in the following story.

Many years ago the famed Golden Dawn Mage Dr. Israel Regardie got into an argument with a Psychoanalyst. The corpus of the argument was about Power and Love. I was there and witnessed the discussion, and as usual put my two cents in.

Regardie's position was that power was neutral, having neither positive or negative moral value. The Analyst's point was that Magick and Shamanism were pre-occupied with manipulation while Psychology, Religion and Mysticism were grounded in Love.

As usual Regardie laughed at such nonsense and I joined in. I pointed out that Love and Power **are not opposites**, but have similar aspects and common roots. The fact is that Love like any other force must be modulated and placed in perspective. When out of control it borders on melancholy, depression, frustration, personal impotency, possessiveness and violence. The analyst quickly responded that it is the **orientation** of Magick (power over events and experiences) which makes Magick more dangerous than Mysticism. Of course the word **dangerous** is a key issue, in that we have to ask "dangerous to whom and to what?"

Dr. Regardie, amused by our discussion, interrupted. He said, "the real issue here is determining whose Will is more powerful. Hyatt, your position is that power is a force which can be used for 'good or evil'. Our analyst simply believes that to think about power as a primal orientation toward life is dangerous in and of itself. If we were to take his argument to its logical conclusion we would not even be having this conversation. I would have died years ago for the lack of antibiotics and surgery and you might have never survived as you were a Caesarian birth. I am afraid that our analyst's position is self-serving, hoping to disarm others of their power while he gets what he wants through subtle word manipulation, rhetoric and appeals to the Christian fear of power."

I continued, "power(s) are simply force(s) which surrounds us, they are everywhere, and man's job if you would is to learn how to use 'them'. The Tree of Life is a good model, in that one pillar stands for mercy, one for severity, and the third for mildness. If you ignore any pillar the Tree collapses. Some Christian occultists have even wished to remove the influence of Mars and the Moon from the Tree."

Regardie interrupted, "The problem with our analyst(s) is that the word Love creates many powerful, infantile and idyllic images, one of which, is that everything would be "Wonderful" if man WAS NOT full of pride, intention and greed. This of course is demonstrated by man's interest in power, magick and science." The analyst interrupted saying that "Love is concerned with **both** the object and the subject, whereas Power is concerned **only** with the needs of the operator." Regardie broke into laughter replying, after he caught his breath, ". . . in order to use Power effectively the greatest respect and concern is necessary." Again he attacked saying, "that the analyst's fear was that he felt he had no power, and that he saw power from the point of view of a chauvinistic male. There are all kinds of power, and if he chose a female orientation, the analyst would be more likely to accept it as love. Males such as our analyst mis-translate female power as love. This degrades both men and women and puts them at war with each other. Recall the cliche 'that men want power and sex and women want security and love.'"

As nothing was getting through I was bored. It seemed that his faith in grammar and words were so powerful that he refused to move off center.

It seems that the preachers of Love usually are the greatest abusers of its power. They tend to divide the earth and its inhabitants into a 'good/bad' dimension based on activity vs. passivity and self/universe centeredness vs. God's will. This is simply another ploy to fool humans into believing that they are 'bad' if they have and use their own power. For them 'power' should only be in the hands of 'those' who 'know how to use it.' The question remains as to who these people are?

Power is something that we have been taught to both want and feel guilty about. Love is something that we have been taught to both want and feel frightened about. Both words create different hypnotic trances and thus fall into the category of the practice of Magick. Religion's solution has been to preach love, while all the time sowing the seeds of impotency by guilt and fear. This tactic has worked for thousands of years. The rememergence of the practice of Magick and Shamanism signifies the return of power back to the people. Dr. Scott's book **THE SHAMAN**

WARRIOR is an excellent text in teaching us that every man and woman is a Star and that each of us has a right to practice our own Magick.

Christopher S. Hyatt, Ph.D.
Santa Monica, CA.
November 17, 1987

Mr. Alli's Contribution

From the perspective of native people, the Earth is a vastly intelligent and compassionate living entity that has chosen to incarnate **as this planet**. The Earth is alive and well. As ancient Chinese acupuncture teaches us, there is a network of "energy points, centers and meridians" interlacing the human body from which the acupunturist is able to diagnose and treat clients. Being the living entity it is, the Earth expresses its own "acupunture" of various energy points, or **power spots**, and meridians or, **"energy leylines"** spread across its surface crust. Throughout world history, primitive phases of most cultures developed some form of "geomancy", or **earth divination**, to detect the precise locations of local power spots for executing their sacred ceremonies and will. These rites served to bond local tribes while providing the basis for a "technology of the sacred" . . . usually an oral tradition of **Earth Magick** passed down from shaman adepts to apprenticing initiates throughout the millennia.

Here and now in the latter part of the 20th Century, there is a swiftly expanding and awakened interest for recognizing the earth as a living being (the GAIA Hypothesis, The Green Movement, Deep Ecology, Etc.) that may, indeed, be **an instinctual response to our potential extinction** via any combination of the current global crises of over-population, pollution, nuclear war, AIDS and so on. Of this newly emerging "tribe", perhaps a miniscule 11% or so have transformed themselves into **self-styled, modern shamans** carrying their own regional tradition of Earth Magick deep into the civilized world . . . like spiritual kamikazi pilots exploding their knowledge into the bloodstream of the masses. It is in this very spirit that Dr. Gini Scott has delivered us, **THE SHAMAN WARRIOR** and Drs. Leary and Hyatt have given us **THE CYBER—SHAMAN** in **THE CYBER—SOCIETY**, and **UNDOING YOURSELF** and I **ANGEL TECH** all carrying their own regional tradition of Earth Magick—Technology.

Americans previously unacquainted with the dark, exotic world of shamanism will read this book and wonder why it sounds and feels **so normal** until . . . it's too late. Her writing style is deceptively simple or rather, "simplex", invisibly flip-flopping our consciousness between mundane and cosmic dimensions while we're not looking. It is in this way and others that Dr. Scott **is** the shaman, despite any claims to the the contrary, and . . . **why this book works.**

As the reader grows increasingly familiar with the shifts in their own consciousness, a gateway opens to their multidimensional nature. It seems human beings possess a veritable spectrum of viewpoints or as Dr. Hyatt says, "rearpoints." We loose our possibilites through our "all too human" dogmatic tendency of getting stuck on one "rearpoint" over the riches of many. The shaman(ess) is an usher guiding us to our seats inside the cool, dark chamber of the Magick Theatre. There, we are subject to our own home movies and a series of non-stop "tapes" running rampant in our heads until a short-circuit breaks the projector down. Then, in the darkest inner recesses of our abyss, we are initiated to a "higher reality" . . . one **undetermined** by our projections and self-created ideological impositions, of "what the world should be." We are **UNDONE!** Here, we confront the primal essence underlying all thought, image, concept and ego . . . the delicious, indescribable black hole center of our origins. What we **do** with this knowledge is as important, if not moreso, than the knowledge itself.

Unlike Shirley MacLaine (who did such a terrific job at ushering mysticism into Prime Time America), Gini Scott is not a celebrity or a movie star but . . . from what I can tell . . . a regular kind of ambitious businesswoman profoundly impacted by **a definite interdimensional collision**. It is to everyone's favor that she has had the resiliance to come around and tell the story.

In concluding, I might suggest that as you read **THE SHAMAN WARRIOR** be aware of the people in your own life it reminds you of. Then, buy them copies. This way, you will have passed through the realm of mere coincidence and embark upon the shamanic journey of turning synchronicity **into a skill**. Psst . . . by the way, timing is everything and timing is believability. Believe in yourself and the rest takes care of itself. **See for yourself**. That, I think, is Dr. Scott's ultimate message.

Antero Alli
Boulder CO.
October 23, 1987

INTRODUCTION

Gini Graham Scott, Ph.D.

Not many people know of the Order of the Divine Flame, or ODF as it is more popularly called. Yet it has developed a unique spiritual approach to viewing and interacting with the world, which is particularly in tune with the current emphasis on personal power. This is what ODFers call the "way of the shaman warrior," which uses spiritual techniques for increasing the power to achieve personal benefits and to help others.

As ODFers see it, the inner warrior exists and/or can be developed within everyone, and the key to success on this path is becoming aware of both the dark, evil aspects of the world and the light, positive side. For then, the true warrior can appropriately confront or flow in harmony with both forces of nature, and thereby "surface in the light and not be engulfed by the darkness."

To achieve these results, ODFers go out into the field at night and call on the forces and spirits of the universe, which are most visible in the darkness. The knowledge and spiritual strength gained from encountering this other reality is used for self-improvement, as well as benefit others.

I spent about a year as a sociologist and anthropologist working with the ODF, and had the rare opportunity to learn their secret techniques for starting on the warrior path. Also, I was able to closely observe members of one ODF group as they worked with these techniques. This book is a report of my experiences and shows how ODFers use the way of the warrior for personal transformation.

I first encountered the ODF at a Magical Encampment one weekend in Marin County, California, July 1984. The encampment, which included about three dozen members of the loosely knit San Francisco Bay Area

EURO MILLIONS ®

Including Millionaire Raffle

7506-019585822-209779

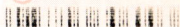

Good luck for your draw on Fri 20 Jul 12

Your numbers

Lucky Stars

A 07 20 43 44 49 - 09 10 LD
B 04 07 12 26 36 - 09 11 LD
C 04 09 14 33 41 - 03 09 LD

Your raffle number(s) for your draw(s)

BWY158122
BWY158123
BWY158124

CHECK YOUR MILLIONAIRE RAFFLE
RESULTS ONLINE AT
WWW.NATIONAL-LOTTERY.CO.UK

3 plays x £2.00 for 1 draw = £6.00

100 UK MILLIONAIRES!

FRIDAY 27TH JULY!

7506-019585822-209779 017404 Term 46785001

[   ] Fill the box to void the ticket

THE NATIONAL LOTTERY®

For information visit the website at www.national-lottery.co.uk or call the National Lottery Line on **0845 910 0000**. A separate MINICOM line for the hard of hearing is also available. A proportion of National Lottery sales goes to the Good Causes. For further information please refer to the Players Guide.

GUIDANCE ON HOW TO PLAY

For how to play and prize structures see the Players Guide, available from retailers, see the website, or call the National Lottery Line. Results can be found through recognised media channels, retailers, the National Lottery Line or the website. Tickets issued in error, illegible or incomplete can be cancelled if returned to the issuing terminal within 120 minutes of purchase and before close of ticket sales from that terminal on that day.

GUIDANCE ON HOW TO CLAIM A PRIZE

For details about how and where to claim prizes see the Players Guide. If you hold a winning ticket you must claim your prize by post, or in person at a retailer, or Regional Centre as appropriate, within 180 days of the applicable draw date, or within this period notify the National Lottery Line of your intention to claim, and then claim within 187 days of that draw date. Claims over £50,000 must be made in person. **If you believe you have won over £50,000 telephone the National Lottery Line.** For all claims over £500 and up to £50,000 please claim your prize at a lottery Post Office, taking a photo ID and proof of address. The Post Office can pay up to £500 cash, above this amount, £500 can be paid in cash with the remainder in a cheque, or the whole amount by cheque if you prefer. Telephone the National Lottery Line on **0845 910 0000** for further details. To claim by post, please send your ticket and your completed claim form, at your own risk to The National Lottery, PO Box 287, Watford WD18 9TT.

SIGN YOUR TICKET. MAKE IT YOURS.

Name

Address

Post Code

Signature

Safe custody of your ticket is your responsibility. If your ticket is lost, stolen or destroyed, you can make a written claim to Camelot no later than 30 days after the winning draw date, but it will be at Camelot's discretion whether or not to investigate and to pay the claim.

THE OPERATOR OF THE NATIONAL LOTTERY

The National Lottery is operated by Camelot UK Lotteries Limited under licence granted by the National Lottery Commission. The principal office of the National Lottery Operator, Camelot UK Lotteries Limited is the National Lottery, Tolpits Lane, Watford, WD18 9RN

GAMES RULES AND PROCEDURES

National Lottery games are subject to the relevant Rules and Procedures which set out the contractual rights and obligations of the player and the game(s) promoter (and operator if different). Games Rules and Procedures are available to view at retailers, or on the website and copies can be obtained from the National Lottery Line. The promoter/operator is entitled to treat a ticket as invalid if the data on it does not correspond with the entries on Camelot's central computer. Players must be 16 or over. **Play responsibly.** If you are concerned about playing too much, call GamCare on 0845 6000 133. **www.gamcare.org.uk**

GM   **Strålfors** TR12

THE NATIONAL LOTTERY®

For information visit the website at www.national-lottery.co.uk or call the National Lottery Line on **0845 910 0000**. A separate MINICOM line for the hard of hearing is also available. A proportion of National Lottery sales goes to the Good Causes. For further information please refer to the Players Guide.

GUIDANCE ON HOW TO PLAY

For how to play and prize structures see the Players Guide, available from retailers, see the website, or call the National Lottery Line. Results can be found through recognised media channels, retailers, the National Lottery Line or the website. Tickets issued in error, illegible or incomplete can be cancelled if returned to the issuing terminal within 120 minutes of purchase and before close of ticket sales from that terminal on that day.

GUIDANCE ON HOW TO CLAIM A PRIZE

For details about how and where to claim prizes see the Players Guide. If you hold a winning ticket you must claim your prize by post, or in person at a retailer, or Regional Centre as appropriate, within 180 days of the applicable draw date, or within this period notify the National Lottery Line of your intention to claim, and then claim within 187 days of that draw date. Claims over £50,000 must be made in person. **If you believe you have won over £50,000 telephone the National Lottery Line.** For all claims over £500 and up to £50,000 please claim your prize at a lottery Post Office, taking a photo ID and proof of address. The Post Office can pay up to £500 cash, above this amount, £500 can be paid in cash with the remainder in a cheque, or the whole amount by cheque if you prefer. Telephone the National Lottery Line on **0845 910 0000** for further details. To claim by post, please send your ticket and your completed claim form, at your own risk to The National Lottery, PO Box 287, Watford WD18 9TT magical community, was held at an old battery nestled between some windswept hills. The site, now part of a national recreation area, had once been a military base, consisting of a long concrete building with a maze of chambers tucked into a hillside, surrounded by two open cement courtyards and a winding dirt road.

A couple who had read one of my earlier books, *THE MAGICIANS*, about a group practicing black magic, had invited me, saying this should be an especially interesting gathering, for it included people from several magical traditions. The organizers came from a school of Christian mysticism and magic, others were involved in Paganism, Witchcraft, and Ceremonial Magic.

When I arrived around 4 p.m. on Friday, the scene was typical of a camp-out by magical community members — a scene of happy disorder, reminiscent of a 1960s love-in. People, mostly in their 30s and 40s, were wandering or sitting around picnic tables in the courtyard. Some had on levis; others wore rainbow-colored shirts, sweaters and ponchos; a few sported long ritual robes and capes, decorated with mystical symbols, astrological signs and foreign-looking alphabets.

A few people were pitching tents or setting up camp in their vans. Some were arranging sleeping bags in the battery's small cell-like rooms. Boxes of groceries, camping equipment, and ritual gear were scattered everywhere. A woman with a lute perched on a picnic table singing bawdy ballads from the Middle Ages, and several clustered around her to listen.

Then, in the distance I noticed a group of four people who didn't seem to fit in, who I later learned were members of the ODF. They stuck out oddly, because unlike the other participants, they dressed in plain black uniforms, which made them look like members of some police group or military service. They wore black pants, black shirts with military insignia, and black boots. After a brief meeting, they fanned out around the perimeter of the encampment and walked about checking security and communicating with each other by walkie-talkies.

My first impression was that this looked like some military troop ready to do battle at a moment's notice, and when I asked some of the people around the picnic table who they were, one man jokingly called them the "psychic boy scouts." A woman, expressing the magical community's general dislike for anything military, characterized them as "the black shirts." Another man criticized them for their youth since they were in their 20s, and objected to their clannish secretiveness. "They're just playing at being magical warriors."

At first, I didn't pay too much attention to this group, and merely thought they added an unusual military note to an otherwise motley and colorful gathering. But that evening I had a chance to see the ODF in action, and became intrigued.

After a fairly leisurely afternoon, the high point was a gala ritual and ceremony at sunset, organized by Lana Woodhue, an aspiring actress and secretary in her early 40s, who combined a dramatic flair with a love of religion and magic. She had turned one of the battery's narrow cement chambers into a temple decked with colorful banners, and she set up a ritual area with a tall white torso-like statue; an altar with chalices, bowls, flowers, and assorted magical tools; and a row of candles along the walls.

As we filed in to experience the ritual, I noticed the ODF leader, Michael Fairwell, and his associate, Gene Perry, standing at the entrance, looking like a military honor guard. Both were in their mid-20s, of medium build, tough, wiry and athletic, and they watched quietly to make sure everything would go smoothly. But, while they were participants, their military bearing made them seem distant and apart.

Afterwards, we filed out, Michael and Gene announced they were going to do a demonstration of their magical techniques and anyone was invited to watch. Michael gazed around the group with a cocky grin, then he and Gene strode off to select a site for their working. As they surveyed the camp, they were joined by the two other ODF members, Paul Stark and Rick Allen, also in their 20s, athletic-looking, and dressed in black.

As we waited, I tried to find out a little more about the ODF. But no one seemed to know very much. As one man explained: "The ODFers tend to stick to themselves, and they have their own magical tradition which is different from anything else in the magical community."

About a half hour later, Michael, Gene, Paul and Rick appeared to announce they were ready. Besides myself, only two others who later joined the group—Teri Barrows and Serge Thomas—responded.

Michael led us to an open courtyard away from the light and sound of people talking and singing by the fire. The full moon, low in the early evening sky, cast a shimmery glow over the area. Standing stiffly in his black uniform, he briefly described what would happen.

"Gene's going to go out and do some work first. He wants to get a sense of the area and evoke what's there. So just watch as he works, and be aware of what you see."

Gene moved towards the far wall and seemed to almost disappear, as his black uniform merged with the night darkness. Then, facing away from us, he stood still for a few moments with his arms outstretched, and soon began to move them up and down and twirl about. I could barely make out what he was doing, but he seemed to be waving his arms up and down, doing a strange, bird-like dance.

As if sensing my confusion about what to look for or see, Michael suddenly broke the silence and explained: "Look in the space around him. You can see some movements there. They look like small flashes or swirls of energy, and some areas appear a little lighter or darker than the others.

That's how you can tell that something is happening—the difference in color, texture, and motion."

I didn't see anything nor did Teri, but Serge and the three ODFers did, and whispered to one another excitedly: "Oh, yes." "That's right." "Yeah, I see it, too."

I strained harder, but noticed only the inky darkness. The ODFers and Serge saw much more, and Michael sought to guide them in their seeing.

"Now look," he commented. "You can see a whitish double forming behind Gene. It has a smoky gray color. Also, in front of him, a little to the right, notice that big mass of dark energy. Gene has evoked an earth elemental, and it has materialized there. Now, he'll direct it around. Just watch, and see what he can do."

I continued to look, seeing nothing. Yet, Paul and Serge eagerly shared their experience.

"He's got it under control now," Paul said.

"Yeah, it's really big," Serge observed.

I was amazed and intrigued. Were they seeing something real out there? Or could this be some kind of group hypnosis effect?

Still, those who saw agreed on what they perceived before Michael spoke, so that his comments generally confirmed what they already saw. When Gene returned to the group a few minutes later and described what he had been doing, his comments further confirmed what the others reported.

Then Michael stepped into the center of the courtyard with a long wooden staff moving about and making circular stabbing motions. When he finished, he returned to our group.

"Great work," Paul said, and Michael explained he had taken a reading of the spiritual activity in the area. "There's a lot of activity out there; a lot of beings watching," he said.

"Yeah, it's busy out there. I saw several pairs of eyes," Rick said.

"One being kept moving around. He had a big hulking shape," said Paul.

This time I had seen a slightly whitish aura around Michael, though I wondered if this might simply be an afterimage—a rim of fuzziness around an object that often appears if you stare at it long enough. According to Michael what I had seen was much more than an afterimage.

"What you're observing is the beginning of *seeing*," he said.

I asked about the Order of the Divine Flame and where it came from. But Michael didn't want to say much about it yet—only that it was a magical society made up of people with a variety of religious beliefs and affiliations with other groups. As Michael explained, the ODF offered a comprehensive program of teachings that involved working with dreams, using psychic phenomena like ESP and remote viewing, experimenting with trance work, communicating with spiritual beings, and much more. The group drew its ideas from various sources, including Tibetan Buddhism, Western Ceremonial Magic, shamanism, American Indian philosophy, Carlos Castanedas writings.

Michael founded the ODF to combine these principles and teachings into the spiritual path of the shaman warrior, because he believed in the strong need for a combination of peaceful serenity, inner wisdom, spiritual truth, and pragmatic strength. With his program, the average person can experience the other reality, without complicated magical formulas and drugs. He discovered that he and others could tap into this reality by going into a secluded area at night to tune into the forces of nature. The door to this experience was learning how to "see" in a special way.

He proceeded to spread the word and form new groups, closely assisted by Gene and Paul, who had each been with the group for about five years.

Michael invited us to take the next step on the magical path of the Spiritual Warrior—attending a basic training class. Of these classes, he would form a new ODF group, called a "weyr" or warrior clan for those continuing on the path.

Deeply intrigued, I wanted to know more. I felt this group merited special attention because of the uniqueness of its message; the unusual military-style costume; and its members' confidence that they could see things out "there," which I couldn't.

I decided to start on the ODF training program. This book is based on the experiences I had as a participant observer, and it has been written with the full cooperation of ODF members, who have read the manuscript.

This book relates my experiences with the group from July 1984 through December 1985. During this time I learned the group's "seeing" process, and moved up from a rank beginner to a third degree in the Order. I describe the group's philosophy, organization, techniques, and I discuss my own and others' experiences on a dozen field trips. Also, I deal with Michael's dramatic personal story which led him to take on ODF leadership.

In writing this book, I have tried to take a neutral participant observer role, difficult as it was. I leave it up to the reader to decide if the spiritual beings and forces encountered by the group are truly real, and then deal with the consequences of this belief system.

All of the experiences related in this book are true and I have used the correct name of the Order of the Divine Flame. I have changed the names and backgrounds of members to protect their real identities, as well as the names of many of the sites described.

CHAPTER ONE

A First Field Trip Into The Unknown

On July 21, 1984, my adventure into other realities with the Order of the Divine Flame began. Michael called to invite me on a field trip, although he usually didn't take people into the field until they had attended a few introductory classes on the ODF's teachings. But since it would be a few weeks before he could organize a more formal group, he suggested beginning with a small field excursion.

Teri, who I had met briefly at the encampment, was able to attend too, and the three of us met about 5 p.m. that July afternoon in a small apartment in Berkeley, where Michael was staying for a few months after his arrival from Los Angeles. Michael had told us to dress warmly, since we would be going to a wooded national park near the ocean in Marin County, and both Teri and I appeared bundled up in ski jackets, jeans, and boots.

When we arrived, Michael was wearing his usual ODF uniform for field trips—the same dress black military-style uniform I had seen him wearing at the encampment, plus a heavy black leather police jacket and black army gloves for warmth. The group used this uniform, sometimes called the "field dress costume," or "dress blacks," since it ideally suited their special requirements of doing magic in an outdoor wilderness environment at night. The clothing was not only tough and sturdy, but the black color blended into the darkness, and the neat trim military or police look of the costume fit in well with the group's philosophy of being—and looking like—a disciplined, controlled warrior. At the same time, ODF members used the shirt for metal or embroidered bars of rank, symbols of power, and personal insignia. Furthermore, the costume helped ODFers in public situations avoid the negative image of the magician or witch held by the general public, since, as Michael put it: "Most people think of magicians and witches wearing long flowing robes or capes. But that's not us."

Before we left, we spent a little time getting to know each other.

Michael talked about having been involved in teaching magic and studying shamanism for over 10 years, since he was 14 and first encountered strange spiritual beings in the woods near his house, then in Mendocino, California. But, at the same time, he balanced his interest in metaphysics with a strong grounding in everyday reality due to his work, interests, and day-to-day experiences. As Michael indicated, he had spent several years working for ambulance companies in the Los Angeles area, and had recently gotten a job as a paramedic for an emergency ambulance service in Oakland. So he had learned to see much of the rough and tumble side of life, as the ambulance responded to gunshot wounds, auto accidents, rapes, and other daily emergencies. Then, too, he developed a very practical approach to life as a result of his interest in camping, target shooting, collecting firearms, and reading about science fiction and his experience of living in a number of tough L.A. neighborhoods as a teenager, after growing up in an ordinary middle-class home as a child. In fact, Michael claimed, some of these experiences had led him to become interested in magic as a child and teenager, because it was a "way to escape and feel powerful." He could use magic to both enhance his personal potential and protect himself from possible dangers. Then, after he had been teaching magic informally for several years and continued to have encounters with spiritual beings, he decided to concentrate on magical development and made a commitment to the shaman warrior path, based on acquiring strength and power to achieve spiritual harmony and peace.

Then, Teri described her own magical interests. In her mid-20's, blonde, and attractive, she was typical of many women who found their way into ODF training. In everyday life, she had an ordinary job as an administrative assistant in an insurance company and came from a solid middle-class background. However, her concern with her own career and women's equality had led her to become interested in some of the ancient magical traditions based on the worship of the Goddess. As a result, she had joined several small women's spirituality circles, and had become an active member of the occult and magical community in the Bay Area. After she heard about the ODF from Serge, she was curious to learn more and find out if it could help her better get whatever she wanted in life, which was currently becoming part of a close-knit community and developing a close relationship with someone special.

Finally, I introduced myself as being interested in learning more about magical principles and techniques, as well as being a sociologist-anthropologist, writer, and marketing consultant.

Once the introductions were over, Michael was eager to get going, and as usual, he carefully checked over the equipment for the trip—flashlight, canteen, and first-aid kit—and he strapped them on his wide leather utility belt. Also, he picked up his staff, which looked like a walking stick with a head of a lion, and inserted it in his belt. This was his most important power object, which he used to direct and control his magical workings.

To drive to the park, we got in Teri's car, a ten-year old Ford that had seen better days. The blue paint outside was rusted in spots; there were piles of papers and books scattered around on the floors and seats; and the car shuddered and chugged like a steam engine. But as Teri commented, the car was usually reliable and it had personality, so she called it "Champ". The drive took about an hour, and we arrived at the park about 7:30 p.m. as planned, about a half hour before sunset. Michael had wanted us to arrive then to give us time to hike to the site where we would be working, so he could show us a few basic exercises before it got dark.

Only a few cars were still in the parking lot when we pulled in—a good sign, Michael observed, since it would be easier to find an isolated spot to work. We unpacked our gear, and Michael led us along a dirt road to a meadow, where he had been on several previous field trips in the Bay Area.

From here, we went up a winding rocky trail, marked "closed" by the park service, to a high meadow that looked out over a network of valleys and hills. Michael asked us to sit down and briefly explained the seeing exercises we would do next.

"They're basic to everything. To do any magic, to begin on the shaman's path, you have to learn to 'see.' It's a way of looking with your eyes, so they're both focused on something, yet unfocused, so you are able to experience other dimensions of reality."

To demonstrate, Michael sat down with his legs crossed directly in front of me and asked me to stare at either the center of his forehead or his nose, but not at his eyes. "You don't want to look directly into the eyes," he advised, "because one tends to have one's attention drawn by the stronger eye. Once you start looking, don't try to do anything. Just let your eyes stare ahead and do whatever they want to do. We'll do this for about 10 minutes. I'll tell you when to stop."

I settled back and began to look, while Teri sat a few yards off to my right watching quietly. After 15 or 20 seconds, I noticed my eyes tearing, and I began to blink several times. I tried staring some more, felt the tearing, and blinked again. At this point, Michael, who had blinked only once during the same period, interrupted the exercise.

"Don't blink unless you have to," he urged. "Try to concentrate on not having to blink."

We started again, and I found I didn't have to blink so much—only once every 10 seconds or so. After about five minutes, I noticed that Michael seemed to fade in and out of my vision and almost faded into invisibility at one point, before his image suddenly reappeared strong and firm again. During this time, I also became aware of a regular humming sound to my left, though I wasn't sure if the hum was in my temple or the woods beyond.

After 10 minutes, Michael called "time" and the exercise ended. As my vision snapped back to normal, Michael stood up and began to talk about the experience. He explained that if we practiced seeing regularly, this would help us see the images that existed around objects and people.

"Each object has an aura or energy field around it, and if you gaze at it with this unfocused concentration we have been practicing, you should be able to see it. Also, you don't have to only sit and stare at something to see it. You can learn to see this way when you walk around, or whatever you do."

Michael pointed to the woods around us and asked us to look. Dusk was fast settling in, but otherwise the woods looked to me as they always did.

As if understanding what we were thinking, Michael went on: "The woods may look very ordinary to someone who isn't trained to see. But once you learn, you'll see an aura around everything. Then, you'll start seeing movements and changes in this luminescence."

I looked around and saw a slight shimmering in the leaves against the deep blue black sky. I noticed a slight bluish haze around the hills in the distance. But that was all.

Michael turned to another key phase of the ODF training—using a power object. He took his staff with the lion head from the baton holder on his belt to demonstrate.

"You can do magic without a power object," he pointed out, "since the staff is just an extension of yourself. So if you want, use your hands to project power instead of a staff. But a staff is a tool to better direct and focus that power, so it becomes stronger."

Teri took out the staff she had found in a local import store to show Michael she had already acquired one. It had a lion's head much like Michael's, and he complimented her on her choice. Then when I said I hadn't had time to get one yet, Michael reassured me.

"That doesn't matter. You can use mine. Many people don't let others use their power objects. They're afraid the energy from someone else will interfere with their own power. But I've charged my own staff enough to protect myself from the energy of anyone else who uses it. My own energy will overwhelm the other person's energy. So, it's fine for you to use this."

However, before I did, Michael wanted to demonstrate a few basic techniques for using the staff to focus and direct power. He led us towards the edge of the meadow overlooking the valley, and as we stood watching, he raised his staff and slashed it rapidly through the air several times, saying as he did:

"Look at the end. See if you can see the faint white sparks and the aura around it."

Both Teri and I gazed at the staff, but we saw only the hazy shapes of the hills in the background.

"It's a little easier to see against a darker background," Michael observed. He stepped forward a few paces and held out his staff, so a nearby grove of dark trees were silhouetted in the background. "Now look again," he said.

This time, I noticed a faint whitish glow that looked like an afterimage towards the tip of the staff.

"The light comes out for about six inches in front of the stick," Michael remarked, although neither Teri nor I could see it.

Then, Michael asked Teri and me to try. He handed his staff to me, and Teri and I began moving our staffs around. I tried to see the light Michael spoke of projecting from the stick, though again, I saw nothing at first.

Still Michael pressed on with the lesson. "Now, as you move your sticks around, notice the differences you experience when you hold your stick in front of empty space and when you brush it past someone else. There's a slight blip of pressure you might feel, when an object or person is in front of you. See if you can feel it."

Again, we felt nothing, but Michael continued undaunted.

"Your ability to use a power object will come over time. Once you have this ability, you can use it for all sorts of things. For example, a power object can help you walk in the dark. It's like you're a blind person using a cane to feel your way about. You learn to sense and feel things that are there, though you can't see them."

Michael pointed his stick at the opposite hill. "For instance, you can use your staff to sense if someone is on the other side of this hill or if someone has been there. You're picking up on their energy—or on the energy they have left behind."

He moved the stick along the ridge and held it outstretched towards a clump of trees.

"You see . . . I'm picking up something now. But it's quite faint, so it's probably some energy that was previously there. The thing is, when you feel that blip or slight pressure that something is there, you should not only be aware of that feeling, but interpret it, too. Also, it helps to check out the experience later, if you can, to get confirmation you were correct. This way you get more sensitive to your feelings and better at interpreting them."

To illustrate, Michael related a previous experience that occurred when he had taken a group of 10 people from Los Angeles into the field. They were standing at the base of a ridge as dusk was falling, and Michael swept his staff in front of him to sense what was there. He felt two slight bumps in the palm of his hand and invited the others to try.

"Most of them felt something," he explained, "and a few even experienced the same sensation. So we cautiously went over the hill to check it out, and it was just the way I felt it. When we looked down, we saw two people sitting next to a car drinking beer in about the same direction where I felt the two blips. So the demonstration was a success. I sent out a beam and picked someone up through the side of a hill. Then, we saw them later, so we verified the sensation."

After this explanation, Michael led us back to the center of the meadow to show us the third major technique in the ODF magical system—drawing magical circles and pentagrams. The purpose of the circle was to create a protective safe space for doing a magical working, and the pentagrams could be created to evoke spiritual beings from the other world.

Michael began by drawing the circle.

"Watch closely," he said, as he leaned over, pointing his staff downward at a 45 degree angle. For a few moments, he held it still a few inches above the ground. Then, holding it steady, he turned in a clockwise direction to make a complete circle, and when he finished, his arm dropped back to his side.

"That's the circle we use. A very simple operation, really. The important thing is putting your own energy into the process, because the staff is only a tool or focus. You could use a knife or any other power object. The point is you have put your energy into it to make the circle real."

Now Michael raised his staff in front of him and began drawing a pentagram in the air. He started at the lower right-hand point of the star, and beginning with an upward stroke to his left, he traced out the five sides of a five-pointed star. As he drew, he urged us to notice the slight sparks at the end of each completed line, and after he finished, he injected a sharp stab of energy with his staff into the center of the star.

"Did you see the sparks when I did that?" he said.

Though I didn't see anything, Teri reported seeing a brief circular flash of light as Michael completed the pentagram, followed by another quick flare when he thrust his staff at it.

"Don't worry. You'll get better at it," he assured me.

Now he invited us to walk around the pentagram to observe the pocket of energy he had created.

"Once you learn to see," Michael continued, "you'll see what happens when people make a pentagram. It's a round area about two inches thick. It looks like a transparent circular plate of light hanging there. So it's important to realize that when you make a pentagram, you've created some new energy form. There's a change in the quality of the air. It's like you've caused the air to heat up or boil a little in the area where you've created the object.

"So that's why it's important to remove any pentagrams, circles, or other diagrams you create. It's not proper to leave these energies hanging about. It's a common courtesy to others, like cleaning up your litter when you leave a site. However, not everyone who does magic is as responsible as we are. So if you're in a situation where other people have left some energy behind, clean it up yourself. It's a little harder with someone else's energy, but if you let it stay there, it will be distracting and can throw off your own magic. So, to remove it, suck the energy back into yourself or send it out and disperse it into the universe."

Having covered the basic techniques we would need, Michael led us back down the path to the meadow. I picked up a stick on the way, and as we walked, I moved it about to see if I could notice the differences in energy Michael described. I tried holding it out several times as we crossed an area with open space and stuck it out a few more times as we passed a nearby bush. Each time I paid attention to what I felt, and I noticed a slight difference. The sensation was very subtle, but I felt a little more heaviness or pressure against my stick when something was near.

Yet, still I wondered. Was I feeling a real difference in energy between an open place and some near objects as Michael claimed? Or was I having this experience, because I was translating my visual perception of these spatial differences into the sensation of different pressures? I didn't know, though the experience of greater heaviness was real.

In any case, when I reported my sensations to Michael, he was pleased.

"That difference is a very routine experience," he smiled. "Keep working at it and you'll feel it all the time. It'll become second nature, like ordinary seeing, talking, and walking. Work with it for awhile, and you'll see."

We walked on for a few more minutes in silence. Then Michael reminded us that we should be practicing our seeing exercise as we walked, and we should use this unfocused seeing to be aware of energies on the path.

He stopped about 10 yards from a shadowy area formed by some overhanging branches ahead of us on the path and asked us to look at it. As we stared, Teri and I noticed some fluctuations in the intensity of the blackness and reported this.

"Yeah, I see it, too," Michael said. "That indicates some things are going on in the area. For example, there are some earth elementals in those trees ahead. You can see them, because they appear as dark, shadowy forms, even darker than the rest of the shadows around them."

I asked Michael to explain a little more about elementals. What were these energies or forms like? What did they do?

"We'll learn much more about them later," he replied. "But basically, an elemental is an embodied manifestation of a form of energy existing in the material world. There are four types of elementals—earth, air, fire, and water—and they represent the lower part of a hierarchy of spiritual essences or beings, which include man who is somewhere in the middle. Also, these elementals are basic expressions of the forces within us in our own consciousness, and that's why we can perceive them and evoke them. These elementals are not just happening in your imagination. These are real forces and energies that manifest in form. So when other people see or sense the same thing, this serves as a confirmation.

"For example, a few months ago, in L.A., I was working with some students in a field, and about a dozen of them were meditating, when a large white spherical cloud suddenly came out of the woods moving towards them. I was concerned it might disturb their peaceful concentration, so I pointed my power object at it, which stopped it. Then, I quickly banished it by drawing a banishing pentagram, doing a banishing chant, and sending out lots of energy. In a few moments, the column dissipated in all directions and was gone. So this shows how you can affect these energies, and I wasn't the only person who saw this happen. Three of the people I was chatting with saw it, too."

We continued along the path, and I pondered about Michael's story. Was this a group hallucination, the skeptic in me wondered? Or was everyone seeing something real? Was there any way to tell? This alternate reality that Michael and the ODFers experienced was so new to me, I felt baffled. Yet it was vividly real to them. I knew if I was to touch this reality, I would have to put such questions away, open myself up to whatever I might experience, and do any analyzing later.

Soon we came to another dark stretch along the path, and Michael asked Teri and me to wait while he walked ahead into the shadows.

"Just watch what happens," he said.

This time as he walked away I noticed that a white radiance seemed to surround him, and it shimmered like an electric force field. For a few moments, this whiteness appeared to grow larger, but as Michael walked on, he began to blend into the rest of the darkness. Meanwhile, to the left I noticed a large amorphous black shape that appeared to hover about in the air, and around it I saw occasional sparkles of whitish forms. Soon, the whole area seemed to pulsate, for a half-minute, with the pulses going faster and faster. Then, suddenly, everything seemed to stop, and Michael reemerged on the path towards us. My first thought was to be surprised by the visual display I had seen. And I was even more surprised when Teri reported seeing the same whitish moving shapes, though she hadn't seen the large black form.

But Michael reassured me there was no need to be surprised, for what we had seen was typical of what people see on a field trip and was a visual representation of the energy movements around us.

"The white aura you saw was the energy shield around me. And the largish black shape is an elemental which appeared on the path and I sought to banish so it wouldn't block our way. So you didn't imagine what you saw."

We walked on, and as we did Michael continued to move his staff back and forth to both clear the way and sense what might be ahead. After a few minutes, we approached another shadowy area where the trees were bunched closely together along the path and numerous overhanging branches formed a web of leaves above it. This time, Michael pointed his staff at the area to send his energy to any elemental forces that might be in the darkness.

As he explained: "These shadowy areas are the kind of places where elementals and other beings are especially likely to be. So it can be helpful to send your energy on ahead so they know you're coming in advance. That way they can step aside and you can move through the area more easily. It's like clearing out the branches that are on a path."

When he finished clearing out the area, he motioned for us to continue and we followed him into the darkness. There was a still, almost eerie hush, as we walked through. We emerged into one last open stretch of the path and in a few mnoments were back on the meadow. It was much darker now, and we could only see the dark silhouettes of the distant bushes and trees against a deep grey-black sky.

Michael had one more experiment to try, and he led us to a large log bench at one side of the meadow to explain. We sat down and he waved his staff across the expanse and pointed to a grove of trees.

"You'll notice some activity there," he said.

I observed a little flickering in the darkness and asked: "Are you referring to the way some dark forms seem to be moving a little?"

"That's indicative," Michael nodded.

"Do these forms only appear at night?" I continued.

"No, they're around at other times. But they're easier to see at night. During the day, they may still be there, but they're very subtle and can get blanked out by the light, so you don't see them. That's why we do most of our work at night—it's easier to see."

Michael stood up and walked a few feet in front of us to begin the experiment.

"I'm going to try an exercise to make myself vanish," he announced. "Watch closely, and you'll find you can look through me as if I'm not there and see whatever is behind me."

According to Michael, ODFers frequently observe others become invisible when they do magical work in the field. It's an indication the magician has stepped outside the mundane world into the other reality and has merged his or her essence with the natural world. Now Michael wanted to give us a taste of this experience.

He moved off about 30 feet into the meadow and again began to gyrate about. He raised and lowered his arms, slashed his staff through the air, and bent up and down in a kind of dance. At first, I saw his form silhouetted against the darkness, with a slight fuzzy white afterimage around him. Then, as I watched, a swirl of darkness appeared to engulf him for a few moments, and he merged into this darkness, until it retreated and I saw him once more. This process of the darkness closing in and retreating continued again and again.

When Michael returned, I reported my experience, which was much like Teri's. She had seen occasional swirls of advancing and retreating darkness, too.

"Great," Michael said, pleased by our reports. "As long as you saw me disappear, that's a beginning."

Finally, Michael suggested that Teri and I try something ourselves. "See what you can do. Do anything."

Teri, who was always eager to try something new, headed towards a grove of trees at the edge of the meadow, stood by it quietly, and meditated on the moon for about five minutes.

"You'll notice some extra activity in that grove now," Michael observed while she was there. He suggested I notice any swirls or clumps of energy indicating that what Teri was doing was having an effect.

After she returned, it was my turn to try something, and I was curious to see if there would be any relationship between what I did and what Michael and Teri perceived. I walked about 30 feet away from them, and as Michael had done earlier, I used my staff to draw a small circle around myself and a small pentagram in the air. Next, facing a grove of trees, I imagined a large lion standing in front of me and visualized a large field of energy around me. I imagined that this energy field was growing larger and I was gaining more power from it. Then, feeling this power, I pointed my staff at the lion and directed it to jump on a stool at my command and sit up on its haunches. Meanwhile, I continued to visualize the energy field around me. After several minutes of experiencing this imagery and the accompanying rush of power, I let the images go and drew a backwards pentagram in the air and a reverse circle on the ground to remove my pentagram and circle.

Afterwards, I returned to the log where Michael and Teri were sitting and asked what they had seen.

Teri apologized for meditating about something else and not watching, but Michael had seen something. "I noticed a wall of energy in front of you and a little to the right."

"That's about where I imagined the lion to be," I said.

As we walked back along the trail in silence, I wondered hard about the experience. I couldn't deny that the phenomena we observed had seemed quite real. And yet a part of me continued to question this alternate reality I had seen. What was real? What was not? I was both puzzled and intrigued.

Hoping to shed some light on my confusion, I asked Michael about his early experiences. How did he get involved in exploring other realities and eventually choosing the shaman warrior path? What convinced him of the reality of the other world?

CHAPTER TWO

Discovering The Path — Michael's Story

$\mathbf{A}$s we walked along the trail, Michael told me his own story, leading to his discovery of the shaman path when he was 14. He spent the early part of his childhood in an affluent middle class family. His father was a successful insurance salesman, and as Michael put it: "We had a maid, two cars, private school for the kids. The whole bit."

But in the early 1970's, when Michael was nine, suddenly everything changed. His father felt dissatisfied with his job, decided to return to school, and wrote a thesis on urban life in the 1960's. As a result, he was intrigued by the lure of the 1960's freedom, decided he wanted something better than his life as an insurance agent, and after some discussion with his wife, Michael and Michael's younger brother, he quite his job, sold the house, got rid of the two cars, and bought a VW van.

After a few months, during which the family lived on the road and in a series of communes, Michael's mother left and subsequently got a divorce. Meanwhile, Michael and his father and brother continued to travel about like gypsies for several years before ending up in Marin County when Michael was 12.

These experiences were crucial for his later development as a shaman, Michael believes, because they helped to dislodge him from being rooted in the mundane world and led him to feel like an outsider in his own country, for he felt disconnected, like someone apart looking in. Meanwhile, to compensate for his own loneliness, Michael began to read voraciously—mostly science fiction at first, and then metaphysics, as a way to make sense of his own gypsy-like life.

The next five years were a whirlwind of experiences all over California.

His father met several members from a large commune with a network of homes and schools in a dozen communities, and after a weekend course on the group's free wheeling and sensuous lifestyle, decided to move into one of their houses in Sonoma County. Then, after a few months there, his father decided to go to Los Angeles to found his own institute, and he pulled Michael and his brother out of school to take them there.

Several months later, the Mexico incident happened that changed Michael's life forever. His father got bored with teaching in Los Angeles and decided to take the family to Mexico. They drove around aimlessly for several days, while his father complained of feeling bored and wanting something to happen. And then something did. His father got arrested by the Mexican Federales for suspicious behavior. He had been exploring on the roof of a house that was under construction, and one of the neighbors reported him for suspicious behavior. The next day about three dozen police officers showed up at their van at four in the morning, woke the three of them up, and with machine guns out and ready, they escorted his father away.

"It was an incredible experience," Michael reports. "My father told us to stay in the car and keep the windows locked, so no one could get in and steal anything. But these guys kept coming over to trick us into getting out. Even the chief of police tried to reach in the window to steal a clock out of the car. But I slammed the window on his hand. It was a vivid realization of the need to be both strong and crafty—two of the qualities which are essential for the shaman warrior."

Finally, after several hours like this, Michael's brother was able to jump out of the car, go to the hotel in town, and call the American Embassy, which urged the local police to speed things up. The upshot of this was that Michael's father was taken to a judge in the morning, and by being resourceful, was able to get the matter dismissed. He pulled out his wallet, showed the judge a card proclaiming him a "Universal Life Minister," and explained that he was a priest and he had been on the roof saying his nightly prayers.

"So they let him go and we left. But we returned from Mexico penniless and broke."

As a result, after traveling for several more months in the van, Michael, his brother and father ended up in a small rural religious community in Mendocino, and it is here that Michael had his first shamanic initiation and committed himself to following the path of the shaman warrior and teaching others to do the same.

The initiation occurred while Michael was going through a Zen training program in 1975, shortly before he turned 15. The experience was much like the classic shamanic initiation where a person typically either goes through a grave illness and hovers near death but survives or has an intense mystic experience in which he or she comes face to face with the energies and mysteries of the universe. In Michael's case he experienced a mystic initiation, and afterwards, he felt that he had been given certain gifts and powers; that he had been chosen or called for this role; and that he could never go back; things could never be the same.

As we continued walking along the trail, Michael described what happened. He was walking alone in the woods, much like the woods we were in now, and he was several miles from home on a logging road. He had been taking walks like this for the past few weeks, because his family had been living a fairly quiet, isolated existence, and he often went out in the woods alone to think and meditate.

"It was strange," he related. "Each time I went out alone, I would suddenly get the feeling that something was coming through the woods towards me, although until the incident happened, I never saw anything. But I did notice other changes in the woods. For example, the light seemed to change. It got gray as if a cloud went in front of the sun. Also, the birds stopped singing and the animals stopped moving, so there was this unnatural stillness. And I felt afraid. I had feelings of terror and anxiety, and the first few times this happened, I ran home as fast as I could to be around other people. However, my fear seemed irrational. There was nothing specific in the woods I saw. I just felt something, and I didn't konw why I was afraid."

So Michael continued to go back into the woods, as if drawn by an outside power to discover and confront this strange mysterious presence that seemed to hang like a cloud over the woods. Then one day in September 1975 the incident happened and Michael met this force when it assumed physical form. Immediately, he felt the encounter was a test, and he had to confront this thing and overcome it.

"Or I would die," he said, and explained what happened.

"I had walked further into the woods than usual. I was about 20 miles away from home, when suddenly the feeling of danger in the air came back. Everything was suddenly very still again, and I was terrified and turned to run. I wanted to go back home as I had before. But this time, I saw my way blocked by a very strange thing—a three foot ball of transparent energy that was hovering about three feet above the road. It sparkled with little golden flashes, and I felt a surge of real terror.

"But there was nowhere to run. I couldn't run forward, because ahead of me there were only dense woods. I couldn't escape to the side of the road, because the hillsides on either side were thick with vegetation. And in front of me, between the woods and my home, I saw the thing. So I felt trapped, like an animal in a cage."

However, then, Michael discovered within himself the power to overcome this thing which was his first step along the shamanic path.

"I learned about my little voice for the first time," Michael said. "It was like a small whisper in my brain, and it told me very gently that this being was here to test me. The voice didn't say why, but it told me the penalty for failure would be death. Then, I asked what I had to do to pass the test, and the voice said that I had to remove myself from myself. I didn't know what to do, but then the voice gave me an example that saved my life."

The example, Michael described, was to think of a railroad track and imagine a heroine tied to the tracks while the train hurtles towards her. Then, at the last minute, the hero comes and snatches her away to safety. This vision came like a revelation to Michael.

"I suddenly realized what the little voice meant. The heroine was my ego or conscious self, which is really very fragile. But the hero, who combines wisdom, insight, and craftiness, was my instinct. And the train, representing power, was rushing at me. It was as if my own unconsciousness was suddenly rising up uncontrollably against me, and the only thing I could do was use my instinct or intuition to combat it."

Thus, feeling he had to act quickly to control that part of himself represented by the strange ball of energy, Michael turned to face the being instead of running.

"I found myself quelling all internal thoughts," Michael continued. "Then, I began getting rid of all thoughts of myself as a separate being from the rest of the universe. So, in a few moments, all ideas of myself were gone, and at this point, I became simply a very aware being that was no longer really myself, but simply an observer of the whole scene. This awareness was at one with all that was happening, but detached from it. It was like being totally opened up and becoming one with the universe."

Suddenly, at this very moment of oneness, as Michael related, the ball of energy came rushing at him, hit him, yet went right through him.

"It felt like a warm wind blew through my body, penetrating every inch of me before passing onwards. After that, the light returned to normal, and I could hear the birds as before. I also had a sense of myself again, and I wasn't frightened by what had happened."

However, the incident changed Michael irrevocably. As he walked back to the farm where he was living, he thought deeply about the meaning of the incident. His life had been full of many changes and upheavals, but otherwise he thought of himself as a very normal person who had lived an ordinary life. But now he felt a sense of calling for a higher, special purpose. He had heard and read about such experiences occurring to other people, and he wasn't even sure whether to believe they were real. But now it had happened to him, and he felt like another reality had opened up to him and he had to explore it and learn its secrets. As a result, when Michael resumed his usual walks in the woods a few days after the incident, it seemed as if the whole world around him had special information to tell him, for as Michael explained:

"Now I could see things in the woods. I saw auras around trees, flashing bolts of energies across trails, glimmers of movement in the corner of my eye, and there were auditory sensations, too. I could hear voices in the woods at times—and after my encounter with the ball of energy, I knew this wasn't just a hallucination. These voices were real."

Michael gave an example to illustrate. "A few months after the incident, I was walking down a trail towards a clearing, when I heard the sounds of a big party. I heard music, pots and pans clanging, people talking and laughing. I was surprised, because I knew the people camping in the area were away at a crafts fair in Oregon, and they weren't due back for several weeks. But I reasoned, perhaps they returned early, and I headed towards the meadow to join the party. However, as soon as I entered the area, all the noise stopped, and the meadow was deathly quiet. Nothing and no one was there. I was standing alone in a deserted clearing.

"But I know those noises were real," he emphasized. "Before the encounter, I might have dismissed this experience as a hallucination. But now I know to trust my own senses—and later, when I talked to others living in the area, I learned they heard similar noises too in the same place. So there's obviously something there beyond the ordinary realm of experience."

Encouraged by such experiences, Michael continued to experiment on his own, and after reading the Don Juan books, he tried several experiments to put into practice some of Don Juan's teachings about seeing and communicating with the powers and spirits of nature, except he wanted to contact the spiritual world without drugs. He began creating his own magical rituals to call on these beings, and soon he felt he had cracked Castaneda's code in describing, but not explaining completely, exactly what Don Juan did to achieve his spectacular supernatural effects.

The next major step of Michael's path to shamanism occurred a couple of years later, when Michael's father picked up and moved again, this time to San Francisco to set up a monastery to teach a mixture of personal development and sensuality techniques. Without telling him, Michael's father advertised a course on shamanism offered by Michael, and so, at 16, Michael began to teach about his experiences in the field. Then, when his father moved the monastery to L.A. a year later, Michael continued to teach. He also started leading field trips with students to demonstrate his techniques for communicating with the spirits of nature.

Then, as Michael continued to read and study, he came to feel that not only was this shaman warrior path the path for him, but that he had a special mission to share it with others. In turn, he decided to go through a self-initiation to formally affirm his commitment to this path and seek a sign that his mission was accepted by the powers of the universe.

As we neared the end of the trail, Michael described his initiation ritual.

"It was a time for commitment, a time to show I was ready to go forward, and that the universe, too, was ready for me. So just as everyone who joins the ODF must go through their own period of initiation, I made that decision to formally acknowledge I had joined the shaman warrior path."

Michael began by taking a cleansing magical bath to purify himself, and put on a black robe, representing the protective powers of the night, which is the time when the shaman warrior does most magical work. Then, standing in front of a mirror with a chair beside him, Michael drew a working circle with his staff, sat down, and stared at his image in the mirror using the seeing exercise he had taught us earlier that night.

At first, though, nothing happened. Michael looked as he always did in the mirror, and he was very disappointed, about to give up, when he saw his first sign that the universe was responding to his ritual.

"A queen ant flew up onto the mirror," he explained, "and I took this as a small omen I had been heard, since the queen ant has always been a symbol of power and productivity to me. Then, since we do so much of our work outside, I felt inspired to go outside to be even closer to the spirit of nature, and I set up another circle in the moonlight. As soon as I finished drawing it with my staff and got ready to work, I knew I had done the right thing, because an owl suddenly flew into the trees, and the owl is a symbol of wisdom and power."

Thus, Michael lifted his arms to the sky and affirmed his commitment to the warrior path.

"I said I would be a true believer; that I would honor the principles of nature; and that I would practice these principles in daily life."

Again Michael looked around for a symbol his vows had been accepted, and again the movements of the owl seemed especially significant to him.

"As I recited my vows, it flew to another tree standing directly under the full moon, which for me is a symbol of fulfillment and completion."

Thus, Michael felt his initiation had been acknowledged. "It was as if I was presenting myself to the universe and saying 'Here I am,' using the symbols that are meaningful to me. And then the universe listened and responded through the owl, as if to say: 'We hear you and we accept.'"

Yet, as Michael emphasized, others who come to this path might bring with them other symbols that have meaning to them. As he told me:

"The warrior path is open to anyone. It combines magical techniques from many different traditions, based on the principle of 'if it works, use it.' The images of the queen ant and the owl have a special meaning to me because of my closeness to nature. So when I saw these symbols, they reassured me that I was proceeding along the right magical route. On the other hand, when someone else initiates themself along this path, they will experience other symbols that have personal meaning to them. You see, the shaman warrior path has many doors, and people can come to it through any one of them. So people can bring along their own traditions on the path. And each person should choose his own way."

Just then the lights of the parking lot came into view in the distance. Our field trip adventure was nearly over, though Michael had a few last things to share about the formal beginnings of the L.A. group, which he started organizing soon after his formal initiation.

He selected a few students from his regular classes to go on special field trips and become part of a small local clan or "weyr." One was Paul, who Michael had met when he studied briefly at a commercial art school in San Francisco. Another was Gene, a close friend of Paul's. And a third was Samantha, who had signed up for one of Michael's classes and showed a special aptitude for magic. I would learn much more about all of them later. But for now Michael simply wanted to emphasize that all of them had started out being somewhat skeptical of what happened in the field, like me, although after awhile the field experience changed them.

As Michael explained: "When we go out in the field, it seems to have an odd effect on people. They see things they can't explain, and that changes their whole way of perceiving the universe, as I found out again and again in L.A. Some people became very scared or spooked when we went out. But almost everyone saw something—and soon they began to realize there was something strange out there, and they wanted to learn more.

"For example, when Paul first arrived in L.A. and I told him about my teaching and the field trips, he thought I was a little nuts. But then, as we were talking in the kitchen, I told him to look around, that there are some things you can't normally see, but if he looked in the shadows, he would see a grayish humanoid shape. When he turned around, he jumped up and turned white with fear, because he saw it too. After that, he looked at me with a new respect, and that weekend, he accompanied me into the field. And that was the trip when we encountered the werewolves, too."

I wanted to ask about the werewolves, but now we were back at the car, and Michael's description of the trip would have to wait for later. We slid in, and as Teri edged the car out into the road, Michael encouraged us both to take the next step on the shaman warrior path—going out in the field alone on a "solo," so we could experience our own personal initiation, much as Michael did when he did a ritual and encountered the owls at night.

He described what would happen. "The purpose of the initiation solo is to be by yourself for an hour or so. The group drops you off at a site, and then we pick you up about an hour later. During this time, you set up your own magical circle, open yourself to be receptive, and experience whatever comes up."

Teri, who had been active in a variety of magical and occult groups, wondered if she should use a formal ritual to set up a circle, but Michael said this wasn't necessary. Just a simple circle with a flick of the wrist or a staff would do.

Then, I asked about the kind of experiences we might expect. Should we expect anything like the ball of energy Michael encountered along the road on his first informal initiation or the animals which appeared when he initiated himself more formally.

But Michael could only be vague, though reassuring. "I can't really say what might happen, because everyone's solo is different. So you might experience anything, since the idea of the solo is that you're making a statement to the universe to say: 'I'm here ... I want to work with you ... I'd like your assistance in the magic I want to do.' But after that, you have to open yourself and allow yourself to be receptive to whatever comes. However, normally, there's nothing to worry about, because usually, the solo is a calm and peaceful experience. Some people have ended up singing, some dancing, and some have simply seen things, like movements of energy, shape transformations, and humanoid beings. It's really very different for everyone. But normally, the solo is gentle. So there's no reason to be afraid."

Teri, who usually liked to have everything clearly spelled out for her in advance, wanted to know what kind of preparations were necessary, and again Michael tried to be reassuring and emphasize how simple the whole process was.

"Just think of it like a shamanic initiation. So the best way to prepare is by meditating and practicing your seeing exercises. Then, once you know how to 'see,' you should go out to a quiet private spot, preferably in the woods or desert, to open yourself up to the surrounding sensations. Also, you should do this with a clear heart and use some form of ritual to address yourself to the divine. In effect, what you want to say is: 'Here I am, a magician or magician-to-be stepping out on my path. Do with me what you will.'

"You see," he continued, "this is like a vision quest you are going on ... so you need to be receptive. Don't close yourself down and accept whatever you see. The intense experience is rare, but possible. More typically, it's a calm experience, and intense experiences will follow later."

I had one last concern. "Does anyone ever fail?" I asked.

Michael shook his head firmly. "No . . . no. I've never seen anyone fail a solo. The only way would be for someone to get up in the middle and leave. But that's never happened. When you stay, you're basically saying to the universe that you're ready to go on. So whatever happens is right."

Michael felt that Teri and I were now ready to do this.

"You both now know the basic techniques of seeing, making a circle, and using power objects. You've had an experience in the field. So if you're ready to go on, the next step is the solo."

"Well, I'm ready," said Teri. "I'm always game for something new. It sounds like an interesting addition to all of the other occult experiences I've had. I always like to learn more."

And I said I would like to go on, too.

"Good," Michael said. "Then soon we'll start your training. And you'll find doors will open that will never again close."

Michael sat back and smiled serenely as he spoke. Yet I felt a hint of danger in his mysterious grin. What would happen as we opened these doors into this strange other world that Michael had been exploring for the past ten years. I was curious, yet a little anxious and awed.

CHAPTER THREE

Solo

Four weeks later, in mid-August, Michael organized another field trip and invited me to do my solo. Normally, I would have soloed a week or two after the initial training session, but Michael was busy getting settled after moving from Los Angeles, so he had to delay starting the ODF's usual weekly program of field trips and classes.

We set off in my station wagon late one Sunday afternoon for the same site as our previous trip, and as usual on ODF excursions, Michael wore his dress blacks uniform and brought his hiking gear. Teri couldn't come, since she had to work, but Serge Thomas, who had watched Michael's demonatration at the encampment, came along. Like Michael, he was dressed in full uniform.

Serge struck me as an enthusiastic eager beaver, who throws himself wholeheartedly into whatever he is doing at the time. Serge had long had an interest in magic, and had previously been in several ceremonial magic groups, one of them completely gay in keeping with his active participation in the gay community. Since Serge showed such intense interest, Michael had met with him privately to discuss the possibility of Serge becoming an assistant weyr leader and teacher of the ODF system. A few days later Serge had gone on a solo on his own, and was now voraciously reading everything Michael had written about the ODF. Tonight he was along primarily to assist Michael in taking me out on my solo.

As we drove to the site, Serge revealed a little more about himself, though it was hard to get him to open up at first, for outwardly Serge was quiet and shy. Yet underneath his outer aloofness, he was a very warm, sensitive person, who cared deeply for others, and was readily hurt when relationships went bad. In turn, these qualities led him to want to help others, and so, since his early 30's—he was now 36—he had worked as a psychiatric counselor in a halfway house for the mentally ill.

"I've always been very interested in the healing arts," he told me. "And I've always wanted to help people become more integrated into society. I guess that's because I always felt distant and estranged from my own parents, and I wanted to be close to others. My father was a very conservative Army officer from the Mid-West, and he was always very rigid and formal. I wanted to be different from that."

Unfortunately, Serge became so different since he became openly gay in his teens that his well-to-do family disowned him, and Serge ended up in San Francisco, where he almost immediately got swept up into the whirl of gay politics and the gay bar and bath scene. But now he felt ready to settle down with a single lover, and he saw magic as one way to help him get his life in order.

"I lived a really wild, fast-paced life a few years ago," he explained. "I used to go to the bars and baths almost every night, and I had dozens of lovers. It was fast and furious. Really an escape from the stilted life I knew in the Mid-West. But in the last few years, I've gotten burned out on all that. It was a phase, and now that's over. After all, I'm over 35, and it's time to settle down. I just want a really good enduring relationship, and I'll be happy."

So far, Serge hadn't found exactly the right person, but he was living quietly with two other gay men, while searching for a close relationship with a single lover.

"And maybe magic will help me find that person and have a good relationship," Serge observed. "Also, I want to understand who I am and my role in life, and I want to better understand others, too. I think magic can help with that."

After Serge finished talking about his background, I had many questions about the solo I would be experiencing that night.

What could I expect? What comes next in the shaman warrior training process? What are the practical applications of developing these magical abilities? And how does the ODF system relate to other well-known magical systems?

Michael answered each of my questions in turn, and he seemed especially concerned that I fully understand. He began by explaining what happens in a solo and the ODF stages of magical growth.

"In your solo," he said, "you're basically making a statement to the magical world that you are there, so you go out alone. Everyone does it differently and has a different experience. But about 90% of the people who go out have a good experience and see the spiritual world as a friendly and comfortable place . . .

"Then, after the solo, the second grade is the selfless magical act. You present yourself to the universe and show you are ready to do a magical act. Then, you open yourself up to whatever comes and listen to the little voice. For example, you may suddenly feel you should move an arm and then your feet. You should do whatever you pick up, and you may find you can do things you didn't think you could, such as seeing a spiritual being and getting it to come to you or go away. For verification, you need to have witnesses confirm what they saw you do. That's why everyone shares on what they experienced after your act. But it's nothing to worry about. So far, no one has failed this test. When you truly open yourself up to the universe, the spirits and forces always respond."

After we stopped for gas, Michael continued describing the ODF system.

"Next comes the third grade level, and to pass that you must successfully do a willed magical act. You decide in advance what sort of act you want to perform, and then you do it, using your inner voice and your seeing to help you.

"For Grades Four and Five, you have to exercise still more control and direction. In the Fourth Grade, you must perfect your ability to do a willed act by balancing the inner and outer energies. You need this balance, because whenever you do magic, you are calling on energies within yourself that affect the world around you, and at the same time, you may experience resistances from this world. So you must learn how to sense what is coming from both within and without to find a balance between the two.

"As for the Fifth Level, that involves balancing the male and female energies in yourself. Each person has both components, and this magical test involves getting in touch with them and finding a balance. The result is experiencing a release that feels somewhat sexual, so if you want, you can do this exercise with a partner of the opposite sex.

"Finally, to pass Grade Six, you have to open up a gate into the other world. And then you have to go through, at least for a few minutes, yourself."

Michael said he had recently achieved a Grade Six himself, and there were more advanced grades—the Order had ten so far. However, he wasn't ready to talk about them until we knew more, so I went on to my next questions.

"How much time does it take to move from grade to grade?" I wondered.

"That depends on the person. Some people can move ahead very fast in a few months. Others take much longer. So it's up to you and the kind of commitment you can make, since you need to practice to move ahead." For instance, Michael had advanced to Grade Six after about ten years of study, eight of them with the ODF, and he had been on over 100 field trips. "So, you see, it takes real commitment, real work. You have to show you can really do something before you advance."

I then asked about the practical applications, and Michael explained.

"Mainly ODFers use these techniques for experimental purposes and to develop seeing. For example, we've experimented with astral projection, ESP, and remote viewing. But you can use them to get what you want. For example, when I moved here from L.A., I used my seeing abilities to help land a job. Other ODFers have used these methods to better understand themselves, improve relationships, and increase their health. So the system is something you can use to put yourself in better balance with the universe in every way, though I'm especially interested in using it to explore new realities."

I also wondered: "How does the ODF compare to other magical systems?" and Michael described it as a kind of personalized synthesis of many systems that made magical development more accessible to everyone.

"In essence, it's really like all other systems of magic, though it's simpler to learn. You're learning how to both exercise the will and tune yourself into the underlying harmonies of the universe. Once you sense these harmonies, you can exercise your will more strongly, because you're acting in harmony with the current balance of things. Otherwise, you're trying to exercise your will against the flow of energy in the universe, which is much harder, since it's like rowing a boat against the current . . .

"It can help to know about other magical systems to intensify your own magical activities. But it's not necessary to learn elaborate systems like ceremonial magic, the Tarot, or astrology, because you can use your seeing abilities to sense the flow of energy in the universe. Knowing these other systems might make you more aware of this flow, so you can better sense it. But seeing by itself works just fine."

Finally, about 8:30 p.m. we arrived at the parking lot. It was rapidly getting dark, so we quickly gathered our gear and got ready for the long walk to the meadow. This time, I had brought my own staff—a long black walking stick with a brass tip—so I didn't need Michael's.

Michael strapped on his heavy utility belt under his black leather police jacket and attached a flashlight, canteen, and first aid kit. Then, we headed towards the meadow. We walked quickly, though quietly at first, to get into the proper contemplative mood for the magical workings planned. I noticed that Michael continually moved his staff back and forth and asked why.

"To sense the energy ahead," he answered. "I especially want to look for changes."

To illustrate, Michael asked me to sweep my staff around the road as I made a 360 degree turn and notice any differences when I pointed it at him or Serge.

I stretched out my arm and started to make a circular motion with it.

"Should I close my eyes?" I asked.

"No. Keep them open. After all, you walk with your eyes open. Now you want to learn to feel for differences."

I continued the circuit and noticed a slightly heavy sensation, a little like a slight blip or pulse in my arm, as I passed each of them, though I wondered if perhaps I felt this because I saw each of them in front of me as I moved by with my staff.

When I reported this, Michael reassured me: "No, the feeling is real. In face, we demonstrated this clearly on a previous field trip. I led about half a dozen people into the field, and I asked one man to stand in the center of the group. Everyone formed a large scattered circle around him, and I asked him to close his eyes and move his staff around and try to feel or sense when someone was there. Each time he did, he felt a little tugging sensation in his hand or arm, really a kind of psychic wrench. Finally, I asked several people to change positions, but he still felt the same pressure when his staff passed by someone. He couldn't see anyone, since his eyes were closed. But he definitely felt something.

"So you are feeling something real," Michael concluded. "Whenever we've tried this circle experiment, people have been able to pick up when someone is in a particular spot, though usually they can't identify who it is. However, some people can make these identifications when they get good. The key to developing this sensitivity is to practice, because this will make you more aware of everything."

The circle demonstration concluded, Michael walked on and we followed. As before, he moved his staff back and forth sensing the environment.

"What sorts of things are you looking for?" I asked.

"Anything that looks unusual," he replied. "Unexpected shadows, white or grey spots, flashes of light, things that move unexpectedly. These are signs that elementals or other spiritual beings are present and active. Then you can check out if the being is ready to be receptive and friendly to you. If so, you can work with it or seek its help for something you want to do."

When I asked how to do this checking, Michael told us to use the seeing technique. "The technique isn't something to only use on special occasions, such as when you practice in front of another person or a mirror. You should learn to employ it whenever you want while you're doing something else, such as walking along a road, like we're doing now."

To demonstrate, Michael asked us to try to "see" as we walked along the path. The way to do this was not only to look ahead at the road, but also to be aware of the things around us through our peripheral vision. "You see," he explained, "to see, you don't simply focus ahead as you normally do. Instead, use a distant gaze in which you look at the energy in the air. Then, you'll be able to sense the changes as the energies and forms move around."

I let my eyes go out of focus, and at once I noticed the fuzziness Michael referred to. I perceived a shimmery quality in the air, as if it was vibrating in front of me.

"Is that what you mean?" I asked, after describing the experience.

"Yes, exactly," Michael replied. "And you'll find these seeing exercises are central to everything else, because they teach you a new way of looking. When you start focusing on the air, you'll discover its energy field in the movements and sparkles you see. Also, you'll begin to see the auras around things and notice how things have very different auras."

Michael stopped again to give us another demonstration.

"Hold up your staffs," he said.

As we extended them, he put his hand next to each of our staffs in turn, then quickly took it away.

"Can you feel the difference when my hand is there and when it isn't?" he asked.

At first I didn't feel anything, and I wondered if my gloves might be a barrier to my feeling any energy radiating from Michael's hand when it was near my staff.

But Michael told me no, "The gloves shouldn't make a difference. Clothing is never a barrier. You can sense the energy whatever you wear."

He urged me to try again and moved his hand back and forth by the tip of my staff.

"Notice the difference in pressure as I move my hand close. See if you can feel that blip."

Again, I concentrated, and this time, I noticed that perhaps there was something, even a slight shift, so my own hand felt heavier.

"Yes," I finally agreed. "I think I felt a little extra pressure."

Then, Michael tried the same technique with Serge.

"I experienced a slight heaviness," Serge said when the experiment was done.

"Good," Michael commented. "What you're both feeling is that feeling of solidity. That tells you something's there."

He raised his staff and pointed it at mine and then at Serge's.

"Now, look all around your staff and in front of it to notice the field of energy."

I looked and reported seeing a shimmering light about an inch or two thick which looked a little like an afterimage surrounding my staff.

"I see a similar luminescence," Serge said.

"Fine," Michael replied. "Now, keep looking, and you might see this light project for about six inches from the tip of your staff."

This time I didn't see anything, although Serge crowed with enthusiasm:

"Yes, I saw it. I saw the light." Then, visibly pleased with his accomplishment, he swished his staff around in the air several times, watching the light.

Michael continued his explanation. "This extension occurs because you're not only seeing the aura of the object, but also projecting your own energy through it and out of it."

Michael then pointed out that this special mode of seeing and feeling could be used while we were doing anything. In fact, he was using them now. "You see," he explained, "right now, as I'm walking along the path talking to you, I'm projecting out my energy to sense what's around us. And it's something I do all the time, wherever I go. For instance, if I'm walking through a dangerous part of the city at night, I'll use my seeing to sense if someone is around who might be threatening, and if so, I'll take some action to evade this person. I know it's probably saved my life several times when I lived in L.A."

Michael gave an example. "One time I was walking along the street, about to pass a dark alley, when I sensed some people were there who meant no good. So I quickly moved to the other side of the street, and just as I did, these three tough characters wearing sweatshirts and baseball caps walked out of the alley. I don't know if they would have actually tried to hurt me, but they sure looked mean, and I sensed they could. One woman I know got roughed up when she was walking on the street, because she hadn't been paying attention to how she felt. So you have to be alert."

We continued walking for awhile in silence, and I focused on being aware and alert. As I had seen Michael do, I moved my staff up and down to see if I observed anything different. Occasionally, I noticed the feelings of pressure Michael talked about; yet I wondered about the source of this experience. Was I sensing some real shifts in energy around me? Or was my own imagination creating this perception? I both wanted to feel the experience Michael described, yet analyze and explain it.

Now, as the main road veered into the dense woods, it became very dark. For a few minutes, we walked on in silence, and Michael continued to move his staff about to sense what was happening along the way. Then, breaking the silence, Michael commented on the darkness.

"Usually, it isn't so dark like this when we go out on a solo, since we like to get there easily and quickly, and when it's still light you don't usually encounter a variety of active energies and beings along the way. But there are a lot more of them out now, since they're more likely to be out and active in the darkness."

To demonstrate the difference, Michael turned on his flashlight. It created a strong tunnel of light that cut through the darkness for about 30 feet ahead.

"Do you notice the shift?" Michael asked us. "You'll observe the energies quieted down when I turned on the light."

"Yeah. I can feel the calmness," Serge agreed.

I didn't notice the shift they were talking about, but I had felt quite spacy as I walked along in the darkness with my eyes unfocused, trying to perceive these energies. However, now, once the light went on, I suddenly felt more centered and directed.

"The light tends to bring us back to the real mundane world," Michael explained. "The spirits are there even during the day. But we can't see them as well because of the light. So the area feels less active."

Michael kept the light down low, and as we walked on, he occasionally called our attention to patches of darker than usual shadows ahead. "They're concentrations of energy that might be an elemental," he said. I noticed that some of the shadows he pointed out seemed to rest heavily along the sides of the path until his light flashed them away. Others looked like small moving shadows and flickering lights, which appeared to shift about as the wind brushed the trees.

Suddenly the form of a deer appeared on the road, and it stood motionless for a moment, before it scampered away.

"A deer," Michael announced.

"A real deer?" I asked, not sure anymore what I was creating in my imagination, what might be part of a shadowy other world, and what was real.

"Yes, it's real," Michael confirmed.

"How can you tell what's real from the animal's appearance?" I asked.

"Well, that can sometimes be a problem. Though you should look to your inner voice if you're not sure."

Just then, as if mocking us, the deer poked its head out on the road and vanished back into the bushes.

Moments later, Serge, walking several feet ahead of me, cried out: "There's the shadow of a cat . . . Ahead of us on the road."

I looked up and saw it, too. It was a small, shadowy shape, that hugged the side of the road and seemed to move in a burst of activity. Then it hesitated for a moment, before darting on.

Serge, like me, was puzzled about what was real and what wasn't, and he asked Michael: "Is that the shadow of a real animal? Or is it some kind of elemental energy form?"

Michael wasn't sure, and he shined his light ahead, though the form quickly darted on beyond the arc of light and disappeared into the woods.

Finally, we arrived and the canopy of trees opened out on the broad expanse of meadow, where we had worked before.

Immediately, Michael, ever the disciplined organizer, wanted to get to the business at hand. "Now, pick a place that feels comfortable for you and do your solo," he told me. As usual, he had selected the general area for the solo. Now it was up to me—as the person having the experience—to pick the specific place that felt right for me.

I made a full circuit of the meadow with my gaze. It looked something like a large oval, perhaps 100 yards across, at its edges, the shadowy forms of the woods surged up, like a dark protective wall. Near the path on a little rise, I noticed a tree with high sweeping branches and I felt it would be perfect for my solo. It reminded me of a lookout point or small fortress; so I felt I would be more protected from anything at that spot.

Michael had one reservation, however. "On a previous trip, we saw some elementals hanging out there, and you should be cautious about this, since elementals often stay in the same place and this is a new experience for you. So you may want to be in a place that's likely to be quieter for your first solo. But if you still want to, you can station yourself there."

Since I didn't see anything unusual about this tree, I said I would do that.

Michael and Serge accompanied me to the tree, and Michael said they would be gone for about an hour, which is common for solos, since they last about 30 minutes to an hour.

But before they left, Michael was quite solicitous that I would be all right, as he usually was with new people. Thus, as they prepared to leave, Michael reassured me: "There's nothing to worry about. We'll be near enough, so if you have any problems, you can call out, and we'll come to help you or get you, if necessary. But otherwise, you'll be on your own."

Finally, Michael and Serge walked off and disappeared down the path. Around the bend was a small clearing with fallen logs where they would wait for me.

When they were gone, I sat down with my back to the tree and my knees crossed in a yoga-like position. Then, I imagined a circle of energy around me embracing the whole field. I wasn't totally convinced this circle would protect me, if a real animal or person should appear on the meadow and attack me. Yet, simply imagining the circle around me made me feel calmer and more secure.

Next I looked around to see if I noticed anything out of the ordinary, and I alternated between using my normal vision and the unfocused seeing Michael had taught us. But I didn't observe anything that seemed different, and felt this was just as well. It was a relief not to encounter anything too weird while I was alone, and I wondered if I was keeping anything out there away by my thoughts. Then, feeling secure, I started meditating quietly.

As I did, I felt a wall of protective energy descend around me, and suddenly, I heard a voice telling me I could ask questions and this voice would answer. So I asked the first questions that came to mind—quite mundane ones really: How should I organize a class I was planning? and What should I do to lose weight? The answers came quickly. "Brainstorm what to include; then decide what to do when." "Take a vitamin pill before each meal to remind you of your commitment to lose weight."

After awhile, the questions and answers stopped coming, and I thought I would try to see things. Thus, I began moving my staff around and I watched as I pointed it, like I was seeing my way around a movie. Soon I noticed some flashing and swirling lights in a grove of trees off to my right. I also observed that the grassy field around me seemed to be shimmering with a greyish-white glow, like a luminescent vibrating carpet in the inky-grey night.

I noticed, too, that it got perceptibly colder, as Michael said it usually did during a solo. He claimed this occurred because, "When you do a magical act, you're usually drawing energy out of the universe around you." Yet, even though I felt this temperature change, I wondered. Is it really getting colder? Am I only feeling this? Is it getting colder because it is later at night? Or am I feeling colder, because Michael told me I was likely to feel this way?

Then, thinking that I shouldn't analyze the experience so much and should simply feel what was happening, I pushed these thoughts aside. "Just experience the experience," I told myself.

Thus, I refocused my attention on the circle I had created around me, and once again I felt an intense calm as I thought of this circle as a protective barrier around me.

After awhile, I had a sense of completion—as if the solo was over for me and I was ready to return, and I started thinking it was time for Michael and Serge to come back. A few minutes later, almost as if they had heard me calling to them to return, I noticed a flashlight beam flicker briefly in the distance, and soon they reappeared.

"How was it?" Michael asked.

"Comfortable," I said.

"Good . . . Then you might want to honor the four directions and thank them for a nice experience before you leave. It's always good to do this as a way of continuing your friendship with nature."

Michael and Serge walked off to a large log at the edge of the meadow, so I could do this alone. As they left, I turned around and faced in turn towards the East, the South, the West, and finally the North. At each direction, as Michael had suggested, I bowed slightly and waved my hand in a salute, while saying a silent "thank you." Then, I joined Michael and Serge at the log.

Michael wanted to know everything I experienced, as he usually did after someone completed a solo. He was particularly interested in finding correspondence between what I experienced and what he and Serge had noticed while waiting for me. His major reason for doing this was to provide further confirmation of the reality of the experience—both for the person "on solo" and for those waiting "on recovery" to pick up that person at the end.

"So what happened?" Michael asked, and I gave my report. Afterwards, Michael and Serge described what they perceived. Both said they felt a distinct energy shift as they came towards me on the meadow.

"I could tell when you had the energy field up and when you took it down," Serge said.

"How did you perceive that?" I asked.

Serge groped for words to describe what he felt. He wasn't used to expressing his feelings in words. But finally he explained: "Well, it was like going into a dark room and feeling I was about to bump into some furniture. Then, suddenly, I didn't feel the furniture was there anymore."

Michael also reported that they had encountered a lot of "active energy" where they were. "However, the energy on the meadow was much calmer. But it's usually like that, because the people who are waiting on recovery are like watchers, and they become a magnet for any activity. So they can help keep things calmer for the person on the solo. It's not always that way, because sometimes the people on recovery have a real quiet time, while all sorts of intense things happen to the person on the solo. But mostly, the active energy stays outside the circle."

When I expressed surprise that the two of them came for me so soon after I felt ready to go back, Michael noted that such an experience is very common. "When you're on recovery, you can pick up when the solo is over for someone. We could sense when you were ready to go, and once we felt it was over, we came for you."

"How do you sense that?" I asked.

But Michael had no words to answer my question. "I don't know. We just sense it and feel it, that's all," he said.

"It's just a feeling of completion," Serge commented. "I felt it, too. But I don't know why I felt that. I just did."

Now it was time to go, and as we gathered our gear together for the walk back, Michael told me I would probably feel differently about myself soon.

"When a person goes on a solo," he said, "they start to feel differently afterwards. The solo may seem like only a little ritual, but it goes beyond that, because you're making a statement about yourself as a magician. You're saying that you're out there as someone to be reckoned with; that you have magical power. And you can't help feeling differently about yourself after you say that."

CHAPTER FOUR

Other Solos

On the way back, Michael reminded us to pay attention to the forces surrounding us.

"Be aware of what's around you as we walk. Sometimes people focus directly ahead as they walk along a path and that's all. But you should be able to see and feel the energies around you."

He suggested an exercise to help us sense things better.

"Be aware of the sides of the path as you walk, and see if you can walk along it just by sensing the sides."

He turned off his flashlight and asked us to try. At first, I saw only the very hazy outline of the path in the grey-black darkness. Then, as we passed through a heavily thicketed stretch, the outline disappeared.

"Now listen to your feelings only," Michael said.

I moved my staff back and forth as instructed, and Serge followed a few yards behind me. Somehow, I managed to stay near the center, though at one point, Michael called out: "You're veering to the right. Go back to the center."

Suddenly, Michael called out a loud, "Stop!" I did, wondering what he had seen. I turned on my light again and noticed I was just about to brush my head against a large overhanging branch full of leaves.

"You should be able to watch out for things like that."

I admitted I hadn't seen it.

"You'll learn," he said. "You can learn to feel these things . . . Now look." He turned off the light. "Plants have their own special aura. Look up at the sky and you can see it."

I glanced up and noticed the leaves above me silhouetted against the sky.

Soon, as I watched, a fuzzy whitish aura appeared around each leaf.

"It's like an envelope around each leaf," Serge exclaimed.

"Good," Michael declared. "Now here's an experiment you can try just before dusk. Go outside and look at the plants. At this time they're especially active, since they are trying to suck in the last energy of the day, and you can see little swirls of energy around them, whereas now, they have a very calm, solid aura. At dusk, though, it's a little like seeing tendrils of energy reaching out to grasp the last rays of the sun."

We started walking again, and now Michael asked us to pay attention to the general tone or feeling of the walk out of the park.

"It's very different than the walk in, as you'll notice. And it's usually this way, because when we're walking in, you're generally more open and receptive. So you experience more energies and see more. But on the way out, you tend to be more closed down, since you've already done a great deal of magical work for the night and might feel tired or be ready to relax. So on the way out it generally feels like walking down an ordinary path at night."

Thus, at Michael's urging we began to walk quickly and soon were out of the woods. As we got in the car, the dreamlike quality of the evening's experience vanished, and I asked Michael what other people's solos were like.

"What's typical?" I said. "How is my experience similar or different from what others experience."

"Everyone's solo *is* different," Michael emphasized. "Usually calm and gentle, but very different, too, since everyone expresses his magical powers in a different way."

To illustrate, Michael related the stories of three people from his L.A. weyr—Gene and Paul, who I had met briefly at the encampment, and Samantha, a woman in her 20's. I noticed that their experiences seemed to parallel their personal qualities. For instance, Gene, a light-hearted, sometimes prankish computer programmer, had an extremely calm peaceful experience. Paul, a serious and usually silent auto mechanic, spent most of his solo in quiet meditation. And Samantha, an unusually flighty person who moved about constantly, had a frightening experience when she encountered dark and threatening beings.

Michael related their stories at length as we drove on through the inky night.

He described Gene's Death Valley solo first. Michael and a friend, Frank, who had been on dozens of ODF trips, accompanied Gene, and soon after they arrived, just before sunset, Michael and Frank hiked around the area to "clear out the aura of the place" as Michael put it, while Gene took a nap in the car. Their goal was to make sure the site would be calm and peaceful, so Gene could have a good, pleasant solo. To do this, they performed various psychic exercises—such as opening up gateways to the other world and doing a general cleansing, so everything would be calm.

Then, when they returned to the car a little after dark, they woke up Gene and led him to a hill above the canyon. There they gave him a flashlight and told him to go down into the canyon, select a comfortable place, and stay there. They told him, "We'll return for you in about an hour," then returned to the car to wait.

Meanwhile, as the fog came in, Gene continued down the hill and turned on his flashlight. As he neared what looked like a black wall of fog, his flashlight suddenly stopped. Yet, he went on anyway, feeling somehow compelled to keep going. Then, when he finally arrived at the bottom, he felt a sudden overflowing sensation of peace, and as the fog moved around him, he spent his solo sitting on the sand, calmly watching balls of energy bouncing around him.

"But, then, it's often like that," Michael observed. "Things can be roaring around for the people on recovery who are waiting to pick up the person. Or the situation can look really tense and scary to an outside observer. But inside the circle, the person on the solo is having a pleasant, enjoyable time.

Paul's solo was more dramatic. Michael lit a cigarette and settled back to describe it. Like Gene, Paul had been on several field trips, since ODFers have to observe on at least one or two field trips, before taking their solo. After hearing about Gene's experience, he expected the same, since he was going to solo in the desert, too. But from the beginning, Paul's solo was quite different.

His experience began on a cold, crisp evening, when Michael and Gene took him to a large sandy meadow. It was ringed by a high cliff on one side and high bushes around the rest of the area, except for a large opening near the path.

"At first, Paul felt strangely scared," Michael reported. "He wondered: 'What am I doing? Why am I here? Am I crazy or something?' Then, he started hearing all kinds of things rustling in the bushes, and he heard a tinkling sound coming from the caves in the canyon. Soon, these noises died down, and he noticed two bright lights, about the size of softballs, four feet off the ground, moving across the desert towards him. At first, he thought the lights might be a car coming towards him. However, as the lights moved closer, they shifted so that one was above the other and they kept on coming.

"Well, car lights don't do that," said Michael. "So Paul realized this wasn't a car, particularly when the light suddenly jumped up about 30 or 35 feet above the desert and hovered there. At first, Paul was pretty nervous. He wasn't sure what these lights were anymore. But then, he suddenly had this flash of insight that the lights meant him no harm—they were just there watching. So he calmed down and glanced away, and when he looked back, the lights were gone."

Paul remained at the site a few more minutes, feeling calm and peaceful, and then got up, feeling it was time to leave. As he walked towards the path, he met Michael coming to get him, which Michael considered a perfectly usual occurrence. "That kind of meeting happens all the time," he said. "I get a sense of knowing when it's time to get someone on recovery. And about 80-90% of the time they're ready to leave. Or maybe they're even getting up to go, like Paul."

Just as Michael finished this account, we passed a truck stop with a few gas pumps and a weathered cafe, and Michael suggested we pull in for some cokes. We did briefly, and afterwards, as I turned the car back onto the highway, Michael related his final story about Samantha's solo journey.

"It was really quite astounding—a rare event. She had an incredible encounter with a series of negative beings, and we think this happened, because she went out into the field without having fully confronted certain negative aspects about herself. So when she began working, certain negative beings were activated or attracted by the exercise. Also, we believe the experience was more intense for her than for most people, since she had a natural talent as a shaman, though she was untrained."

Though I immediately wanted to know the details, Michael felt it crucial to explain why even a negative experience can have value.

"The solo is really like opening a window on yourself," he said. "It helps to show you where you're at and what's important to you at the time. So even a negative experience can give you insights and open doors, which is what happened for Samantha. Though negative, her solo was a valuable learning experience. It may have seemed a little frightening at the time, but the experience was a valuable one for Samantha and the group, since it was a test of harmony and balance. It showed her that one needs to have internal harmony and balance in confronting raw power, and it showed the group it needed harmony and balance, too, to deal with a potentially dangerous situation."

Michael lit another cigarette, and thoughtfully began to explain, by first giving me a capsule biography of Samantha.

"Well, really, she was always kind of a drifter. She came to us after she fled from her family in New England. They were always very strict and repressive, and when she turned 18, she decided it was time to get away. So she hitchhiked out to California, and had a series of jobs as a waitress and short-order cook. She also moved around a lot. She lived with one guy and then another. She was really quite attractive you see, and guys were always falling for her. But then, she would get bored and move out.

"So when she turned up in one of my classes, I picked up immediately that she was someone who was very restless. Yet, she was searching for stability.

She wanted to know who she was, and she felt an incredibly low sense of self-esteem, because she really wasn't sure. So we were working with her to try to build that up. Plus, I sensed she was a natural magician, though she had practically no training. She just had this intuitive sense. She seemed to attract all sorts of energies to her, just like people, and yet she never knew exactly what to do with them. Thus, things in her life were always seeming to blow up, and then she would move on.

"Well, the event that happened to her in the desert was much like that, and it helped her see where she was going and what she should do. It was really an amazing encounter, and it started with a potentially dangerous experience in a restaurant that was like a mirror of the spiritual confrontation she later experienced. The four of us were there—me, Gene, Paul, and Samantha. Samantha was looking especially good. She had just gotten her dress blacks, and with her long blonde hair, she looked quite striking.

"On the way, we had stopped at a run-down, old-fashioned truck stop, sort of a 'good old boys' redneck hangout. While we waited at the counter for our order, one of the truckers came over and started to come on to Samantha. He asked her: 'What are you hanging around with these other guys for?' Then, he stood there, looking grim and foreboding, as he waited for her to respond. For a few moments, you could almost feel the tenseness in the air, as Gene, Paul, and I watched him intently, ready to act, should a confrontation be necessary. Meanwhile, across the room, the other truckers were watching this guy, as if they were ready to charge across the room, should he give the signal.

"But fortunately, after Samantha didn't say anything, he backed down and walked away. Still, the potential for a dangerous confrontation was there, and Samantha was a little unnerved by the scene. She realized the danger as we did."

Thus, before the group even arrived at her solo site, they felt a sense of potential danger that made everyone feel especially cautious and tense.

"It was like the incident was a possible warning," Michael suggested. "Perhaps a signal that we should be especially alert."

Yet, determined to go ahead with the solo, they drove on. For a time, the summer heat of the desert was especially intense. Then around dusk, there was a cool breeze, and they welcomed the cool of the night. Around 10:30 p.m. they headed to the top of a barren hill overlooking a series of desiccated valleys and hills.

Michael described the scene as "surreal . . . It was like being visitors to another planet, where everything is dry and devoid of life. Yet, as we looked around, every warm breeze, every shadow or cleft in the low alien hills felt filled with life. We could sense the energies and beings that were waiting to show themselves when we descended into the canyon."

The four held a short conference about what would happen that evening, and afterwards, Michael led Samantha down a steep, thin, almost invisible trail towards the bottom. Although Samantha had been nervous about the solo before the trip and even more anxious after the restaurant encounter, now that she was going to start the experience, she was calm, ready for whatever might happen.

Michael walked with her for about half a mile and stopped at a small ledge near the bottom of the hill. He gave her the usual last minute instructions, wished her luck, and returned to where Gene and Paul were sitting to wait for her.

Soon even this waiting time became a dramatic event. As Michael described it, "The wait seemed like hours. As we waited, the breeze gradually began to pick up velocity, until it was difficult to stand; and soon we saw all sorts of figures moving around us, while the canyon below became darker. Some of these figures were barely visible, just whispers of form, but others seemed to be composed of more solid and definite shapes. At one point, when the winds were at their fiercest, we saw a large luminous being, like a solid sheet of phosphorescent energy, fly nearby overhead. It was like having a confrontation with pure power as Samantha was doing her working."

Eventually Michael felt it was time to get Samantha and started down the hil. As he neared the site where he left her, he heard what sounded like her voice calling his name. But he was suspicious that he was being tricked.

"Her voice seemed to be coming from the wrong direction, and it sounded somewhat different than usual. I wasn't sure what was wrong, but I sensed that some entities might be trying to lure me away from her. So I continued on to where I had left her, since years of working in the field have taught me to trust my heart."

However, when he arrived and shined his flashlight at the ledge, he saw only Samantha's hat. Startled, he moved forward cautiously to inspect the area, holding his staff aloft in the event of any danger. "I felt I needed to be ready for anything," he said. "These beings can sometimes be very wily, and if so, you need to be prepared to outwit them."

Finally he spotted her near the edge of a precipice, looking over the ledge, and he was terrified she might go over it, since as he approached, he saw a face floating in the darkness just beyond the edge.

"It looked sinister—it had a pale white deathly look—and it seemed to be calling to her. But then it retreated rapidly as I walked up to her."

Meanwhile, seeing Michael, Samantha began to back away from the ledge towards him. She had been moving towards the ledge, she explained later, because she saw two large evilish faces that were trying to lure her out on the cliff by telling her she could walk on the air. But when Michael appeared, they suddenly went away. At first, Samantha didn't trust her own experience of Michael and hesitated before going to him. Was he just another illusion, she thought.

In turn, Michael wondered if this was really Samantha, since he had nearly been misled by a voice that sounded like hers. Then, he noticed her hat, picked it up, experienced a sudden feeling of release that told him everything was fine now, and he walked up to her. After he led her back, he gave her the first silver bars to acknowledge she had passed the solo, and he heard her report of the event.

"It was incredibly frightening," he said. "And significantly, it was consistent with my experience of what was happening. She said the winds started up suddenly after we left her, and she tried to control them at first by asking them to calm down, though she felt she only managed partial control. Then, she noticed that the ledge she was on appeared to flatten out, and she saw what appeared to be two rocks on this plain. However, as she looked at them, one seemed to vanish and reappear, while the other changed into the disembodied face I saw when I arrived.

"It tried to tempt her," Michael went on. "It beckoned her seductively, urging her to step out over the ledge onto the plain. But, of course, that was just an illusion. She resisted as long as she could, but the pull was strong, and as time went on, her determination began to fade. So she began to back away from the ledge, and she was about to step out onto the plain when I arrived. Thus, she survived what could have been a very dangerous experience."

"Whew. I would have been terrified if that had happened to me," Serge said nervously. "I'm not sure if I could have handled it. I'm always so impulsive. I probably would have jumped right in and thought about whether the plain was real later." He shivered a little contemplating what might have happened.

"Has anyone else had that kind of experience?" I asked.

"No. Nothing as dangerous or dramatic as that." Michael said. "It definitely is a rare experience. But the point is the event was a valuable lesson about harmony and balance, and it occurred because of Samantha's own negative situation which provided the space for those entities to manifest."

"What do you mean?" I said.

"You see, this cliffhanger was a potentially dangerous situation, just like what happened in the restaurant earlier that day. But in both cases, the people on the field trip were able to handle the situation well. They had balance, and as a result, harmony developed out of what could have been an unpleasant, dangerous experience. It's an approach basic to the philosophy of the ODF. We feel everyone should learn how to turn something that might be dangerous or unpleasant, any sort of challenge, into a valuable lesson, a chance for positive growth."

"So why should Samantha's negative situation produce a potentially dangerous experience?" Serge wondered. "If I have a bad day, does that mean I have to watch myself magically, too?" He had been having difficult times recently with his two roommates and was concerned how this might negatively affect his magic.

"Could be," Michael said with an impish smile. "Because our thoughts create our reality. In Samantha's case, she was insecure about herself as a person and her relationship with others. She also used a lot of drugs in a self-destructive way. And she had a love-hate relationship with men, where she both resented them for coming on to her like a sex-object, yet felt dependent on them and liked their attentions, too. So those kinds of conflicts can create explosive situations, when a person presents him or herself to a responsive universe.

"You see, these things and the beings we experience in the world around us are real. Some of them appear because they are manifestations of our own consciousness and energy. If, for instance, you have a negative attitude, you tend to evoke that, which is what happened with Samantha . . ." Michael paused thoughtfully. "Yet, it's okay to bring forth such beings, because once these things surface, you can deal with them. For example, when Samantha asked why these weird things happened, the experience brought up many of the problems she had, but was trying to avoid. Then, as we talked about her problems we were able to show her that she needed more balance in her life, since her lack of balance was so destructive for her. As a result, she resolved to work on that, and really started settling down. She even got involved in a fairly steady relationship with a man she met at the restaurant where she worked.

"So the solo seems like an experience of self-discovery, a lesson," I noted.

Michael nodded in agreement. "Yes, you could say exactly that. You make a magical statement that helps you find out who you are, then take your first steps on the beginning of the path. We believe the solo shows you have achieved a certain level of knowledge on the path, and you should be recognized for it. Then, when you want, you're ready to move on."

"It's scary, and yet it's a real challenge ahead," Serge commented. "I just hope I'll be worthy."

"You are if you make that commitment," Michael said.

He lit up another cigarette, and I concentrated on driving. We were almost back to Berkeley, and there was much to think about. I had begun to open the door on the ODF's vision of another reality. I wanted to learn more.

CHAPTER FIVE

Moving On

On our return, we headed for Micki's, Michael's favorite pizza parlor in Berkeley, to unwind from the intensity of working with another reality and to discuss any questions. The restaurant, noted for its rolicking student beer garden atmosphere, had a large open dining area, with about a dozen long tables and heavy oak beams along the walls and ceilings. A few large beer barrels were scattered here and there for atmosphere, and near them were several hanging plants. A few video games were in the corner, and often the noise of students playing them richocheted around the room. But now, late at night, it was quiet, and only a few tables of students lingered over pizza and beer.

We ordered a large pizza at the counter and returned to our table with salads and a big pitcher of beer.

Michael began our after-trip gathering with a little ceremony to celebrate my passing the solo. He unwrapped a set of small silver lieutenant's bars from a piece of tissue paper and handed them to me.

"They're your bars for passing your grade. You're now a Scout in the Order. Congratulations."

He fastened them on my collar, and told me it was time to get my long-sleeved black shirt, which ODFers consider the most important part of their uniform, since they normally wear it on field trips and on other official occasions, such as the encampment I had been on. He explained I could easily get one at any police or military supply store.

"And now you can start working on your next grade in the Order," Michael said. "You can move ahead as far and as fast as you want to go. We encourage everyone to set their own pace, since everyone is different."

45

Our pizza arrived, and Michael settled back to talk about his own experience in creating a Gateway into the other world, which he had done in passing the Sixth Degree. "Now I'm working on my Seventh," he remarked. "It involves going beyond the Gateway."

I found the conversation a strange juxtaposition. On the one hand, we were surrounded by the mundane reality of being in a pizza parlor with beer barrels, hanging plants, and a scattering of students. Yet at the same time Michael began talking very matter-of-factly about the mystical other world he had been exploring for much of his life, and the very strange experiences he had in this world as a result. Now his report was even more bizarre than anything I had heard before. But he spoke quietly, assuredly, with the conviction that everything he was about to say was true, no matter how weird or strange it sounded.

"My encounter with the Gateway happened the night after we met at the encampment in July. The demonstration you saw was my way of preparing for that. We were testing out the setting, seeing what kind of beings were out there, making sure this was a receptive environment . . .

"And that's important in going through a Gateway, because it's a potentially dangerous experience. You're stepping into an unknown reality and you don't know what might happen. So you need the best possible friendly, receptive environment to do it in to make it more likely to succeed."

Michael took another slice of pizza, and continued. "You see, a Gateway is basically a bridge between this world and the spiritual world. Usually, we meet the spirits and beings who have come through into our world. But in the Gateway experience, we actually go through to the other side ourselves. It's a risky undertaking, and if a person doesn't do it correctly, he's not going to come back . . . So you have to be completely prepared to do this. It takes a true warrior."

Unfortunately, Michael claimed, he hadn't been ready when he made several earlier attempts to create a Gateway, and so he had failed.

"It was a real fizzle in the past," he said. "Gene and I had been trying to get through for months before I finally succeeded. The problem was we knew the possibility of making the Gateway and going over to the other side existed. But we didn't know exactly how to do it or what would be the best way. So we kept making mistakes and having near misses. For example, one time when Gene and I were driving on the desert, we tried imagining a gate, but we just ended up driving through a lot of smoky grey energy. Another time, I visualized a Gateway with a small triangular shape in a wall of energy. But it was only big enough to put a hand through, not big enough for a person to get through, and I couldn't make it any larger."

But then, the night before the encampment, Michael had, he claimed, a conceptual breakthrough, which gave him the understanding he needed to break through to the other side. He was in a Greek coffee shop drinking coffee with his friend Turner, a stage designer in his 40's who belonged to a mystical Christian group. They had been speculating about a number of metaphysical possibilities concerning the meaning of life and death, when Turner suddenly began discussing the Egyptian structure of the soul.

"What he said was amazing," Michael commented. "All at once I realized he was giving me the information I needed to break through the Gateway. Basically, he said that the ancient Egyptians believed the soul comes into the body at birth from the plane of death, and is overlaid in life by the person's *ka* and *ba* which represent the personality and physical part of that person. Then he compared these outer forms to the leaves of an onion, and he suggested that going through a Gateway might be like a near death experience, in which these outer rings were stripped away, so the person could experience the bare essence of the soul.

"I felt that was the breakthrough or vehicle I was looking for. As a result, the first night of the encampment, I decided to check out the energy and get ready, which is what you observed. But what you didn't know is that while I was doing this demonstration, I noticed an image of death standing by himself near a gate, and immediately I realized that that was the symbol of what I must do to go through the Gateway and return. I needed to combine the symbol of death and the Gateway into a synthesis of life and death."

"How do you do that?" I asked.

Michael gazed at me thoughtfully. "Well, it's as if you have a double of yourself that represents you in death, and that double is your soul essence. You separate that essence from yourself and send that across into the other world through the Gateway. Of course, you have to be able to pull back that essence from across the Gateway, or you could die . . . because you could never get back."

"That sounds like it could be dangerous," said Serge. "I'd be concerned about doing something wrong and screwing up."

Michael grabbed another slice of pizza and wolfed it down, and I thought about how incongruous the discussion of death seemed in the midst of this very ordinary and clamorous pizza palace setting.

Michael grinned cockily at Serge and replied, "That's why you need to learn to become a warrior, and you need the courage to do this. At the same time, you have to be extremely careful in going through a Gateway to know what you're doing. Besides, it takes a great deal of intense energy, since there are so many steps you have to concentrate on at the same time. For example, not only do you have to prepare to make the Gateway and get across, but while you're over there in the other world, you still have to take care of the basics of keeping your ritual going properly in this world, so you don't get hurt or have trouble getting back."

"What basics?" I asked.

"Well, keeping the circle in place for one thing. Also, you need to keep out elementals that might interfere with what you are doing. And you have to keep the double of yourself, the soul essence you have sent over, connected with your physical self, so you can get back."

"That's quite a bit to think about," Serge gulped. "I'm not sure I could keep it all straight."

"Well, that's why it takes time to work on this. You can't do it overnight. You have to build up to it with plenty of practice and discipline. We did." Michael took a few swigs of beer to wash down the pizza.

"So how did you create your Gateway?" I queried.

Slowly, carefully, Michael began to explain. First, as he described it, he started off by making the usual circle with his staff, surrounded himself with the usual pentagrams, and called on the elementals around him for assistance as usual. "Then," he added, "I called on the image of death I had seen the previous night, and I visualized death and the Gateway as one. Next, I projected a cord of energy from my belly, the power center, to the Gateway to form a pathway on which I could walk across."

Michael paused, breathing heavily. He looked almost tired from his description of the experience. Then, pressing on, he observed: "Of course, all this took an incredible amount of energy—creating the pathway, walking across it, keeping the Gateway open, and all the while, staying linked to the everyday world. Then, as I walked through the Gateway, the experience was incredibly intense. I noticed a large flat black obsidian plane. But nothing else. It just seemed to hang there in the middle of nothingness, and I had a sense of profound emptiness. It's as if that was death—just blackness, nothingness, a dark and empty plane.

"Yet there was something very compelling about this space. I could feel it enticing me, pulling me, like it didn't want to let go. But I knew I had to pull away, or I'd never get back. So finally, I forced myself to do it and I turned away from this image and returned along the cord I had sent out. Then, when I felt like the double I projected had fully returned to my body, I pulled the cord back in and closed my circle. Afterwards, I collapsed on the ground, totally exhausted. Later I learned this experience had lasted about 20 minutes, but it seemed like hours and I felt all my energy sapped away.

"Really, I felt this incredible feeling of heaviness," Michael explained. "It was like a pile of rocks on top of me, holding me down, and I could feel my heart beating loudly and rapidly. I was almost gasping for breath, and I lay there, wondering if I was going to make it. At the same time, I wanted to tell others about my experience, so at least, if I was going to expire, I could share what had occurred."

"But then you did it. You made it back," Serge put in. He glanced at Michael with a mixture of admiration and awe.

Michael simply grinned with his cocky grin and continued. "Anyway, at this point, Paul and Gene who had been watching, rushed over and as they helped me up, I told them what I had seen. Then, they got me inside to a mattress where I could lie down, and after perhaps a half hour, I felt okay. When I woke up the next morning, I found everything around me much more intense than ever. The colors, the sounds, the birds singing—everything felt suffused with energy, and it was as if I could feel a greater intensity now, because it was in contrast to the empty world I experienced on the other side of the Gateway."

"That's fantastic," said Serge. "I hope I can develop that kind of courage, so I can do that sometime."

"If you're committed to the path you will," Michael said firmly. He took a few more swigs of beer and picked up the last slice of pizza.

"Did your experience affect you in everyday life?" I asked.

Michael eyed me thoughtfully. "Why, yes. Of course. As you gain more control over the spiritual world, you gain more control of yourself. And that's the whole point of all this. You're not just interested in producing mysterious phenomena. You're interested in working with the phenomena you're producing, because it's coming from you. You're manifesting your powers in the physical world. So what you experience is real. You're creating it; it comes from you. And the more powerful you become as a magician, the more you can create—not just in the field, but in your own life as well."

"How?" Serge asked. "What sort of changes can I expect to create? For example, will these techniques help me find a new lover? Or can they help me get back together with my old one? It really hurt me the way he suddenly left."

"Possibly," said Michael, "it depends on how you apply these techniques from the field. Let me explain it this way. There's spiritual control and there's personal control, and they seem to develop together. For example, when my friends and I started experimenting with these things when I first joined the ODF, we often had to run to our car to escape the entities we had created. We would start evoking things—elementals, wolves, owls, other beings, and when they appeared, we didn't know what to do with them. So we ran. But gradually, we developed control, so that's not a problem anymore. We acquired the power to be in charge of the entities we evoke, and so we can call them up or banish them at will. The secret, we learned, is developing the will to attain this power. Then you have to know what to do with it, and it's the same in everyday life.

"For instance, when I found a job I wanted, soon after moving here, I used a projection technique to convince the man to hire me. I did a ritual in which I imagined myself being hired and working on the job, and soon after, I got a job offer. Also, I frequently create a shield of invisibility to protect myself if I'm walking along a potentially dangerous street, and one time when I sensed it would be an especially bad day, I was extra cautious.

"You can't stop doing normal things. But you can learn to be extra alert and resourceful with these techniques. For instance, one time my job as a paramedic took me to a tough part of town and someone shot at me. But he missed. One more step, and I would have been in his line of fire. But my intuition suddenly told me to wait, and I did. So he didn't get me."

Serge complained that he didn't have to worry about a job or evading gunfire. What he was concerned about was relationships. So Michael described some techniques for controlling or influencing relationships with other people. "You can project your energy to get into a person's dream. Or you can direct your will to a person and visualize him doing something you want. For example, try this . . . "

Michael shifted slightly to the right and gazed at the back of a stocky male student in a sweatshirt at a nearby table. In moments, the man paused while holding a slice of pizza to his mouth, looked up, and glanced quickly around the restaurant before taking a bite.

"You see," Michael exulted, "when I projected my energy at the back of his neck, he felt something, and he looked around to see what it was.

"Now, you try." He glanced at Serge and then at me.

In response, Serge and I each picked out someone to stare at for a few minutes. I chose a golden-haired woman in her 20's who was talking animatedly with a man who looked like a football player. Serge selected a thin man in glasses who looked like a professor in a serious discussion. But nothing happened. The two people we selected kept on eating and talking as normal. We gave up and turned back to the table.

"You've got to project harder," Michael admonished us. "You have to get the hang of it. But you'll learn. It just takes practice . . . "

He glanced around the room and continued. "These techniques can also help you feel the things around you more intensely. For example, when someone enters a room," he pointed to four students coming into the restaurant, "if you pay attention, you can feel a subtle energy shift . . . You can also pick up when things are going to happen. And you can sense people from a distance.

"For instance, one evening I was expecting some friends to come over but they were late. It was perhaps an hour or so after they were supposed to arrive and that wasn't like them, so I was concerned. Maybe there was an accident. So I tuned in on their energy on the freeway to see if they had an accident or were on their way, and I picked them up a few miles away. So I knew they were okay. Then, based on where I picked them up, I estimated when they would arrive, and a minute or two before I expected them, I went to the doorway. Just then, they pulled up on the street. 'Were you waiting long for us?' they said at the doorway. But I told them, 'No, I knew when you were coming.'"

"Well, I sometimes have that happen," Serge said. "I think about calling someone and they call. Or I want to meet someone at a party, and without my saying anything, they come over."

"Exactly," Michael said. "These kinds of things happen to people all the time. And sometimes these events might seem like coincidences when they happen only occasionally. But the difference between what happens to most people, and what happens for us is these events happen again and again, and they happen consistently because we learn to get control over the process. In other words, we work on doing something to project the will or express a desire for something, and it happens. Well, that's confirmation. And when it occurs over and over, you know what you're doing works."

Michael finished his beer. "You'll see, as you start working with these techniques. You'll do something, and you'll feel the charge of power when you do. And that's why . . . " He paused and looked at me and Serge intensely. "That's why you have to be responsible in how you use this power. There's a real potential for abuse when you develop this ability for control. So we believe there's a real need for morals and ethics on the warrior's path. You can't go using these techniques to hurt people. Sure, you should do everything you can to protect yourself from others and gain benefits for yourself. But you've got to be ethical, too, and make sure you use these powers to the good . . .

"Some magical groups don't take this responsibility, and when that happens, people can get hurt—and not just the people these magicians are trying to control. For they can seriously hurt themselves, too. That's because when you use these powers irresponsibly, your workings can produce negative energies that come back to hurt you. So you can lose control . . .

"However, as long as you work with these powers responsibly, you have nothing to worry about. You can expect to encounter all sorts of difficulties and obstacles along the warrior path. There are always problems and challenges to overcome when you're seeking knowledge. No one gets this knowledge easily. It's hard work, and you really have to work for it. But if you go at it with a good heart and with a sense of moral commitment, you won't have to worry about making your way more difficult or dangerous, and you won't have the problem of cleaning up all sorts of magical debris."

And with that, Michael ended our magical discussion for the evening. It was late, almost 1 a.m., and Michael felt we had covered enough for the night.

As we stepped out on the street he told us: "Now you've had your first taste of the basics in the field; and now you know the potential risks and dangers. So now you're ready to take the next step if you're willing to go on."

We said that we were, and he said he would contact us about the first ODF class soon.

"You'll see," he said as we parted. "This is only a beginning, and there's so much to learn."

CHAPTER SIX

Seeing and Dreaming

Several weeks after my solo, Michael began his first series of classes in the Bay Area. It was a Saturday evening in late September—coincidentally the date of the Fall Equinox, which many people in the magical community consider a time of new beginnings.

Michael held the classes in his Berkeley apartment, which he had set up for teaching. Trunks and boxes of information lined the sides of the room like file cabinets, and a small blackboard hung on one wall.

Both Serge and Teri were present, plus a new person—Harvey Fox, a chubby computer programmer of 23, who looked like he had gotten over a bad case of acne as a teenager and had a strange intense look in his eyes. As I arrived, Serge, who was dressed in his full black uniform, and Teri, who looked like a 1960's hippie in her rainbow colored serape and levis, were comparing their experiences for the past week. Serge complained he was having problems with his roommate who was not only inconsiderate, but now things had escalated, so his roommate was trying all sorts of subtle forms of sabotage, such as turning on the alarm clock in Serge's room to ring at 3 in the morning. Teri, in turn, griped about her boss, who had caught her making several filing errors, and now wanted her to fix them up on her own time. "It's not fair," she complained. "I don't get paid enough anyway, because they pay all the women in the office less than the men. I'd like to quit if I could, or at least tell them off. But my friends say to cool it. Still I've been thinking about doing a ritual to get a promotion or transfer to another department."

Meanwhile, at the other side of the living room, Harvey, dressed in faded jeans and a T-shirt that said "X-Rated," was bragging to Michael, in official

ODF dress, about the high rank he had attained in another magical group and his extensive knowledge of European ceremonial magic. "Ever since I've been a teenager," he said, "I've always been interested in the occult. It started out when my parents moved to a new town and I was the new kid on the block. So nobody wanted to have much to do with me. Well, I decided to learn magic to show them. And pretty soon that whole high school scene didn't matter, because I was learning to become a powerful magician. I think I must have read just about everything on European ceremonial magic in my local library, and then a few years ago, I joined several magical groups. One of them has the reputation of being into black magic," he grinned with a slight smirk and mentioned a group with a bad reputation in the magical community. "But the other is mainly into white magic and they made me a Sixth Degree, which is almost as high as you can get. Well, I believe you should know both—so you can choose the right magic to use in a given situation. And that's why I'm interested in the ODF. Another type of magic I can use."

Harvey plopped down on the couch, and Michael glanced at him skeptically, not especially impressed by Harvey's bragging.

"Are you sure you can manage being involved in several traditions at once?" Michael asked him.

"Sure," Harvey said with an arrogant smirk. "It'll be a breeze."

Michael wasn't so sure, and later he told me he was skeptical of Harvey making it, because he so often rubbed people the wrong way with his arrogance. Also, Harvey tended to be a fairly lonely person, who had difficulty making friends, though he came from a very social wealthy business family. Now, after several years of studying engineering in college, he lived at home, and spent most of his free time alone in fairly esoteric pursuits—studying the occult, playing tactical war games, and reading science fiction. But Michael had decided to give him a chance because "He was having so many difficulties fitting in with people, and I learned what it was like to be different from others when I was a teenager. So I wanted to help Harvey find a place for himself if I could."

Now it was time for the class, and at a few minutes after 8 p.m. Michael strode over to the blackboard to begin. Everyone pulled their chairs around into a circle and listened intently.

"We'll be talking about seeing and dreaming tonight," he announced, "since they're so basic to everything else we do in the Order."

He placed two wicker chairs facing each other in the center of the room.

"We'll start with the seeing exercises. You should start practicing these regularly."

I had previously experienced this exercise briefly, when Michael had led

Teri and myself on our first venture into the field. Now he wanted us to learn to work with this process in a systematic way.

"Incredible things can happen when you learn to see," he said. "Besides being able to see the auras of things in the field, you'll develop new insights into other people. You'll be able to see into their essence and discover who they really are."

Michael sat down in one of the wicker chairs and asked Teri to sit across from him so he could demonstrate. Meanwhile, Serge set up a Nikon camera on a small tripod, so he could capture on film anything special that happened.

Michael asked Teri to get comfortable, and following his example, she planted her feet firmly on the ground and let her arms hang comfortably at her sides, while holding her head erect.

"Now," Michael told her, "look directly at my forehead. But let your eyes go out of focus, as I showed you in the field. Then whenever you see anything unusual happen, raise your finger, so the others can see if they notice anything unusual happening and Serge can take a picture. We'll see if we can get anything unusual on film."

Teri nodded and shifted around slightly to get comfortable. "We'll do the exercise for 10 minutes," Michael said, and I volunteered to keep time.

Serge dimmed the lights so the apartment looked like it was illuminated by a few small lanterns, and the exercise began. Seated across from each other, Michael and Teri gazed at each other motionlessly.

Now and then as I watched, my image of them faded in and out of focus, and from time to time, I noticed that Michael's shadow on the wall seemed to expand and contract. A few times, Teri lifted her index finger briefly and Serge snapped a picture.

So far I hadn't seen anything especially out of the ordinary—nothing which I couldn't explain by my own vision getting tired from staring at the same space for several minutes. Yet, when I looked at my watch, I got a sensation of time standing still. It was as if the minutes stretched into hours, so the exercise seemed to go on forever.

I kept glancing at my watch, thinking surely the experience must be over and not wanting to let it go on longer than requested. However, each time I looked, the watch counter had barely moved, and I had an eerie feeling that my perception of time had changed.

Meanwhile, Teri and Michael continued to gaze firmly ahead at each other, like two motionless statues. Serge snapped a few more pictures, and finally the 10 minutes ended.

"Time," I called out, and Teri and Michael turned away from each other.

Michael shifted in his chair to face us, "Well, that certainly seemed like an eternity." He turned back to Teri. "What did you experience?"

Quietly, Teri described what happened the three times she raised her finger. With each description, Michael described his simultaneous visualizations and psychic projections and commented on the parallels between what he did and what she reported seeing. Then, when Serge reported on his observations, Michael pointed out the parallels, too.

"The first time," Teri began, "I felt a red energy radiating around the room. Then, for a moment, I had the experience of your clothes disappearing from you, and your body was surrounded by a bright greenish aura of energy."

Serge commented: "I noticed a new shadow on the wall in front of your chest for a few moments, although there seemed to be nothing different about your body to cause it."

Michael smiled impishly on hearing this report. "Interesting . . . interesting. That's what I usually see when we do these exercise—the room radiating red energy. It's like the energy of these exercises that produces that glow." Then, turning to Serge, he remarked: "It's interesting you should see my shadow, because I was experimenting with it, and you can do this, too. I visualized it moving around me; and I shifted it up and down and expanded it in and out. What I was doing is like changing the shape of the aura around you, except you're doing it with the shadow you project."

He turned back to Teri. "So what else did you experience?"

"Well, I felt my bodily responses and perceptions were slowing down at the same time that your body motions seemed slower. And then I noticed my responses started speeding up again, and you seemed to do that, too."

Again, Michael grinned broadly. "Yes, exactly. I was trying to raise and lower your respiration. I did this by radiating my energy at you from my sternum, which is the power center. It's like using a battery with a light. I focused on sending out more energy to speed you up; then I concentrated on projecting less energy to slow you down."

Finally, Teri reported: "I saw your facial features change. For a moment, you seemed to disappear, and afterwards I saw your mouth and nose blend together and become a snout."

"Yes. Yes. Very good," Michael said. "What I was doing then was projecting my face onto yours, and I was also thinking of the image of the snout . . . You see . . . " He stood up to continue, "What you do psychically can effect what the other person sees. You can play with thought projections, and the visualizations become real. If I imagine what I am thinking about strongly enough, she'll see it."

"Well, I didn't see anything," Harvey huffed.

"That's often normal," Michael replied. "Not everyone can see easily when they start working with these methods."

Thus, Michael described a visualization technique he used to help people see. "It's designed to intensify the experience, and it really helps when someone is new or having trouble seeing. There are three ways to do it. I imagine myself split in two, imagine the other person split this way, or I imagine a big wall of energy between the two of us, and cut a big hole or Gateway in this wall. The idea of these visualizations is to disrupt the other person's energy or intensify what you are projecting so they can see things. To make a split, I visualize a blade coming down through the top of the head, splitting me or the other person apart into two. Or I see a knife appearing to cut open the Gateway. After you imagine this happening four to six times, the other person will begin to see, which is what happened with Teri. She saw me disappear and reappear again."

"Why didn't you tell us this before the exercise?" Harvey grumped.

"Because you need to discover what you need to learn for yourself."

"How does this more intense seeing happen?" I asked.

"Well," Michael continued, "when you use this splitting process on yourself, you open yourself up so your vital energy rises up in you and goes out to the other person through the Gateway you have created. I know when I do this, I feel something wash over me like a wave, and I feel a cool breeze of energy sweep over my face. Then, I experience that energy going out to the person. Or when I visualize the other person splitting up, I'm breaking up their personal reality which stands as a defense against them seeing. That happens since some people put up resistances to seeing into another reality, because it can be really frightening to learn the mundane world isn't all it seems.

"As for the third option of creating a Gateway. That's a little more difficult, so I don't do it as much, because it involves dealing with three-dimensional space. But essentially," Michael looked back at Teri intently, "when I use it, I work on creating a cloud-like form of intense energy between us like I'm doing now. As we look at each other, that energy forms. But, instead of letting that energy dissipate around the room, I'm focusing on making it stay together in a ball or wall between us. In fact, you can see things fogging up right now. So now, I'm imagining a knife cutting a clear channel through this energy, so we can both look right through it and see."

Meanwhile, as Michael demonstrated, Serge clicked away on his camera.

Then, the demonstration finished, Michael signalled for Serge to stop taking pictures. "Well, it'll be interesting to see if the camera picked up any of that," he told Serge.

Michael then pointed out that we each had our own personal colors or energy vibration, and others could tune into this with the seeing technique. He cited Teri's first perception of the aura around him as an example.

"Remember when Teri was seeing the light around me. She said it was green. Well, that happens to be one of my colors. The other is a brilliant purple, almost a white violet. We all have our personal colors, and when you're tuned into someone else, you'll see the color of their universe. That's why when Teri was looking at me, she saw a lot of green."

Michael sat down again across from Teri. "On the other hand, when I was looking at Teri, I saw her colors. I observed lots of bluish grays and some yellows. So when you sit with a person, you can tune right into them, and their colors will tell you a lot about them. When you first start looking, you may see a lot of superficial changes, such as movements in their aura. You may see their face go invisible, too. For example, a few times I've suddenly experienced seeing the back of a person's shirt and reading the label on his collar. So, as you keep looking, you can really sense who a person is and how they feel from the color of their energy.

"In fact, when you get really good . . . " Michael stood up to emphasize the point, "you can pick up the colors of someone who has been working magic in the area. You can see or sense the colors that are there. It's like the person has left his own personal calling card. So whenever you do magic anywhere, it's like leaving a fingerprint of you."

"How can you tell what your own colors are?" I asked.

"It's what you seen when your eyes are stressed. It's the first reaction you get when you see some visual phenomena, such as gazing into a very bright light. It's very spontaneous."

I glanced at the light next to the couch, then gazed away. I closed my eyes, and noticed a violet red afterimage that lingered on, as it danced around in my closed eyes.

I mentioned this and Michael recommended, "Try doing this a few times to see if you continue to get the same visual effect." He walked over to the side of the room abruptly. "Look, let's do an experiment."

He leaned down and pulled out a large fishing tackle box from under a shelf, rummaged about in it briefly, and pulled out a thin small flashlight.

"Sit here and I'll show you."

He lined up two chairs next to each other, and asked Teri and me to sit in them and close our eyes. He explained that he would tap on one of our eyebrows and shine his flashlight at it. When he did, we should open that eye, and gaze at the light. Then, he would turn it off, and we should notice the afterimage.

When he did this, I noticed the red violet image again, and Teri reported a violet and blue image.

"So, you see, you saw the color I saw around you," he told Teri. "And you saw the same color again when you looked at the light," he told me. "So that's a pretty good indication those are your colors. Though experiment for awhile. See if the same colors keep coming up consistently, and eventually, you'll be certain of your resonant colors. They're the colors that represent you. Once you know them, you can use them to work magic in the field.

"For example, say you're just meeting someone or you want to tune in on them when they're someplace else. At first, as you mentally come into their air space, you'll notice a whitish, yellowish light around them, which makes up their inner aura. Then, around their outer shell, you can pick up their resonant colors, which will help you experience who the person really is. You're gaining this insight because this technique enables you to deal with people as energies, rather than just bodies. As a result, when you see these colors, you're picking up the energies which people give off.

"You can use this technique to feel better, too. Suppose you have an emotional crisis. You can use your colors to get back your strength. To do this, gather your resonant colors around you and feel their strength radiating out to you. Also, you can increase your own resonance by creating a personal coat of arms with your colors . . . And be aware that you're radiating out your own colors when you do magical workings. For example, when I do workings, I often see an intense green energy coming out of a voilet field all around me."

"Is it like the energy radiating out of our staff of other power objects?" Serge asked. He held up his own staff and gazed at its tip.

"No. It's very different. Usually the energy you see radiating out of these power tools is a bluish white or a dark amber color, which is a working color. The color will be pretty much the same for everyone, though it depends on the intensity of the energy you're putting out. The colors get brighter and deeper the more energy involved. But that's different than your resonant color. That's the color that represents you."

We took a brief break for pizza at Micki's, and when we returned, Michael began talking about dreaming. He asked us to each start keeping a dream log to become more aware of our dreams. Then, he told us: "Report back every few weeks on how your dreams are changing—or perhaps, more accurately, how you are changing them. You need to become more aware of your dreams," he explained, "because all shamanistic cultures have used active dreaming. These are states of consciousness where the person experiences reality unbounded by the normal limits of the body. Most people see dreams as a kind of fantasy play. But dreams can be much more than simply reflecting on your past experiences and recombining your visions in new ways. They can be very real, and you can use your dreams to affect and change things in everyday life."

Michael wrote the phrase: "share dreams" on the blackboard and underlined it. "For example, in our experiments in L.A. we've found it's possible to share the same dreams. You can meet someone in a dream and experience a spontaneous event. Then, when you share what happened, you'll discover you both experienced pretty much the same thing. It's like agreeing to see someone on the street. We both meet, and later we can agree on what happened there. Similarly, dreams are just another form of ongoing reality, so it's possible to have shared interactions with people in dreams, and we can manipulate what happens with them in the dream. Then this can influence how you relate in everyday life.

Michael paused to sense our reactions, and for a moment, everyone was very quiet, pondering what he had said. Aware of our uncertainty, Michael interrupted the silence. "Yeah, I know these ideas may sound crazy and unusual. They may contradict your traditional beliefs about dreams and the way reality works. But it's true. Let me give you a few examples. For instance, one time when I was teaching in Los Angeles, a student dreamt about being in his friend's kitchen, and he knocked over a vase in his dream. When he woke up, he felt a little spooked by the dream, like maybe this event really happened in real life, as well, and he called his friend and asked him to go into the kitchen and check. When he did, he discovered the vase was actually broken. Now, I know, there are all sorts of explanations for why the vase might break. Maybe the wind could have knocked it off the table. But what shows the power of the dream is the man felt certain the vase was broken, and he felt this certainty so intensely that he called his friend to make sure."

Michael also urged us to pay attention to dream coincidences as another example of the close connection between dreams and everyday reality. "Such dreams are very common. You dream about someone, and the person suddenly calls. Or a dream turns out to be true. For instance, one of my students in L.A. dreamt about an elderly uncle who wasn't too well. He saw his uncle riding on a horse beside him and several friends in the desert, when suddenly his uncle's horse stumbled and he fell on the ground. When he tried to help his uncle in the dream, he found his uncle had broken his hip. Then, the next day, the student got a call from the hospital to say his uncle had fallen in his kitchen and was now in the hospital. In another case, a student dreamt that her sister, who was in bad health and living in another state, was sick, and she called to express her concern. The sister told her not to worry, that everything was okay. However, soon after the woman woke up, she got a call from a relative saying her sister had died. It's those kind of stories which let us know our dreams are talking to us, sometimes to give us important information."

"I know, my dreams are always talking to me," said Teri. "But what I don't understand is how do we get these communications in our dreams? How do our dreams acquire this information to give us?"

"Well, basically what happens is the person you're dreaming about has had a bad experience in real life, such as an injury, and in your dream, he or she is symbolically injured to reflect this real life injury. You're simply being very sensitive to this experience, so you're picking up what happened unconsciously and then you're translating your perceptions of real life events into the language of dreams." Michael wrote the words: "seeing the future" and "personal control" on the blackboard and continued.

"Another common type of dreaming we work with is precognitive dreaming. You dream about something that hasn't happened yet, and afterwards it happens. For instance, I've heard at least 50 stories like this. A student tells me he dreamt about a friend he hadn't spoken to in years, and in the dream he asks his friend to call or write soon. Then, about six weeks later, he gets a letter from his friend saying the friend was recently thinking about him and decided to get back in touch.

"Also, you can make things happen in everyday life with your dreams. Suppose you can't work things out with someone on a conscious level. Sometimes you can create a dream about the situation to resolve the problem. For example, one friend had a boss who introduced a new policy at work which my friend didn't agree with, and the other employees were upset by it, too. My friend told his boss about these reactions, but his boss was determined to institute the policy anyway. But my friend was convinced he should chance it, so over the next few nights, he directed himself to dream of his employer, and finally he had a dream in which he talked to his boss and got him to see things his way, which you can do in your dream, since you control it. Then, when my friend went to work the next day, he discovered his boss had changed his mind and was willing to listen and reconsider his policy."

"What about other explanations?" I asked, not quite ready to give up my traditional views about dreams being reflections of wishes and fears, leading me to search for more everyday explanations.

Michael quickly replied to support his claim for active dreaming. "Sure, there could be other possibilities, such as the dream and the events occurring independently by chance. But after you hear these stories again and again, and you personally direct your own dream by deciding what you want and ordering up a dream to create it, you'll become convinced you can shape your reality with your dreams."

Michael glanced around the room to make sure we were still with him and offered a few more suggestions on how to use dreaming.

"Sometimes it's helpful to get information from dreams about the people you know or care about. You can either pick up an experience they have had; or they can get a message to you, and you become aware of it in your dreams. But, by the same token, people you don't want in your dreams can invade them, and the occurrence can be unpleasant. For instance, this happened to me a few years ago in L.A. I noticed I was starting to have nightmares about bad things happening to me — like the gas being turned off during a freezing winter or finding a burglar rummaging through my possessions. I hadn't had a nightmare since I was thirteen, and every night for a week, I experienced one."

"Couldn't you get rid of it by willing these things to go away?" Serge asked.

"Yes, if it was an ordinary nightmare which I created. But as I thought about it, I had a feeling that someone else who understood the dreaming process did this, and gradually I zeroed in on a group of magicians in L.A. who didn't like some of the techniques used in the ODF. They were doing some rituals to send me bad dreams. I discovered this by using astral projection to project myself mentally into the astral plane to see if any negative forces were around me, and when I encountered them, I tracked them back to their original source, which turned out to be someone I knew very well in this magical group. I went to see him about the situation and learned he was angry because of some of my spiritual views. Also he enjoyed the rush of power he experienced in affecting my dreams.

"I asked him to stop, but since he wouldn't, I did a ritual to defeat him. I went into the desert with Gene and Paul, and I did a ritual to return what he was sending out back to him. It wasn't the usual sort of ritual I do, since I prefer to work with the more friendly, healing spirits of nature. But this situation called for a strong negative response to fight fire with fire. Thus, after I found a suitable open field to work in, I erected an especially strong protective circle around myself and used very ancient incantations to get the response of the darkest, most sinister elemental beings. As in most magical conflicts, they already knew this problem was brewing, and they were already waiting on the astral plane until one of the people involved in the conflict called on them to act.

"In any case, I called on them first, and they appeared near my circle as dark humanoid-like shapes. When they came over, they brought a distinct chill in the air and were surrounded by a sulphur-like smell. I explained the problem, which they already knew about, and I asked them to frighten the man who was sending me the bad dreams, so he would no longer pursue me in my sleep and the beings agreed. Then, I sent them off into the night to deal with this man, and as they left to confront him, I saw an explosion of black light followed by birds flying into the sky.

"After this, I took down the circle and returned to Paul and Gene. They felt confident the ritual would be effective and said I smelt like sulphur, which further confirmed my own experience. A few days later, after we returned to L.A., the nightmares disappeared, and soon after I learned from a mutual friend that the man bothering me had been attacked in his waking consciousness by the evil beings he created. It happened when he was meditating in his own temple. Suddenly, he saw a monster-like apparition enter the room and stand gazing at him. He realized at once that I had sent this being, and as a result, he abandoned further attempts at influencing my dreams.

"So you see," Michael concluded, "you really have a lot of power to control your own dreams and the dreams of others. Most people aren't aware we have these abilities, but these techniques work because there's an intersection between what happens in a dream and real life, and we can shape this interaction process by our own actions. We've come to these conclusions in the ODF after years of reading about shamanic dream states and experimenting, and we see dreaming as an important avenue for working magic. Dreams don't have to just happen to us, for we can direct them, control them, and use them for working magic."

Harvey interrupted with a comment. "Good. I know exactly who I'd like to get back at in my next dream. And there's this woman who won't give me the time of day. Maybe I could get her to pay attention to me."

Michael glared quickly at Harvey. "That's not exactly the best use of this technique."

Then, he went over to the blackboard and drew a small stick-like figure with the outline of a ghost next to it. "Now put anything you may already believe about dreaming on a shelf and I'll explain why this works . . . You might look at it this way. There's the real self . . . " he pointed to the stick figure, ". . . and there's the dream self," he pointed to the ghost. "Usually our dream self remains in the world of our dreams. But it can enter into everyday life, too. When that happens, other people may think they have seen you when your physical body is somewhere else, because you are projecting your dream body into everyday consciousness and it appears very real. That's because this dream self can become visible to some people when it enters normal reality, so you get the phenomena of the double. In other words, our dream body becomes the vehicle on which we travel. Usually, we move on it through our dreams, but when it intrudes on our everyday space, that's when ordinary people may see it.

"In fact," Michael went on, "our conventional reality is no more or less valid than any dream. And we've found working magic in the field very much like a dream. We visualize another reality, project our thoughts to create Gateways, use our imagination to call forth spirits and beings—and these manifest as a physical reality. It's the same with the dream.

"You might think of it this way. There are numerous layers of reality in the world, all existing simultaneously. Most people aren't aware of these different places, because they're tuned into the usual everyday level. But as you use different faculties and change your level of being, you become aware of these levels. You realize reality is unboundaried, and it depends upon your perceptions what you see.

"For instance, if you can tune in on it, you'll experience several different types of energies existing in this room. It's like there are several different worlds in contact, and they're overlapping with each other at the same time. There's the physical reality we're accustomed to. And there's the level of energy where you can experience cosmic rays, auras, and spiritual beings. All this energy comes from one underlying source. You might imagine it streaming out from a single pinpoint of light into hundreds of shapes and forms. However, as this energy source becomes heavier and more diffuse, material existence occurs, and we see what we usually do.

"So you can think of dreams as existing on one of these levels. You can move your consciousness there and operate from that level. Then, because of this shift, you can use the dream to influence what happens in your waking space."

Michael circled around the room watching us, making sure we were still understanding him. When he saw we were listening and waiting, he went on.

"People can do a lot with dreams. Even if you don't try to control your dreams consciously, you can have some effect. It's like the domino effect, such as when you dream about a person, and he calls. That happens again and again, and the more it does, the more sure you can be about this intersection of dream and ordinary realities. It may be you picked up that the person was going to call you. Or perhaps your dream helped to prod that person to call."

"What about coincidence?" Teri asked. "What if you were both thinking about each other at the same time, and that led you to have the dream and the other person to call?"

"Sure, that can happen. But in the cases I'm talking about, there's a conscious willing going on. It's more than coincidence. When you actually see someone's double outside of a dream, you know you didn't just imagine it. Likewise, when you plan to have the same dream with someone and it happens, you know that's not a coincidence either. Look, let me give you some more examples."

Michael hunched over the back of the chair, much like a tiger getting ready to leap, and continued.

"One incident happened when I was living in an apartment building in

L.A. One day I was painting my own apartment, and the apartment across the way was unoccupied. Then, suddenly, I saw one of my students who lives upstairs looking at me from the window of this unoccupied apartment. I wondered why she was there and went to check. She wasn't in the apartment where I saw her. But when I knocked on the door where she lives, she answered the door wearing a bathrobe and told me I had just woken her up. She had been in bed asleep, and had just had a dream in which she was looking out of a window.

"A similar event happened to a friend. He was sleeping in bed, when he heard a noise in the kitchen and went to investigate. He saw his wife near the kitchen sink, and as he approached her, she left the sink and disappeared around the corner. He followed her, but when he turned the corner, she wasn't there, and there was no place she could have gone, since the hall doors were closed. Then, when he went upstairs, he found her in their room asleep in bed.

"So, people experience these kind of things where they see psychic doubles again and again while they're in a state of normal waking consciousness. I know I was certainly awake when I was painting the house. There was paint around me, brushes, a half-painted wall. So I know I wasn't dreaming. And the man in the kitchen was wide awake, too. He left a handprint on the refrigerator that showed this. Likewise, when we hear other stories, we look for confirming evidence to be sure the person reporting the incident isn't dreaming. As a result, we know these things really happen.

"They happen because the mind of the dreamer can project thoughts which are potentially visible to waking people. The dreamer can do this because thoughts are things; so that mental energy can manifest as something real in the physical world. Thus, there's really no difference between everyday reality and the dream. They're both aspects of the same reality. Only sleep separates the waking and dream reality. But both are equally real—and that means the waking person can enter the sleeping person's dream space, too. It works both ways."

Just then Harvey broke into Michael's presentation cackling: "That sounds ideal. I know a few women's dream spaces I'd like to enter." For a few moments there was absolute silence in the room as everyone glared at Harvey for interrupting with such an off-the-wall sexist comment.

Then Michael, pretending to ignore Harvey's comment, gave a few more examples to illustrate. "Another L.A. friend, Jerry, had a very successful dream experiment with me when he said he would concentrate on having a dream that night, and I told him I would try to drop into it to see what he was dreaming. We also agreed to take notes. In the morning we compared what we wrote and found we had reported pretty much the same thing. Jerry dreamt about being on a beach and walking along it, and I saw him swimming near the shore.

"Another student, Susan, wanted to try dreaming with me, and we agreed to meet in a forest in her dream. In the morning, she claimed she saw me there as we planned.

"But most of all, I saw the power of dreams turning into reality when I dreamt of meeting an Indian sorcerer in L.A. The dream was so powerful that I drew a picture of the Indian. Later that day, a Mexican who was working nearby stopped at the house, and as we talked, the Mexican mentioned he had a friend who was a powerful healer. So of course I wanted to meet him, and a few days later, when I did, I discovered that this healer not only looked exactly like the Indian sorcerer in my dreams, but he was also aware that I had the dream. And he knew that because our dreams are real, and he was sensitive enough to pick up my dreams.

"Then, too, you can use your dreams to communicate with other people. For example, my friend, Mark, got in touch with someone through a dream. He wanted to locate a friend who had borrowed his book, so he had a dream about getting it back, and one day later, the man with the book called, saying he had the strangest dream. He dreamt Mark asked him to call and left a phone number. He felt really weird after the dream, like it was a special signal to him, so he wanted to call to share his dream.

"In short," Michael said with finality, "I think the evidence is pretty conclusive in showing our dreams are real. So we treat them accordingly in the ODF and use them for magical purposes. But you have to understand, I'm not talking about any dreams. We all have random dreams, where we turn over the events of the day that have psychological meaning for us. No, what I'm talking about here are special dreams, which take on their own reality and become a vehicle for magic."

Teri broke in. "So how do you know which are ordinary dreams and which are special dreams? I have lots of dreams. How do I tell the difference?"

"You just know," Michael said. "These dreams have a special symbolic quality; a special compelling power, so you can simply feel it.

"Also, these special dreams show us that dreaming while we're asleep and when we're awake are the same. So when we're in the field doing magic, we're using the same meditative dreaming processes to create the magical circle and get in touch with any entities out there. For instance, creating a Gateway is like having a waking dream. It's the same process. We're projecting our thought forms whether we're asleep or awake to create something tangible and different in the world around us.

"Which means . . . " Michael made a few circuits around the room as he talked, " . . . we have to be concerned about the matter of ethics and privacy when we dream." He gave Harvey a hard look as a result of Harvey's earlier comments, and went on. "That's because when you get good at magic you can start invading other people's dreaming and waking space. Or alternatively, other people can invade your space when they're doing magic or dreaming. Now, I don't like my privacy invaded, and other people don't either. So, if you're not careful, you can end up in fights and get hurt on a real or psychic level, because people can see you magically invading their space; or they can sense it's you."

To illustrate, Michael described a few incidents where he invaded someone else's privacy in a dream and had negative results.

"Once, before I knew any better, I used a dream to spy on a teacher I knew, and I made the mistake of telling him what I learned about him in my dream. I dreamt he was fooling around with a student, which is a real no-no for teachers, and the next day, I went up to him and told him: 'I know you've been at least dreaming about fooling around with this girl,' and he looked like he wanted to cream me for being aware of this. I had pegged him accurately in my dream, and he disliked me afterward as a result. So the knowledge I gained from dreaming wasn't worth it, and I realized the problems that can result when you learn things you shouldn't about someone else through your dreams.

"Another time, I thought I'd chase someone in my dream, and when I woke up, I saw him standing there at the foot of my bed, looking really annoyed. It was just his double—a projection of his real self. But I felt this was a warning—telling me if I didn't stop doing what I was doing, he would come after me for real.

"So you see," Michael said, sitting down and folding his arms in front of him, "the best rule is to be respectful of others when you dream and mind your own business. You don't go bursting in on people's privacy in real life; so you shouldn't do this when you dream. Instead, it works better when you get permission to contact someone in his dream space, or if you set up an arrangement to meet in a dream. Another good possibility is to use dreaming to get some basic information about someone. For example, sometimes I dream about a person to get a sense of where they're at. But I don't go beyond that to avoid stepping on people's space. For if you do, you'll find out they can come back at you in some way—either psychically or in the real world. It's like anything in life—you put out negative energy, you do something to hurt someone, and you'll get that back."

Now, having explained the basic principles of using magical dreaming, Michael wanted to show us how to develop these abilities. He wrote the words: "Conscious Lucid Dream" on the blackboard and announced:

"That's the kind of dreaming you want to develop. You want to be aware when you are dreaming, so you can guide and control your dream. To do this, you need to become aware of your own consciousness. Then, if you want, you can decide what to dream about and can change the direction and content of your dream.

"However, it takes time to develop this skill. Start with first things first. The first step to remembering your dreams is paying more attention to them. Think about wanting to dream before you go to sleep. Then, when you wake up, notice if you had any dreams. If you do, write them down."

Michael continued, "The next step is to be awake in your dreams. Then, you can influence what happens in your dream, and by extension, what happens in the real world."

"How can you tell your dream is really having an effect?" I asked.

"Easy," Michael said and he recommended we use some experiments to verify our attempts to direct our dreams. "Two of you could decide to meet one night in your dreams. Then, the next day compare notes to see if you have similar experiences. Or maybe you could decide to dream about something which you can verify independently later. For instance, try dreaming about driving along the freeway and look for crack-ups. Then, see if there is any report of an accident in the next day or two."

Michael also advised us to look for correspondences between any dreams we had without trying to control them and other events in our lives. "These dreams are just accidental, but you may find they're telling you something if you look. You might also try projecting yourselves into someone else's dreams while you're awake, and he or she is sleeping."

Michael claimed he used this projection technique once with very dramatic success at a magic encampment in Los Angeles. "It was a real reconfirmation that I could affect other people's dreams. There were about 45 people at the encampment, and everyone was asleep. I went up to the top of a hill and visualized an eagle soaring about and entering the dreams of the people below. Then, feeling I had done this effectively, I went down and knocked on a friend's camper to wake him up and see what he was dreaming about. He woke up groggily and wasn't particularly delighted to see me. 'What are you waking me up for? It's three in the morning,' he said. When I asked him what he was dreaming about, he told me: 'A dove flying around; now let me go back to sleep.' I felt delighted that my experiment was confirmed since I had been thinking about a flying bird, too; and later, when I heard others talk about their experiences that night, many of them also described dreams with birds."

Michael jumped up, slapping his hands together with a sense of finality, as if he felt he had proved his case.

But Teri, who often liked to be critical just to play devil's advocate and show off what she knew, brought Michael up short when she piped up, "Yes, but I thought you said it wasn't right to go into other people's dreams without their permission. Didn't you just do that? You talked about the problem of invading people's privacy and the question of ethics."

Michael hesitated for a moment. "Yes, of course, that's true, generally. And my experience with the teacher shows the possible problems when you don't use good judgment. But at other times, it may be appropriate to go in, such as to help someone or to handle some situation which will have positive results. For instance, suppose someone's ill. You might go into their dreams to influence them to get better. Or if you are having a conflict with someone, this could be a way to get them to stop.

"For instance, one time, some people kept showing up in my dreams, and when they did the dream turned unpleasant. I finally confronted them about this, and they said they were doing this because they didn't like some of my ideas, and they wanted to make things more difficult for me and perhaps change my way of thinking. It was their way of trying to undermine and manipulate me. But I caught them at it, and they admitted it, though they didn't agree to stop. As a result, I had a conscious dream myself, in which I fought with them in hand-to-hand combat and finally overwhelmed them. After that, they stopped doing what they had been doing, and my bad dreams stopped. So that's the sort of situation where a dream invasion is quite ethical. You're doing it to protect yourself."

Michael returned to the blackboard to describe some useful techniques.

"First, start keeping a dream log," he recommended. "Record whatever you dream, and it'll help you pay attention to your dreams, and you'll remember them better, too . . .

"Secondly, use wish-fulfillment. During the day or before you go to bed, say to yourself several times, 'I'd like to have this dream,' and describe to yourself what you want this to be about. Also, when you're doing your seeing exercises, this is a good time to formulate and affirm what you want to dream about. Just say to yourself in a firm directed way: 'I choose to have a consciously-controlled dream about this particular experience, and I choose to remember it." Also, tell yourself: 'I will wake up at the end of the experience and record my dream.'

"Then, for recording, I like using a tape recorder, since I find that easier than waking myself up to write something. Though use a notebook if you prefer. In either case, there's one main drawback to waking yourself up to record your dream; the experience might be so intense, you could be awake all night. But eventually, you'll strike a balance, so you can wake yourself up just enough to write up your dream; then you'll go back to sleep right away."

Finally, Michael had some recommendations about how to give ourselves suggestions on what to dream about.

"The most powerful time to influence your dreams is right before you drift off to sleep. This is because as we relax, we gradually shut our bodies down, and soon we get into a hypnogogic imagery state, where we experience all sorts of images. You may feel you're sinking or rising; you may feel you're floating free of your body. It's a little like being in a neutral space between consciousness and unconsciousness, where you're consciously aware that you're drifting into unconsciousness. If you keep on drifting, you'll drop off to sleep. But if you take advantage of this moment when you're still lucid, that's when you can do important magical work. This is because now, if you're lucid enough, you can make a specific request of what you want to dream about, and at this time, you're most powerfully able to influence your unconsciousness, because you're right on the edge of it.

"However," Michael cautioned, "this is also one of the most difficult times to give instructions, because the pull of the unconsciousness is so irresistible, and the hypnogogic imagery can easily lull you to sleep. So there's a tendency to lose this chance. Thus, you need to use your will power to stay awake in the process of going to sleep. You need enough conscious control to exercise your will, so you can give the command to shape the content of your dream. Then you can relax and have the experience.

"And that's why seeing is so important. You need it to quiet your mind and be aware of your mental processes, so you know where you are on the way to falling asleep and can open the way to exercising your will."

"That sounds like it could be fairly complicated," Teri put in. "I have enough trouble just trying to keep things straight at the office and remember what I'm supposed to do when. I'm not real good when it comes to being disciplined and organized."

"Well, it may be a little complex at first," Michael agreed. "But as you work at it, you'll get the hang of it. It's like everything in life and magic. You've got to practice to get any good."

Then, Michael continued with an explanation of how we should use our aware consciousness to observe our dream.

"Once you're in your dream, look at your surroundings or any objects in your dream until they become solid. Often, when you first start looking, you may find that objects suddenly vanish or alter their shape. But by looking at them till they become solid, that helps solidify your dream. . . . Also, when you're in your dream, look around and remind yourself you're awake in your dream. Then, continue looking at different objects to make them more solid. If you see something changing, look back at it again to keep it firm. And don't settle for anything less. For example, if you see a doorknob in your dream and reach for it, it should be cold, hard, and metallic. If it isn't, reach for it again to re-experience it more fully. Finally, will yourself to wake up after you have completed the dream, so you can remember it and write it down."

The class over, we adjourned to Micki's Pizza Parlor, where we had many questions to discuss.

CHAPTER SEVEN

Questions and Answers

After we ordered and sat down with our pizzas and beer, Harvey erupted with the first of our many questions.

He wanted to know about the dream persona, since he was already struggling to come to terms with how others perceived and related to him in everyday life. "Do you have the same personality in your dreams or can you be different? And if you change your dream personality, can this change your personality in everyday life?" He said the words with a certain intense wistfulness, as if he hoped that if he could change, maybe his relationships with others would be better; maybe people would like him more; maybe he could have better luck with women. He didn't say these things at the time, but as I got to know Harvey better, I realized that this concern about getting along better with others was never very far from his mind. He constantly kept trying, but never seemed to know how to do it exactly right.

Michael, sensing Harvey's inner struggle, was encouraging. "Sure, you can change. You can use your dreams to become more the person you want to be. Also, you can gain more insights into who you are now, and what other people are really like. For example, a person can seem quite nice and quiet on the surface. But in dreams, that person's double can be quite tough. The difference is because your deeper dream self is coming out. In turn, you can decide if you like that inner self, and then work on making it the outer you."

"But what if you don't like it?" Harvey said.

"Then, you need to work on changing it. You can change anything—the inner you, the outer you, whatever you want. The point is you want to have your inner and outer self in balance, even if they are different; and by getting insights into your inner self through your dreams, you can decide if that's who you want to be, and if you wish, you can change."

"Then there's hope for you," Teri said, glancing quickly at Harvey and looking away. He glared back at her, and it looked like she was about to make a nasty reply, when Serge, ever the peace-maker, quickly cut in, and the tension between them dissipated.

"What effects do your dreams have on your daily life?" Serge asked. "How much of it carries over?" He explained that he was having problems with one of his roommates, who was extremely noisy and inconsiderate, and he wanted him to leave. "So if I have a dream about my roommate leaving, does that mean I'm picking up something that may happen in the future? Or if I work on having that dream, will that help make my roommate leave?"

Michael considered Serge's question carefully. "Yes, dreams do have a great effect on daily life, since dreams and life are part of the same reality continuum. However, some dreams have more power to affect your daily life than others. As you get more sensitive and more in control of your dreams, you can tell which ones. For example, in describing his experiences with Don Juan, Castaneda says he hit a sorcerer in his dreams and afterwards the sorcerer was near death for a few days. So you don't want to go around hurting people or getting people angry at you in your dreams.

"By the same token, you can use your dreams to do some exploring, and sometimes this can help prepare you for going there later in real life. But if you do any such exploration, be careful where you go and what you do there. Say you go to a strange new place. It's best not to drink the water or eat native foods. Of if you're in a place you don't want to be, just stop the dream. You can discover some really hellish places in your dreams, and the best thing to do is to avoid them."

"So what kind of places have you been to yourself?" Teri asked. "And what makes them so hellish?"

Michael paused thoughtfully, and glanced at the ceiling, as if remembering. Then, he began describing some strange unearthly places that sounded like a forbidden landscape from a science fiction movie. Yet, he described these places as if they were quite real—and he pointed out that not only had he visited these strange sites, but other ODF members had done so in dreams, too.

He pulled out a napkin to illustrate one such site and sketched a high mountain with three peaks, surrounded by a long concrete road. Towards the front was a big park.

"Many ODFers have shared this place in dreams," he explained. "We've each gone there from time to time, and when we come back, we share what we've found. It's a little like being visiting anthropologists or explorers. Then, we keep this information, so if it becomes relevant—say someone really goes to a place like this—we've got the information from our dreams on file and can compare it to see how accurate we were. Anyway, the people we met there were really very nice. Quiet, very friendly, and good food . . . You might go there sometime yourselves if you want."

However, another world he described visiting with other ODFers was more unusual and difficult to enter. It was a place where almost everything was green.

"The first thing we noticed was the big green sun," Michael said, sketching on a napkin as he spoke. "It took up about 80% of the sky. The place also had a big ocean with low waves and very dense gravity. We noticed little rocky islands in the middle of the ocean, but otherwise the place was very flat. Also, we noticed some large standing crystals on the island plateaus. On meeting the inhabitants, we discovered they were composed only of light, like smoke in a field. They seemed to appear in front of the crystal mountains, and soon faded back into the glass, which was like an energy prism. As we watched, we saw a tremendous flash of light and one of these smoky beings flashed by us into the sky like a rocket ship taking off."

"Do you consider this dream vision real?" I asked.

Michael looked startled, almost annoyed by my question, as if I should accept such things by now and not question their reality. "Why, of course, they're real," he said. "They're just visions in our dreams right now, but eventually, we believe, these places will be discovered to exist in a physical form. In the meantime, we want to explore them as much as we can by guiding our dreams to take us there. Then, too, we sometimes use trance and astral-projection to explore these worlds while we're awake."

As Michael continued to discuss the process of exploring other realities, his explanation seemed stranger and stranger. He described the process as if we were to learn to be anthropologists or explorers visiting a real country with real people.

As he commented: "You don't want to interfere with the local customs in a dream. It's just like in real life. You don't want to disturb the people or things you see. For example, I once dreamt I was in a town in the desert, and I saw people in white robes with red crosses on their head. Suddenly I saw them stoning another villager, and feeling heroic, I tried to step in and save this person. But, as soon as I did, the people started stoning me, and I barely escaped. So you want to stay out of it, particularly since your dreams can affect you in real life. For example, if I hadn't escaped as I did, I could have woken up to discover I was cut and bruised."

His comments made Serge, who was often ultra-sensitive, nervous. Serge was afraid of possibly finding himself in trouble if he didn't know how to dream the right way, now that Michael made him aware there was both a right and a wrong way of dreaming.

"Do you have any suggestions about where we should go in our dreams?" asked Serge. "What would be pleasant and safe?"

"Well," Michael replied, "you might think of yourself as a tourist or traveler, and go the places most tourists go. For example, some good dream worlds to visit are deserts or local street scenes in U.S. and foreign cities. Seashores and forests are nice and peaceful environments, too. When you go, you'll probably meet up with other dreamers or the natives."

I was still trying to make sense of this new reality. "If you meet up with other people in your dreams," I asked, "are they likely to be having the same dream at the time, or do you expect to meet up with them later outside your dreams?"

"Possibly both," Michael said, "since the images from others' dreams can intrude on your real life. For example, when I was in L.A., I saw a girl on the street turn a corner and disappear. There was nowhere she could have gone, because it was late and everything was closed. She was just gone! What happened is the same phenomenon as the phantom hitchhiker which some people report. In that situation, a person is driving along a road, usually at night, and thinks he sees a hitchhiker. He picks the person up, but then, all of a sudden, the hitchhiker vanishes. Say he turns to talk to the hitchhiker and suddenly he isn't there. It can be really unnerving to experience this. You think you're nuts. But what's going on is you've met a visitor from somewhere else—from a dream reality—who has stopped by to visit. And we're like part of the dream to them."

I looked around the table, and I noticed that Serge, Teri, and Harvey were listening raptly, intent on capturing every word.

"Look at it this way," Michael went on. He drew another illustration on a napkin, starting with three cubes on top of each other. He drew a small stick figure of a man in the center one, and pointing his fork at it, he explained: "This middle box is our normal awareness. The bottom box is for the physical environment around us. The top box represents our dream projections and our other altered states of consciousness, like meditation and trance. In a dream, the dreamer projects himself to an adjacent space, and as he does, the energy of that image or thought goes outward, so it not only affects the dream level, but the adjacent physical level, too.

"Thus, when you have a pleasant dream experience, that tends to carry over into your real waking life. Likewise, whenever you do something negative in an altered consciousness state—whether it's in a dream, trance, or magical working—the negative energy you release tends to rain down on the physical. So you'll experience something negative happening, or maybe get a negative response from others."

Harvey shuddered a little. Michael's comments about negativity appeared to be hitting home. He quickly cut in to change the topic: "Well, if dreams can affect our future, can we use dreams to find out what that future will be?"

"Definitely," Michael said. "You can experience the future in your dreams. In fact, you can program yourself to have a precognitive dream, if you can stay conscious on that edge between waking and dreaming, so you can tell yourself to have such a dream. I've had many of these dreams myself. For instance, one time I heard voices as I fell asleep, and the next day, I heard people talking about the same things as in my dream.

"Then, too, you can change any future you dream about, because you're only seeing a probable future. The future is *likely* to happen that way, given what's happening now. Yet, if you don't like what's likely to happen, you can intervene and change it. Or if it's a future that involves a lot of people, you can change your own course, so it doesn't happen to you."

Michael stopped talking and drew another diagram on a napkin. Everyone watched intently as he placed a large dot in the center of the napkin, labeled it "the present," and drew a half dozen lines and branches radiating out from this dot.

"That's where we are now," he continued, pointing to the dot. "And these are all the probable futures around it." He pointed to the lines and branches. "We have a choice of where we want to go. However, as we move towards a probable future, we experience it more intensely and are more likely to notice it. But you still can avoid it. For instance, as you move towards a critical event in your life, you may have recurrent dreams about it, and the closer you move to it, the more likely you are to have such dreams, because you're feeling the event pull on reality more. Yet, until the event actually happens, you still have the power to resist the pull.

"For example, once before Gene and I went on a field trip, we both dreamt about a truck on the road. In my dream, it was bearing down on us rapidly and in Gene's dream we got into an accident with it. Thus, the next day when we left on our trip, we were especially cautious, and when we saw a truck like the one in our dream, we quickly steered away from it, so the accident didn't happen. In short, your precognition abilities, which turn up in dreams as well as in other parts of your life, are valuable to indicate what's likely to happen so you can steer around it. . . .

"You may not be able to stop the event from happening entirely, but you may be able to prevent it from happening to you. For example, Gene once dreamt about a light airplane crashing on a freeway in Los Angeles, which was followed by civil insurrection and several of his friends were killed. Immediately, Gene interpreted this as a dream about a probable future, and we discussed how to avoid the situation in our group. Samantha, who had that experience in the restaurant, commented that she had a negative attitude, which resulted in many negative things happening to her and others around her. So she decided she needed to change her outlook and did. Then, about two weeks later, the paper reported that a light plane crashed on the freeway. But there was no insurrection, and none of us were affected in any negative way. So we believe the change we discussed helped to protect us from what might have been a dangerous probable future. Part of the dream came true, since the plane did crash. But we weren't involved."

As I listened, I considered how Michael's ideas might sound outlandish to an outsider. Yet there was a certain logical consistency in what he was saying, since the effects he described seemed to flow logically out of his underlying premise—that the dream world and material world are integrally connected, so one can influence the other. Accordingly, as Michael proposed, if a dream could provide insights into the future, then if a person changed that dream or him or herself in response to it, he or she should be able to change the future, too.

Meanwhile, Teri and Serge seemed convinced and were whispering among themselves: "Far out . . . I never realized dreams were so powerful . . . I'm going to go home and do some heavy dreaming tonight."

Michael continued. "These times when we can make powerful changes are full moments that happen to us. These can occur in dreams or in a waking state. What essentially happens is you suddenly become aware of the importance of the moment for changing things. It's as if reality becomes like a fan at this instant, so a small act can have a major effect on what happens next. For example, we often experience full moments as big events, when we have to make a major decision like whether to move or take a job. But a full moment can be really subtle, too—even something as minor as dropping or spilling a glass of beer. So, recognizing this, you can counteract the effect of that moment by taking some action to counter it—for example, pushing your glass of beer forward so it doesn't spill."

Harvey held his hand out so his mug of beer teetered back and forth on it. "But how can that be so significant?" he asked, teasing Michael with the possibility of the mug crashing to the floor at any moment. "Why should something major be affected by whether you spill a glass of beer or not?"

Michael pretended to ignore the teetering mug, and after a few minutes Harvey put the beer back on the table.

"It's not just the beer," Michael commented. "Sometimes you spill things, and it's not a big deal. The key difference is that at certain times, you get this feeling—it's a gut level thing—that this event has a special significance. So your feelings are telling you that you have to act to take charge, because this is a full moment. Then, when you act, you can pull yourself out of ordinary time to create and affect your probable future.

"And it's the same with dreams. When you're aware, you can tell if a dream is merely processing unimportant material from the day, or is a significant event you should pay attention to.

"In short," Michael concluded, "it's important to be aware of your dreams. It's like watching radar. If you're not careful in magic, it's easy for all sorts of things to come in through the back door. But as you pay attention, you'll discover that many significant things show up in your dreams. Then, you can use them to guide and affect your life . . . and to see your probable futures. That way, if you don't like what you see, you can make a change. But it all starts from your being aware of not only what happens around you, but of your dreams, for everything is part of the same reality. They're just different levels, that's all."

CHAPTER EIGHT

Seeing With The Mind's Eye

During the following week, I experimented with Michael's technique for controlling dreaming. As I drifted off to sleep, I thought to myself, "Okay, tonight, you're going to give yourself a command at that edge between being awake and asleep." But each time, as I approached that point, I promptly forgot my intention and fell asleep.

At our following class meeting, the others didn't report much better success.

"I had a lot of things happening at work," said Teri, "so I forgot about practicing most of the time. There was a mess up in a mailing, so my boss promptly blamed me, and we all had to work overtime to get it out. Then this women's magical group I belong to was organizing a big ritual to celebrate the changing of the seasons. So I didn't pay much attention to my dreams."

Serge reported he had a bad week, so he was literally afraid to be in touch with his dreams. He was concerned if he had a bad dream, it might make everything that was happening even worse. As he explained, "My roommate has been putting up a big fight. I think he knows we want him to leave, and he wants to leave, but he's trying to show us he can stay if he wants. Meanwhile, I'd like to find a lover and settle down—but everyone I meet is just so . . . " he paused, searching for the right word. " . . . Well, promiscuous, the way I used to be when I was young. I wish I could dream up the right lover, but then, I'm afraid if I did, he could hurt me like my last one. So I guess I didn't feel much like dreaming this past week."

As for Harvey, he had tried and tried unsuccessfully. "I thought I'd visit an old girlfriend, but she wasn't at home in my dreams. Then I tried to dream about getting some girl to fall for me. But the image was real blurry, and I can't remember if I scored or not. I'd have to rate the whole experiment about a two on a 10 point scale."

Michael tried to be reassuring. "Well it just takes practice to get that control. Keep working on it if you can."

Then, he turned to the subject for tonight—"geoteleportation" a process

Then, he turned to the subject for tonight -"geoteleportation"- a process dream." The technique involved using conscious mental control to trigger the subject matter of a dream. Michael explained how to do this: "You need to learn to relax your bodies completely, so your higher or astral self can leave your body and travel wherever you direct it. Then, you can experience things on the astral or soul level, just as you can in dreams.

"The astral is the level of reality occupied by the soul, and astral projection is a really common phenomena. The words may sound unusual. But all of us do it all the time. For instance, when you're lying down and feel your body vibrating and have a floating, drifting sensation . . . that's a form of astral projection. Your unconscious is beginning to move out of yourself. But usually, the shock of this changed reality snaps you back into your own awareness, and you're suddenly back in yourself.

"Thus, what we want to learn is how to go past that point of snapping back, and that takes a lot of concentration. You need to use a very intense form of relaxation, and you need to prepare your subconscious very fully for the process, because without this preparation, you'll probably just go back into your body.

"Then, once you can use this technique to go past yourself, the goal is to use it to get the knowledge and see things. You want to do that in dreaming, too. But with geoteleportation, you're awake; so you have more control of the process. Also, with this technique, you're only using the mind's eye for seeing—not the whole astral spirit as in full astral projection; so there's more protection and less risk of a shock to the body. That's because you're not in a trance, as in astral projection, so you can easily get right back into your body."

"Is it like remote vision?" I asked, referring to a technique some parapsychology researchers use to test people's abilities to pick up information mentally from far away.

Michael nodded. "I guess you could say that, although we focus on physical objects and use a different process to achieve a relaxed state. Also, we believe anyone can learn to do it—not just someone with special psychic gifts."

Michael proceeded to explain how to do it. "Geoteleportation begins with having a picture in your imagination of a site or scene you want to go to. Then, allow whatever images you perceive to come through. They may be smoky or fuzzy at first, but as the picture clears, notice where you are. For instance, pay attention to whether you're in a city and what one. Notice the time. Are you on a particular street? Be as detailed as you can. In the beginning, you may find that not everything is true. But as you practice and get more sensitive, you'll find that what you pick up is closer to the real situation.

"Once you learn to do this properly, you can use it to see with others— through their eyes. You can also use it to anticipate what's likely to happen in general or at some place where you are going. For example, before I enter a room, I imagine what's going to be there, so I know better what to expect. Plus you can use geoteleportation to monitor where people are or what they are like. You pick up intuitions and impressions about them.

"However," Michael cautioned, "be careful when you're doing this not to get too close. You want to be close enough to observe people, but far enough away so you're not sucked into their space. Also, avoid situations that are unpleasant or too morbid, or you'll end up in an adjacent reality which you don't want to be in. So stay away from negative forces and places like graveyards, or bodies and bones. You want to explore, but you want to do so safely—particularly when you're getting started and don't have much ability to control yourself if you get into anything that's hard to handle."

Michael paused and rummaged around in a large trunk by the side of the room. He pulled out a small black notebook in which he had drawn a series of geometrical designs.

"Now the way to get good at this technique is to practice by getting verifiable information . . . So that's what we'll be doing this week."

He explained he had drawn some targets in the book. Our task would be to discover that they were using the mind's eye technique.

Michael continued: "You should start by memorizing this apartment now, so you can easily project your imagination here. I'll put this book out each night on the table and turn it open to the appropriate page. It'll have a geometric design on it. Then, each night, imagine yourself coming here and looking in the book, and record what you see. At the end of the week when we get together we'll compare the results and see how close you got."

"What sort of images should we look for?" I asked. "And how do we know if our impressions are right?"

"Well, after you do this for awhile, you'll get an intuitive sense of what is true. The way to get to this point is to really pay attention to any impressions you get, no matter how subtle. Then continually seek to verify their accuracy, until you get that intuitive sense. It takes time before you get that sensation, but eventually, with practice, you'll be able to clearly see that you're really seeing what you're seeing, because your perceptions are true. And that's the point of this exercise—so you can get verification by checking out your impressions against the symbols I've drawn."

Michael then went on to explain that we weren't limited to using geoteleportation to see physical objects. "As you get more experienced, you can use it to pick up spiritual projections and images of other people. For instance, that's what Gene and I did when we went on a field trip to Yosemite. Gene couldn't go but he said that during the afternoon, he would project an image of himself to wherever I was, though he didn't tell me when he would do this or what this image would be. Then, that afternoon, suddenly I looked up and saw a hawk, a real one, and I felt that image was significant. Later, when I talked to Gene, I discovered he had been projecting the image of a hawk to me, about the same time that occurred."

Michael had other suggestions about the process. "You can also use geoteleportation to make a person do something, like call you. If you concentrate on the person doing this enough, if your belief is strong enough, their subconscious will be receptive, and they'll call. It's like having a waking dream and projecting that energy at a person. Your dream becomes a strong tool for getting someone to do something when it's focused correctly."

"What if someone resists you?" Harvey asked. "Suppose they don't want to call." Harvey complained that he frequently encountered this situation in everyday life, and he wondered if using magical techniques would make things better.

"Sure. You can change things," Michael reassured him. "If you feel a no, just repicture them saying yes. Or talk to them in your mind's eye. You negotiate it, so they freely decide to call. The idea is not to force someone to do something they don't want to do. You're not trying to do something unethical. But basically, you're trying to connect up with someone; you're trying to get them to respond to a message you're putting out. That's all."

"In fact," Michael stated, grinning broadly and bringing his hands down with a flourish to show he was about to put forth what he considered a radical conceptual breakthrough, "we've discovered you can use this technique to communicate with and influence spiritual beings. For instance, on one field trip, we got some spirits to cooperate that were showing up in the form of wolves. We were going to take a group of students out in the field, and I wanted to impress them by having them see these wolves. So we put out a message to these creatures through geoteleportation. We told them: 'We want you to show up and do things.' And soon after we got to the site, there they were waiting to perform as requested."

"Are you talking about real wolves or spirit wolves?" I asked, wondering if perhaps Michael was talking in metaphors.

But he made it clear he wasn't. "Oh, they were very real. You could see them. They took on a real physical form. But they were spiritual beings, too."

As I wondered whether Michael and his group really saw the wolves or only imagined they saw them, Michael, as if anticipating my questions, emphasized that these beings took on real form, became visible, and could be contacted and directed through the mind.

"What's important is the wolves showed up and the students could see them. Then when we asked the wolves to leave, they did, so we were in charge. If you're not, these beings can become dangerous. So you want to be careful not to draw something out which you can't control."

I noticed Serge, Teri, and Harvey listening almost motionlessly, as if awed by Michael's unusual account. Then, like a preacher who has brought his congregation to a climax of emotion, Michael suddenly switched gears to show how this technique could be put to more mundane uses.

"Of course, you can use geoteleportation to pick up ordinary information about someone, just as if you were making a phone call, and we've done some experiments along this line. One time a former ODFer and I tried to imagine how each other was dressed, and we were usually accurate. In fact, one time when we were in separate rooms and I changed my clothes, he picked this up.

"The trick is to keep practicing," Michael emphasized. "With practice you can pick up information more accurately, though you may still miss on some things. And the beauty of this technique is you can split up your attention. It's not like you're in deep trance where you can't do anything else. So you can use geoteleportation while you do other things. "It's a little like daydreaming . . . "

Michael returned to the blackboard and drew an elongated triangle, with a series of horizontal lines through it. He added a curved arrow that projected up through the triangle and back down to the bottom.

"It's like you're slingshooting a message out in a dream and it comes back again," he explained. "But to get a hit, you have to focus on where you want that message to hit. You want to have a direct idea of what you want. It's like sending out a laser beam, rather than turning on a flashlight."

As an example, Michael described how he used this technique to get his job when he moved to San Francisco. He combined geoteleportation with a ritual, and though he could have used the technique alone, the ritual was designed to intensify his focus and direct more energy towards his goal. He began by making his usual circle, requested the assistance of the guardians of the four directions, and appealed to the spirits for help. Then using geoteleportation, he pictured himself in the office where he wanted to work, imagined himself being interviewed, and saw the interviewer saying "yes."

"I pictured it very clearly," Michael stated firmly. "I poured all of the energy of the circle into that, and I used geoteleportation to select the reality

I wanted. It's like dreaming when you're wide awake, and you externalize it. So, after imagining what I wanted very clearly, I focused on believing that what was in my mind would take place without a doubt. The ritual was designed to increase the energy I put into this, to make it even more certain to happen.

"In short, to get what you want, you've got to picture what you want very vividly and precisely and focus all your energy on achieving that. And whether you're using the technique in daily life or for ritual work, it makes no difference. It's that concentration of energy and vision that makes the technique effective. In fact, when you think about it, you realize there's no difference between dreaming and normal reality. We're literally in the midst of a dream. For whether we're awake or asleep, we can use our ablty to see in the same way—to bend and shape reality to get what we want."

Michael paused for questions.

"Are you saying there's no difference between using this technique in the field and in everyday life?" I asked.

"No, none at all. In every major working, we use it, and we also use it to take care of day-to-day realities. For example, when I did the Gateway for my Sixth Degree, I used geoteleportation to imagine extending my power through the Gateway, and then I used it to picture the future. Likewise, I use it regularly at work. For instance, say I'm very busy, and I don't want anyone to call. I'll picture silence, and there won't be any calls. Or if I have something to do and can't meet with someone, I'll picture a link between us, and I'll give him the message not to come to the meeting. So he won't show up, and I won't have to explain why I can't make it. Or, typically, the person will call to say that something came up and he wants to change the date.

"So you can use this technique to affect the future as well as see the past. And it works because we live in a world with probable futures. I know that's really difficult for some people to accept, because most people live in a linear system where one thing leads to another, and they think the present is all there is. But reality is very complex, and nothing is firmly determined—just probable or not probable. So we can do magic to influence the outcome of probable futures."

"So are some futures more probable than others?" Teri asked. "Like is it more probable for me to leave my job than stay there?"

"Sure, some things are definitely more likely," Michael said. "And you can sense the probabilities as well as push them in one direction or the other to make things more or less probable. It's like being in a movie, which can be influenced by yourself or others. Thus, you need to be aware of shifts in time and space, and if you see things turning adversely for you or sense something happening that you don't want, you can act to change it. Or conversely, if you like what's happening, you can act to make that continue even more strongly.

"Think of it this way. Everything you do influences everything else. So if you're aware of that, you can learn to control your attitude, and you can feel more connected to the web of things, so you're better able to affect things. It's like you're interrupting a circuit by your action. For instance, suppose you make even a very slight movement—such as throwing something. That breaks up a circuit that's already connected and creates another connection. So that breaks up one probable future, because it makes something else happen."

At this point my head was spinning a little. The reality Michael described was so radically different than the reality most people take for granted. However, it had a certain tight logic, though it was based on different premises than ordinary reality. As he described it, everything was inter-connected—time, space, personal reality, and the world around us, much like a spongy rubber ball with masses of fibers clustered inside it, so that a movement anywhere on the ball would produce movement along another part. Also, any fiber could initiate a movement that would affect every other movement in the ball.

"Then, if you say everything is interconnected, does that mean that anyone can have as much effect on changing things as anyone else?" I asked.

"Oh, no. Of course not," Michael stated firmly. "Sometimes magicians can feel too self-important. They can develop the feeling that everything revolves around them." He glanced momentarily at Harvey, who was sitting up stiffly, with an arrogant far-away look, as if he was off on some fantasy of personal power. Almost immediately Harvey snapped back to pay attention and Michael continued. "But that isn't the case. Your movements have an effect, but there are also a series of larger movements all the time. There are planetary movements; movements on the level of society; movements on the level of individual races and groups. We can all cause ripples. But there are other factors. If you're sensitive, you can feel what's in the air. So, while we do have a conscious choice, there's an internal reality that shapes us, too. It's a reciprocal process. Sometimes you can influence things; but at times, these stronger forces are so much more powerful that things should be left as they are, and if you try to act against them, you'll get flattened."

Michael gave an example of when it was best to move in harmony with these external forces. "I was preparing to go on a field trip to the desert with Gene and Paul, when a storm came up. At first, we set off anyway, thinking: 'We're magicians; we should be able to decide when it's time to do something or not.' However, as the storm closed in, it dumped several inches of snow on our path, and we finally decided to turn back, realizing this storm was stronger than we were. In fact, we barely made it back through the pass. If we hadn't turned back, we could have been frozen in for the weekend.

"So this is an example of a time when a probable future is so likely, you can't alter reality. You just have to sense the momentum and bow to it. It's like the desert was giving us a very clear message: 'It's time to go.' So we did."

"How do you know?" Teri asked. "When does the momentum become so irresistible that you know you should go with it, rather than try to change things the way you want? Like at work or with other people—how do I know when to keep pushing versus when it's better to cut back and lie low?"

"You can feel it," Michael said. "You listen to that little voice inside. For example, when I first began exploring this stuff many years ago in L.A., I started thinking I could do something about anything. So sometimes, I let myself get into dangerous situations which I know now to avoid. One time, for instance, I was going to Watts on an ambulance run, and I felt I would be in danger. So as I was driving, I started picturing a safe day using the usual geoteleportation technique. But once I arrived on the scene that afternoon, I passed only a few yards away from several guys who were taking pot shots around them. It was like they were playing at being at a shooting range on public streets. Fortunately, I was far enough away, so I wasn't hurt. But it sure gave me a scare and showed me I should listen to my little voice inside me.

"So, after that, I started to listen when that little voice began telling me to be aware of inevitable movements. That's why later, when I stopped at a liquor store in a dangerous area, I didn't go in. My little voice told me it was time to leave, so I moved on. And I'm sure glad I did because another guy who was walking behind me stopped at the same store to look at a newspaper, when suddenly a robber entered, and he was killed.

"Thus, it's best to flow with things or get out of the way if you feel the inevitable is happening. Because if it's inevitable, it's too strong for you to change. You must adapt to it. And that's the key ability a successful sorcerer needs—the ability to adapt, as well as use power when it's appropriate."

"How can your little voice tell you such things?" Serge asked. "How do you know? I get feelings all the time, but I'm never sure which one to trust. Like I thought for sure my ex-lover was going to stick around. And then, all of a sudden he left and I felt devastated."

"You simply learn to feel it and you become more sensitive to distinguish that voice from all that inner mental chatter. If you listen, if you're open to that little voice, you can tell when there's real danger. That little voice comes from your subconscious. It's that part of us which is linked to the rest of the universe and to the movement of things. It's connected to the collective unconscious, so if we tune into it, we can feel all sorts of things.

"For instance, this is the reason animals can sense earthquakes. They listen to this inner sense. People have this ability, too, although most people don't use it. We've lost that with the coming of civilization. But we can get in touch with it again. I don't know how to explain it any better, but essentially, the feeling you get is of a sensation of truth. You just know what is so. Thus, if you feel that certainty, that feeling of truth, while listening to your voice, that's the time to go with it. Trust your feelings and you'll be right," Michael concluded on a note of firm confidence. "You have to learn how to trust."

Serge, Teri, and Harvey nodded in agreement. In principle they agreed, yet they seemed confused, unsure about when to trust and when not to do so.

"But how can you know that you know?" Serge finally asked. "How can you be sure you're correct in trusting your feelings? What do you look for to be certain you're right?"

Quietly, gently, as if talking to a group of small children, Michael tried to explain. "It's being aware of the texture of the voice which tells you that what the voice is saying is true. It's a gut sensation, a tone. It's like the Zen mind that talks to you, and you know it speaks the truth. It's so hard to describe. But you feel a certain calm steadiness that pushes through all the conscious chatter. And you feel totally certain. I don't know how to explain it any better than that.

"I just know." He looked at me directly. "It's basically an intuitive sense of knowing, and to experience it, you have to put the usually logical part of yourself that wants explanations aside. You have to learn to accept and trust. And that can be a difficult process, since it often conflicts with a desire to rationally know."

I nodded knowing that if I expected to go on with this training, I would have to do this. I knew I had many questions about the very premises of this alternate reality Michael described. Part of me kept doubting the essential reality of this "reality," and the inner voice and seeing process Michael used to relate to this world. But I knew if I was going on, I would have to leave such questions and doubts on the shelf. The rational and intuitive were in conflict. To learn more, I would have to leave the rational behind.

Meanwhile, Michael continued with a few last points. "In short, you need to listen to those intuitive hunches and follow that inner voice. Whatever you're doing, when you're practicing your seeing exercises, when you're out in the field, in everyday life, let your conscious mind go in order to hear that voice. Your conscious mind tends to blot it out, but your voice is always right. So fight against any inclination to edit it, deny it, or disbelieve. One of the major purposes of the ODF training is to stimulate your interaction with this voice and make you more intuitive. You want to be better able to listen to it, hear it, and act from its instructions.

"And that's what your Second Degree is about. It's a self-less act of magic, in which you have to listen to your heart for what to do next. The seeing exercises are designed to help you get in touch with that voice, too, because when you do them, you're monitoring what you're doing and feeling, and you aren't thinking about it. So you've got to practice letting your conscious mind go to tune into that small quiet voice. Then, keep reconfirming what you experience as you go along. You have to prove to yourself that the method really works to use it with confidence."

The class was over now. Michael reminded us to practice our seeing exercises, and he suggested we experiment with geoteleportation using the small design targets in his book, which he described as black and white geometrical forms.

"I'll lay the targets on the table each night with the book open to that page. Just get relaxed and guide yourself here. Then, look at the target. After you return, draw a picture of whatever you see, and at the next class, we'll compare what you saw with the diagrams."

But before that happened, there was a magical encampment, where we would all have the chance to show what we could do in the field and work toward our next degree.

CHAPTER NINE

A Magical Weekend

Like other magical encampments, this gathering, planned by the ODF and several other local magical groups, was a chance for people involved in magic to get together. Also, some groups planned to perform special magical workings and group rituals.

The ODF considered this an especially important weekend because Paul, down for the weekend from L.A., had decided to take the oath to become a formal ODF member. Also, Michael had decided that I was ready to try for my Second Degree. Teri, Serge and Harvey, who had recently joined the group, wanted to go on solos, so that was on the agenda, too.

The encampment was held at the abandoned battery where I first met Michael. I arrived shortly after 6 p.m., as the people organizing the encampment were settling in. Lana, who planned a gala Greek ceremony for the following afternoon, was putting the finishing touches on the temple, which she set up in one of the barracks. She had already put out some candles, incense and statues, and hung some large banners on the walls. Meanwhile, Anthony and Sally, an older couple with a long-standing interest in magic, were having a picnic dinner in front of their car. Several other people were moving equipment, sleeping bags, and bags of food around, getting ready for the group dinner or for camping that night.

I found Michael patrolling the grounds with Gene and Paul. As at previous encampments, they were wearing their official dress blacks and were helping out by welcoming people, showing them where to park cars, and assisting in setting up equipment.

They were also watching for stray tourists, so they could greet them in a friendly way, but keep them from entering and disturbing the encampment.

As I approached, Michael was holding a walkie-talkie and completing a message to Paul.

"Yeah, check. All clear down here. Copy and over."

He turned off the walkie-talkie and came over to me.

"Lots of exciting things happening tonight," he said breezily. "Paul will be taking his oath in a little while, and afterwards, you can take your Second Degree. We'll also be taking Harvey out to do his solo."

Just then, there was another crackle on the walkie-talkie, and after a brief exchange, Michael told me: "Well, gotta go."

He headed up the hill, and I went to my car and unpacked. Since I couldn't stay overnight, setting up was easy. I got out my potluck dinner contribution and my magical gear—the long black staff I used as my power object, my dress black shirt and slacks, and the athame or knife with a black handle I wore strapped on one side. To pass the time while waiting for Michael to return for Paul's ceremony, I joined Anthony and Sally by their car, and they invited me to share their picnic.

After a while, I saw Michael, Gene, and Paul gathering outside the barracks, along with Serge and Teri. Harvey wasn't expected until the following day.

I joined them, and Michael told us to wait in the temple, so we could observe Paul take his oath of commitment to the ODF in a secret ceremony.

It occurred in a long dark room, lit only by a few candles and gas lights, and surrounded by colorful ODF banners. An altar with candles and assorted magical objects, including a chalice of water, incense burner, wine and flowers, was at the far end.

After the ceremony broke up and we left the temple, I asked Michael about the meaning of the initiation. When does a person decide to take this step, and how does it affect his or her role in the group?

"It's definitely a serious step of commitment," Michael replied. "And the person must ask for it. They must really want it. But first they must have at least passed their Third Degree. They must show they can produce and control magical phenomena. Then, they must decide that this is their chosen path. That's why a person has to wait at least two weeks after passing the Third Degree before asking to make this commitment. They must be sure this is their way."

Soon we joined the others around an open barbecue pit for dinner—a rollicking community affair with a large pot of stew, broiled chickens, a big salad, and several platters of homemade bread. Lana bustled around fixing the chicken, while Turner ladled out the stew. Anthony, Sally, and several others scurried about cutting up bread, pouring wine, setting out silverware.

Shortly after we finished eating, as dusk settled in, Michael motioned for the ODF members to meet him by the road into the camp. "It is time to take Serge for his solo," he announced. "Then, when everyone returns," he told me, "you can try for your Second Degree and do a self-less act of magic."

Then Michael and Paul set off with Serge up the windy road into the nearby hills. The night was foggy, and a deep night chill was already settling in. Owls hooted in the distance as the three of them disappeared into the fog, and I recalled my own solo which was so different, since it occurred in an open meadow on a clear, warm night. My own experience had been very calm and peaceful, and I wondered if Serge's experience might be quite different, since the cold dense fog and hooting owls made this night seem eerie and forbidding.

Along with the other ODFers, I rejoined the group around the barbecue to wait to do my Second. Everyone was singing songs, and Sondra, a hefty, motherly-looking woman in her 30s, provided the accompaniment on a small thin lute. As I waited, I thought about the contrast between this lively singing group, bathed in the warm glow of flickering candles and the night darkness that provided an opening into another reality for the ODF.

When Michael and Paul returned, I was ready. They motioned for me to join them, and holding my staff, I followed them to a flat concrete area on the other side of the bunker, away from the noise and lights of the barbecue. Gene and Wendy, a woman of about 20 who would later go on some ODF field trips, were seated on a picnic table waiting for us.

"What should I do?" I asked Michael.

"Just listen to that little voice inside you and let yourself respond to it to perform a magical act. The whole point of the Second Degree is to open yourself up to the magical forces, and then work with them to produce some results. We'll be looking for some phenomena—some indication that the magical universe has heard you and responded."

"What kind of phenomena?" I wondered.

"Well, maybe you'll call up an elemental, and we'll expect ot see the form of this being appear. Or if you work with the wind, we'll expect to see the wind rise up or die down. Every person's experience is different. Just do what you feel inspired to do and produce a response. The way it usually works is if you're open and receptive, you'll do the right thing."

With that, I walked away from the group towards the center of the flat concrete area. A large cement wall loomed ahead in the darkness, and I stopped before it.

Then I hesitated, not certain of what to do now, despite Michael's description. I also felt extremely self-conscious, since the four of them were sitting on the bench watching me. Even though I could barely make out their forms in the darkness, I very much felt their presence, and I wasn't sure if I could produce any results, much less make the appropriate movements.

"Should I create the circle first?" I finally called out.

"You can, though you don't have to," Michael said. "There are no specific procedures you have to do. Just do what you feel. And don't worry. Not all people make it the first time. So don't worry if you don't. You can always do it again."

I turned away from the group towards the wall, feeling a little less self-conscious that way. Then, trying to remember what Michael did, I started making a circle with my staff. I leaned towards the ground and holding my staff just above it, I turned in a clockwise circle.

Afterwards, not sure what to do next, I stood waiting for a few minutes. Suddenly, the thought came to me that I should try to create some energy in front of me, so I imagined a stream of energy coming out of my staff. Next I tried to draw the outline of a person before me. As I did, I saw this person take on form. Then, waving my staff, I mentally directed him to move around along the walls, go to a barbecue pit, about 20 feet away, come back, and kneel in front of me. As I did, I felt a surge of power, as if I was really controlling this imaginary being, and I wondered if Michael and the others could actually see this person in front of me, or if they would see me merely moving around and going through the motions.

Yet, despite my uncertainty, I continued. I did a reverse drawing over the outline of the person I created to send him away, and next I visualized directing a stream of energy through my staff to one corner of the cement walls. After this, I suddenly felt very tired and not sure what to do next. So I simply reversed the circle with my staff and returned to the group. Had I done enough to pass, I wondered.

"Did you see anything?" I asked.

Michael shook his head. "Not much. There was only the glimmering of something happening. I feel like there was a block in your energy."

Gene nodded in agreement. "I didn't see anything either, and I felt that block, too!"

I was puzzled, not sure what they were talking about. Hadn't I imagined this form out there? Didn't I visualize it moving around? What should I be doing differently?

Michael got up from the table, interrupting my thoughts, and Gene told me:

"Okay, now watch Michael, and he'll demonstrate how to do it."

Michael strode over to the wall and Gene positioned himself a few yards away. Then, Michael walked in a circle near Gene, explaining as he walked: "You see, the idea is to be open and receptive. Just listen and do whatever the little voice tells you to do. You don't have to do anything complicated. Just walking around, being receptive is fine."

Michael continued walking silently for about a minute, and I could barely make out his dark shape in the darkness. Then, waving his staff in the air, he began again:

"Some people may start the process by moving a hand. Some feel they should do a dance. Do whatever comes."

Michael stopped and turned towards Gene. I noticed a pale whitish aura gradually take shape around him. Then, as Michael pointed his staff at Gene to direct energy at him, his aura appeared to grow larger and a big smoky ball of energy seemed to engulf Gene. A few moments later, Michael pulled back his staff and the ball of energy seemed to dissipate into the atmosphere and disappear. Then, the demonstration over, Michael and Gene returned to our group.

Had others seen what I observed, I wondered as they walked back. Michael wanted to show that there was a connection between what he had demonstrated and what we observed, and so he asked everyone to share their observations.

"I saw a big puffy cloud around Gene," said Wendy.

"It looked like a large energy mass around both of you," Serge said.

Thus, when everyone finished reporting, there seemed to be a good match. We all had apparently seen much the same thing, and Michael commented to me:

"You see, the energy we produce is real. You can see it. Now, go try again."

So once more, I headed out towards the wall, determined to let myself go and really experience the energy this time. I would try to release my rational mind, stop questioning what I was observing, and let the experience just happen.

This time, as I walked around, trying to imitate Michael's easy fluid style, I started to feel some warm energy radiating out of my staff, and I noticed a hazy whitish glow around it. Then, as I moved my left hand over to touch it, I experienced a slight pulse of energy against my hand. Soon I felt this energy expand like a big round ball. Its edges were barely perceptible—more of a sensation of slight pressure than anything else—and I moved my hand outward as I felt it expand.

Now, feeling in control of this energy, I imagined it coalescing and shooting out through the tip of my staff, and I directed it to go to the corner of the wall and form into the shape of a large glowing ball. Slowly, I aproached it, and as I stepped into this energy mass, I felt it warm and glowing around me. Then, when I lifted my staff into the air, I suddenly felt like I was in a stream of energy which radiated up and fell down upon me, and I closed my eyes, feeling as if I was taking a shower with sparkles of energy instead of water.

When I looked up, I noticed Michael standing in front of me.

"Okay," he said, "you can cut it now," and he led me back to the group.

"I decided to interrupt," he explained "because you left an energy double of yourself behind you while you were in the ball of energy. Gene and I saw this double wandering about towards you. So I wanted to stop things before you got into trouble."

"What kind of trouble?" I asked.

"Well, if the double actually got to you, you could get sick, or maybe nothing would happen. But I didn't want to take the chance."

Michael explained why this double effect happens. "It's what we call a doppelganger—a ghostly counterpart of the real person. It's really quite common when you're doing magic. It happens sometimes when a separation occurs between the physical body and the magical self, when the magician isn't fully involved in the magical act. So part of himself separates out. To prevent this from happening, it's important that you step fully inside the magical act, and don't leave that part of yourself outside."

However, in spite of this problem, Michael told me I passed.

"Sure you did," said Michael. "You did produce some phenomena. The other people watching saw it, too. Still, you've got to be careful, because you may not be able to control the energy you produce. So you can open yourself up to all sorts of dangers. But it's a beginning."

The others congratulated me briefly, and then Michael and Paul anounced that they had to pick up Serge from his solo.

"Can I come, too?" I asked.

"No," Michael said, explaining, "Taking people out is the easiest part, because things are usually pretty quiet. But the recovery process can be very difficult, because you don't know what the person on the solo may bring up. There can be all sorts of weird things out there, and you have to be able to handle them. You need more experience for that."

As I waited at camp for Serge's return, I talked to Gene about his early experiences with magic. "I've been experimenting on my own for about ten years, since I was 17," he told me. "Then, about five years ago, I met Michael who was teaching about the ODF and I decided that this was to be my path, too."

When Serge returned, I was eager to hear what happened. However, Serge wanted to be alone for a little while to think about the experience, since it had been so powerful for him. Later that evening, though, Serge was ready to talk, and he described his encounter with the other side in detail.

As he explained, the solo turned out to be a continuation of an experience he had one week before when he was meditating alone in the woods by the Russian River, about two hours north of San Francisco. Once again he was in an emotional crisis, because he had just broken up with a person he felt very close to, and he needed some silent time by himself. While he was quietly meditating, he heard something large crash through the woods towards him and felt anxious. But then, calling on his earlier training in ceremonial magic, he did a brief banishing ritual to get rid of whatever was there, and the sensation of its presence ended. In his solo he confronted the same crashing being again, as well as a series of temptations which he resisted.

These temptations began soon after Michael and Paul left him in a secluded spot in the woods near the ocean. Serge made his circle and suddenly a large hawk with a 20-foot wingspan appeared out of the fog and tried to lure him out of his circle. It flapped and whirled above him, like some ancient dinosaur-like bird.

"But I resisted the urge to leave," Serge said.

However, in a few minutes, another temptation appeared.

"This time, I saw a large rectangular hole open up in front of me, and I could see it led to an underground passageway. It was lined with glittery gems and marble. And I was really tempted to leave the circle and go into the hole to explore. But I knew it would bring disaster."

So again, Serge listened to his little voice and resisted. However, after a few more minutes, he heard a child crying for help.

"And again, I was tempted to step outside the circle and go help, but I didn't. I felt it was another dangerous or evil presence, so I concentrated on meditating to make the sound go away." And once more it did.

Soon after this, Michael returned to pick up Serge, and he led him down the hill to meet Paul, waiting a short distance away. As they walked back, they both heard a large thing crashing through the woods, which sounded much like what Serge heard a few weeks before at the Russian River.

"I thought it might be the same thing," Serge said, "back to test me again."

Thus, Michael was especially concerned about the possible dangers, and he asked Paul to stay behind to deal with the being, while he led Serge back to camp. He felt Paul would be better able to deal with this mysterious unseen being than Serge, since Paul had been on the ODF path for about two years and had become a full member that night, whereas Serge was just beginning.

Then, Paul went back to where Serge had been, and when he returned he reported that he heard the same crashing noises and sobs of a child crying for help. "However, he wasn't tempted like me," Serge said. "He simply banished the beings and calmed things down."

Then, after Paul returned from doing this, Michael complimented Serge for a successful solo. "As Michael told me, I opened myself up to the magical universe, resisted all temptations, and I sure got a response."

Once Serge concluded his report, the magical activities for the night were over, and we returned to the group around the barbecue. Some people were still near the fire talking and singing, and a few were toasting marshmellows. Others had drifted off into the bunker and were setting up sleeping bags and preparing to retire for the night.

I had to return to the city to do some errands, and when I returned the following afternoon around three, people were sitting around talking quietly or lazing in the late afternoon sun. I spotted Michael, in uniform as usual, talking to Teri, who had arrived wearing a long gypsy-like dress.

"Things are really quiet," Michael advised me. "Paul and Gene are off exploring the area, and Teri and I are going to walk around the area now to select a site for her solo tonight." In the meantime, he suggested I should just relax.

Michael and Teri wandered off, and shortly after they returned around four, Harvey suddenly came running into the encampment area. He was breathing heavily, his hair was disheveled, and he sounded frantic.

"Where is everybody?" he gasped. "I've been rushing all over the place, trying to find this camp for two hours. I was searching everywhere...." He pointed to a distant barracks on a hillside. "And I must have spent almost an hour combing the place, before the ranger told me to try over here... I can't believe I finally found you. I nearly went home a few minutes ago in total disgust."

Harvey panted breathlessly and he glared at Michael, as if Michael or the ODF were at fault and should give him an apology. But instead, Michael merely tried to calm him.

"Well, you're here now. That's the important thing."

Harvey grimaced and sat heavily down on the picnic bench. "Well, I nearly didn't make it."

Again, Michael ignored Harvey's attempt at getting sympathy. "So, you're up for a solo tonight. Are you ready for it?" he said cheerily.

"I don't know," Harvey grumped.

"Anyway, we'll be doing them right after dinner."

"Okay, okay. I'll think about it," Harvey said.

For the next few hours, his participation seemed in doubt. He continued to grump about his two hours of trying to find the encampment, and during dinner, he whined at Lana, until she told him: "Look, why don't you just shut up." Thus, by the end of dinner, he was in a terrible mood. The whole experience had only revived his frequent insecure feelings about whether people really liked or accepted him, and now he felt intensely rejected and alone.

Still, Michael tried to be encouraging. "Just put yourself out there. Relax. Let yourself go. You can do it."

But Harvey was still unsure. However, as the other ODFers—Michael, Paul,

Gene, Teri, and myself—assembled by the roadway to leave on a field trip, Harvey came rushing to join us.

"I decided to try for it after all," he said.

"Fine," Michael said. "Then, we're all ready." And we set off.

At the top of the hill, Michael asked Serge and me to wait, while he took Teri to a spot overlooking the ocean for her solo. Meanwhile, Paul led Harvey to the top of an old tower high on a hill near camp.

A few minutes later, Michael and Paul returned. Now Paul was ready to do his experiment, which involved calling up his "allie" or spiritual helper and inviting him to interact with Serge. If Serge did this successfully, he would pass his Second Degree. Normally, a new ODFer wouldn't take the Second Degree so soon after the First, but Michael was so impressed by the phenomena Serge produced on his First Degree, that he felt Serge was ready to try for the Second the next night.

To begin the test, Paul walked across the road and stood in front of a small rise, with his back to us. Serge followed and stood about ten feet away from him on the opposite side of the road.

Then, lifting up his hands, Paul wordlessly called on his allie, Ethan, to appear and make himself known to Serge. As he appeared, Paul and Serge later reported, the hillside was bathed in radiant white light and they saw a large purplish form emerge from this glow. Then off to Paul's right, Serge saw another hulking form advancing. It was a friend of Paul's allie, as Paul later explained.

Meanwhile, as I watched, I saw the two shadowy forms flicker a little, and at times they seemed to merge completely into the hillside. As Paul called on his allie, I observed a whitish aura radiating around him.

Once Paul felt Ethan was fully present, he instructed him to interact with Serge, and in moments, Serge felt a force pushing against him, forcing him backwards down the hill. At the same time, I noticed that a whitish misty projection of energy seemed to flow from Paul to Serge. For a few moments, Serge tried to push back, and then backed down the hillside and returned to where Michael and I were watching.

"It was pushing against me," Serge said as he approached. "I felt like it wanted to push me off the hill."

Michael smiled mischievously. "Yeah, sometimes they try to do that. They get a little uppity and try to play with you."

As Michael spoke, Paul finished bidding Ethan and his friend goodbye and returned to our group.

"Nice work," Michael commented. He praised Paul for his skill in bringing forth his allie and setting the stage for the interaction with Serge, and he complimented Serge for feeling its presence and reacting appropriately. As a result, Serge had passed his Second Degree.

I asked why I had seen Paul and Serge disappear at times, and Paul explained, "That kind of disappearance is common in magical workings, because it means the person is stepping into another reality. Thus, anyone watching may cease to see him for a time."

I also wondered about the lights and colors I had seen, which Paul and Serge reported, too. Did Michael also see them?

"Of course," he said, "they're real. We may not all see exactly the same thing, but the energy forms trigger a reaction, so we'll see generally the same sort of forms, or we'll see them in roughly the same place. We'll see different things because we have different experiences, different ways of interpreting things. But we always get enough agreement, so we know what we see is real."

Then, as I started to ask myself questions about what really was real and what was an illusion or group suggestion, for I was having a hard time accepting this new way of seeing, Paul suddenly noticed a quick burst of light in the air and said to Michael, "Hey, that's a signal to you. It's time to do your thing."

Paul pointed up in the sky to where he had seen the flash, and Michael walked about ten feet down the road and positioned himself under that spot.

Quickly, he drew a circle, then raised his staff to create a Gateway in the sky. He made several stabs in the air as he called forth a hawk-like bird. Once it appeared, he did a kind of dance with it, in which he guided it around through the sky, as he shifted and darted about using quick, yet flowing, graceful movements. As he worked, Paul pointed up at the sky and urged Serge and me to look.

"There's a lot happening up there," he said. "Look up and you can see the bird. It's a big, circling thing."

"I see it," Serge cried out ecstatically, though I only noticed occasional flashes of light in the sky about eight feet above Michael's head.

Finally, Michael directed the hawk to fly about 50 yards to where Harvey was standing for his solo to see that Harvey was all right and let him know we were thinking about him. When the bird flew back, Michael banished it with a few thrusts of his staff and returned to our group. "I had to banish it when I finished working with it," he explained, "so it won't fly around and do who knows what."

Then, Michael wanted to show us a technique for creating Gateways, so we could evoke beings through it from the other side, too. He raised his staff and moved it around in a triangle shape several times to create a small triangle of energy a few feet above the road.

"Now look at the area and feel the energy," he told Serge and me. "Do it like this," he said, demonstrating. He put his hand through the triangular area and bent over into it, as if he was leaning out of an open window.

Serge stepped over and did the same. Then, returning to our group, he described what he saw on the other side.

"It looked like a large cliff drop—a little like the hole I noticed last night on my solo. Also, the area felt colder and filled with energy."

Michael and Paul nodded with recognition. "Yes, usually, these areas do feel colder," Michael said.

Then, it was my turn to try. I stepped ahead a few paces and moved my hand slowly around the area, trying to feel something. Soon my hand felt slightly warmer and tingly. I also noticed a slight triangular glow, but as I moved my head towards it and peered through, the glow disappeared and the surrounding area looked much as usual.

"Just keep working with it," Michael said in response to my report, and he banished the shape with a few waves of his staff.

"You see," he concluded, "it's possible to put up these Gateways all over, and they're especially good on a foggy night. Then, you can experience all sorts of things, depending on where you put a Gateway."

It was now about 45 minutes after Teri and Harvey had started their solos, and Michael said it felt like about time to go get them. While he and Serge went to pick up Teri, I accompanied Paul to get Harvey.

The walk was quiet, and Paul attributed this to the fog. "A foggy night tends to be more peaceful," he explained, "because it tends to conceal much of the activity that's going on. It's like a curtain is drawn over the activity one might normally see, so it looks like nothing is happening. But even so, the beings are out there doing things. So that's why a Gateway can be so helpful on a foggy night. It lets you tune in on that activity."

As we approached the bottom of the hill below the tower, Paul asked me to wait, so he could retrieve Harvey himself. He wanted to go himself for the same reason that Michael only took experienced people with him on recoveries or went alone: "You just aren't sure what kind of activity the person on a solo has produced, so it's best not to have a relatively inexperienced person along."

As Paul walked up the hill, I saw Harvey silhouetted against the sky by the tower, standing stiffly like a statue. As Paul approached, he began waving and calling out, "I've been watching you. I wanted to make sure you weren't going to sneak up on me or pull something funny. So I've been really alert."

It was a strange response for someone on a solo, since the ODF's policy is to leave someone alone and not interfere with their solo in any way. However, Paul ignored Harvey's comments and quietly told him it was time to go back.

"What happened?" I asked Harvey as we walked down the hill to camp.

At first, Harvey shook his head and gruffed, "I don't want to talk about it." But as we neared the camp, he relented and described his experience.

"I felt scrupulously ignored," he complained.

"In what way?" I asked.

"I put up a circle to protect myself and waited. But then nothing much seemed to happen, and I felt a little disappointed. I noticed it got a little colder, and I had a feeling of aloneness. At one point, I noticed a bird overhead, and I felt it had come by to watch me, but that was pretty much all."

As Harvey mentioned the bird, I recalled how Michael had evoked a bird and sent it to fly by Harvey. An interesting parallel, I thought.

Just then, Michael appeared on the road with Teri. She reported that nothing much had happened to her either, though she found the experience mostly calm and peaceful. She thought about her close feelings to some of her friends she had known for years, and felt a sense of recommitment to her desire to have a successful career.

"For many people, it really is a calm experience," Michael observed. "For others all sorts of things go on, but the important point is you both stayed with it and experienced whatever you did."

Thus, both had passed the First Degree, and we returned to camp to celebrate everyone's progress. Michael said he was encouraged and felt we were ready to move on, since there had been two successful solos and two new Second Degrees. Also Paul had evoked his allie, and several successful experiments at creating Gateways were performed.

"I'm proud of you all," Michael said to me, Teri, Serge and Harvey. "You're really well on your way to becoming shaman warriors."

CHAPTER TEN

The Path of the Warrior

$\mathbf{N}$ow that our group had some successful field experience, Michael felt we were ready to learn more deeply about the ODF's philosophy and the shaman warrior path. Then we could move on to more advanced degree work. Thus, our third class was devoted to this purpose. As usual, our small group of regulars—Serge, Teri, Harvey and me—met in Michael's apartment, and he led the class dressed in his usual dress uniform.

Michael started off with the basic principles of the ODF. "We believe in duty beyond service. The warrior should not only become strong and powerful to help himself, but to help others to the best of his abilities."

He gave some examples. One time he rescued Samantha from spiritual beings trying to tempt her over a cliff. Another time, he stepped in to calm down a man who was threatening another with a gun. At a weekend camp-out, he intervened to keep two friends in an argument from coming to blows. "We don't believe in staying apart from the world, but feel we should step in where needed," he explained.

Also, as Michael warned, "The warrior should expect to be tested to make sure he or she measures up to the task. For instance, when I went on a field trip to Death Valley, with Gene, Paul and Samantha, we encountered numerous difficulties. Our car broke down several times, and no one would stop to help, but we got it started again. Also Samantha was tempted several times on the cliff before I arrived, but each time she had resisted. Finally, when we returned to town, the gas station attendant was amazed we actually made it through the desert at all, because he told us, 'Your bearings and brakes are really shot. By all rights, this car should have broken down.' "

These were all tests, Michael explained. Yet they had passed through each difficulty successfully because they took it calmly, or "gracefully" as Michael put it, and tried to work out a solution.

"You see, we feel these things happened," Michael said, "because we were being tested to see how balanced and how powerful we were in dealing with them. The point of being a warrior is we can take repeated exposure to difficulties and come out richer for the experience, rather than being mentally hurt by it, as others might be."

He used his experience in breaking up the camp-out fight to illustrate. Two friends had gotten into an argument when the ODFers camped out one weekend in L.A. When one threatened to hit the other, Michael, Gene and Paul stepped in. They sensed that the person making the threat was tormented by some personal problems and perhaps even personal demons. Thus, they acted quickly to calm him down and prevent any violence from occurring. Afterwards, they did a banishing ritual to cleanse the area where the man who made the threat would be sleeping.

"Some people at the camp felt really wiped out by the experience," Michael observed. "But we performed well in resolving the problem quickly. So we came away pleased at our own performance, rather than feeling terrible about what happened."

Michael paused, looked at us thoughtfully, and went on.

"In a way, being on the warrior path is a little like a game. The energies in the universe are really responsive to what you are doing. So if you are doing good things, they will support you, though occasionally, they'll throw you a curve, to see if you can handle it. As you move up in grades through the Order, the challenges get bigger and bigger. But it's easier to deal with them, because you have more knowledge. Also, as you are better able to deal with daily problems, you can better deal with the unknown. And it works the other way, too. The more you know about the unknown, the better you get at dealing with everyday life.

"And yet . . ." Michael hesitated again, looking at us with a firm, penetrating gaze and measuring his words carefully, ". . . not everyone can make it. Perhaps fewer than one in ten can do it, because it takes work and commitment. You have to learn to be strong and be committed to staying on the path."

"That's all right. I'm willing," Serge commented.

"And so am I," Teri said.

When Harvey and I nodded that we were ready, too, Michael continued.

"Okay, then. Let's begin. A basic idea of this training is to discover your true will and act from it. You need to live from a certain balance or center inside yourself. Our job as shaman warriors is not only to evoke elementals and other beings in the field, but to apply that work into developing more control and power in everyday life—both to help yourself and to help others. It's important to build the person as well as the magician."

He paused briefly to see that we understood and went on.

"People need certain qualities to withstand the impact of the unknown. For example, in daily life, we experience both good and bad events, and both can be difficult to deal with. The bad, for obvious reasons. But a good event can be difficult, too, since it can easily throw a person off the path, if a person can't deal with it properly. As an example, take a lottery or major promotion. Some people don't know how to deal with success; so they blow it and lose control.

"I've seen many situations which create stress that people can't handle. Or they get distracted from their real purpose in life. When you set out on a path, though, you should make a commitment to yourself and to whatever higher beings or beings are important to you. It doesn't matter exactly what your commitment is. Whatever your path, you have to stick with it, or you'll fail.

"Thus, it's important to be on guard against any situations that can trip you up and cause you to lose your direction. For example, suppose you get into a fight with someone. It can be easy to get upset and forget your commitment to the path, which includes staying centered and working things out as smoothly and efficiently as you can. Instead, when difficult situations arise, you should air the problem, solve it, and move on with the least conflict possible to something else. Thus, when you have a problem, ask yourself, 'Am I getting through this as efficiently as possible? Or is something holding me back?' "

Michael then had some suggestions on how a shaman warrior should deal with stress. "Because of who we are, ODFers frequently get into stressful situations. You can't help encountering stress if you try to move through challenges and grow yourself or help others do the same. There's no way you can be a warrior without opposition. If you get victory after victory, it's easy to become weak or burn yourself out. You lose perspective and maybe come to take the world or your situation for granted, when the world isn't like that. So you aren't prepared when disaster comes, and you can be destroyed by your own success.

"Thus, a warrior needs the ability to be flexible and bounce back, whatever happens. You should work out any problems that come up quickly and move on to something profitable. That's the warrior path . . . having the ability to adapt, handle any situation, and move on. It doesn't matter whether the situation is a very serious one or a minor one. Whether it's a man with a gun or lost keys, you should be able to handle it and go on.

That's the difference between the warrior and other persons—the warrior combines the ability to adapt and control, as well as the ability to move on and grow."

Michael also distinguished between the shaman warrior and other types of spiritual leaders.

"Many spiritual people, like saints, try to respond to situations by remaining at peace or being non-aggressive. But that's not the warrior way. If you try to withdraw from things, you can be very insulated, and we believe in the path of action. You should try to be as integrated as possible in all of your aspects. It doesn't guarantee you'll experience peace. But you can deal with things more profitably and efficiently. . . ."

"In fact . . ." Michael grinned slightly at the thought, ". . . we really have a very capitalistic attitude. It's like spiritual capitalism. You want to do things that will profit you and other people as efficiently as possible. For example, when I teach, I get a lot of satisfaction from seeing a person do something well, because I feel my investment of time and energy has come back to me. Similarly, when you do something for others, you make people feel good, and they'll want to do something for you."

Michael compared what we were doing to the acts of leaders of large corporations. "It's like being a captain of industry. You have the same kind of power over yourself and others, except you're directing that power and control to a different end—to your own personal growth and the growth of others. . . . At the same time, you have to learn to work with others to help them along the path."

"So how much commitment is required?" Harvey asked. "What do you have to give up?" Since he was involved in many other magical groups and activities, he was concerned about how the ODF path would fit with the other things he did.

"Well, this isn't an aesthetic path," Michael replied. "So you may not have to give up anything. We believe it's appropriate to get what you need to take care of your own well-being and your body. But don't overindulge. Basically, you want to further your own evolution and the evolution of others on the path with you. But you also have to recognize your own limitations and the limitations of others, and start on that level. So we believe in acceptance and compassion. Yet you should help people move on and evolve yourself.

"It's not always easy. However, when you feel this bond between yourself and the cosmic that develops, you get a sense of strength from the idea that you're committing yourself to a great work. It's like the search for the grail. Ultimately, after you search for it for some time, you accept that commitment, it becomes lasting and binding. You gain the feeling of being a knight for life. Then, as long as you continue to feel and keep this commitment, things will continue to work out well. But if you turn around on the path, you're doomed to live an ordinary life . . . and that can be very difficult. It's like you tried, gave up, and failed. So to be a true warrior or magician, you must make that commitment and surrender yourself to your quest for growth. Then, once you have done so, you must have faith."

"How do you know it's worth it?" Harvey asked. "It sounds like you could be committing yourself to a big struggle."

"You know it's worth it, because once you make that commitment, you come to feel there's a power out there that loves you and is concerned about you. Then, if you encounter any challenges or problems, this belief pushes you through any growth experiences, so you grow. Sure, you'll be faced with things you almost can't handle. But that's how we grow—by surmounting challenges and obstacles. And extending your trust, making that commitment helps you do so, because it removes the fear of failure or death. Sometimes you'll find this love of the universe can be a harsh love, when you have a particularly challenging experience. But that's part of the path . . . and part of everyday life. So you learn to become stronger and go on."

Harvey frowned a little and his brows raised up with a hint of skepticism. But Michael continued, not letting Harvey's resistance bother him.

"Look at it this way. You're seeking knighthood by proving yourself to you and by affirming that power or godhood within—whatever you want to call it. The path of the shaman warrior involves the process of getting to know this inner strength and who you are. If you encounter adverse situations in life or in the field, your only choice should be to welcome that situation and deal with it to the best of your ability. You may have a lot of doubts and ask yourself: 'Can I measure up?' But you go forward, hoping you will succeed in overcoming the challenge, and certain that you should do this and will have the help and support of the powers that be. . . ."

Having outlined the reasons for the ODF way, Michael was ready to talk about the "steps on the path." He passed out a sheet of paper entitled "Grade Insignia," with pictures of gold and silver bars and stars. These represented the symbols of achievement along the ODF path. Michael had briefly described some of these steps to me before I took my First Degree. But now he wanted to give us a detailed explanation of the ODF system.

He pointed to the first illustration of a single silver bar.

"This is the insignia of the Scout, and it's earned by the solo. You go out on a mini-field trip by yourself, or we drop you off somewhere. Then, you do your seeing exercises, open yourself up, and experience whatever comes, though that's usually mild for the person on a solo. It's like the power out there shields him, so he can easily handle the experience. Essentially, what you do on the solo is show you are willing to trust. It's like you're initiating a cycle when you first step out on the path and say to the universe: 'Here I am. Accept me as I am."

He glanced around the group. "And that's what all of you did. You went out there and let things happen, and you all did fine."

He moved his finger over to the picture of the double silver bars.

"This is the level of the Ranger, which some of you have done." He nodded at Serge and me. "This is the act of selfless magic, and for this grade, you need observers. You open yourself up to your heart and wait for that little voice inside to speak to you, or you ask it for instructions on performing your magical act. Then, we expect you to do something beyond your normal capacity to show you have tapped into the power of the universe, such as evoking some energy or beings, as happened on the encampment." He glanced at Serge and me again. "It's relatively simple, if you can let go."

"But what if problems develop?" worried Harvey, who had not yet gone for his Second Degree, and typically adopted the attitude; if anything can go wrong, it probably will to me.

Michael tried to reassure him. "Well, if you've done your solo right, probably nothing will happen. Or tell yourself, 'No hassle, I'm not going to let it bother me,' and go on."

Harvey made a skeptical grimace, as Michael pressed on.

"In any event, we watch carefully when a person goes for their degree to see what happens. Some people do unique and powerful things. For example, when I passed my Second, I opened up a Gateway, and on his, Serge looked through a Gateway to the other side. It doesn't matter if you create a plan for yourself or not. Sometimes a general plan can help you direct your energy in a certain way, but you don't want to be restricted by it. For instance, sometimes people plan, but when they go out to do it, something takes control and they do something different. One fellow, for example, expected to open up a Gateway, but got pushed back by something, and was surprised at this barrier he encountered. But whether they plan or not, people usually discover they know how to do things they haven't done before. So the idea is to open yourself, listen, respond, and do it."

Next Michael pointed to the gold bar on top of the paper.

"Now we come to the Third Grade, the Knight. This time the idea is to both open yourself up and have a preconceived idea of what you want to accomplish and see it through. You do this by seeking power to help you perform your task. For example, when I first opened myself up and passed this grade, I felt this power come to me spontaneously, and I knew what to do. Once you have this experience, you can tap this power in the future. You'll feel it around you. Then, when that little voice inside you tells you to move or do something, you should jump."

"How do you feel this power?" I asked.

"You just do. You sense it, you feel it. I can't really explain it. You just know it's there. Then, as you need it, you can draw on it and crank yourself up to channel that power to get what you want. . . .

"It's like . . ." Michael paused, and gazed around the room thoughtfully. "It's like there are two major patterns in life working in tandem, and the Third Grade helps you realize this. On the one hand, you have control over life. Yet life also has control over you. So, there is a constant play between the two. You have some self-determination; then, after you exercise that, life has something to say.

"Thus, we strive to balance these two elements for the Third Degree. You must say to the universe, 'This is what I want to do if you help me.' Then, if you are ready and receptive, the power you need to do what you want will come. You don't need any special words to do this either. Some magicians seem to think that the power lies in the word, so you have to use magical words to command this power. But we don't believe that. We believe you need to express your control through your heart, using whatever words you want, or even none at all. Your thoughts and your will are all you need. Then, listen for life to speak back to you, so you can respond. That's how you find the balance between your personal will and the power out there."

Michael claimed it was possible to achieve these results without any special training.

"All you really need is to be aware you must balance your personal control with this receptivity to outside power. Then you can achieve results. For example, we had one member in L.A. who wanted to evoke an earth elemental on his Third Degree, though he had never done this before. And he went out and did it, though he didn't have any training. Thus, it's just a matter of deciding what you want and asking. You can do it once you open up."

Still Michael had a few cautions for us after we passed the Third Degree.

"You can expect something to happen about a week or ten days after the Third. We find that's when a person is typically made or broken on the path. We're not exactly sure why, but we think it's because you reach the limits of what you are doing or think you can do. So some people drop out at this point. They decide it isn't their path. But those people who go on normally stick with it. So that's why we wait to make someone a full ODF member. Before the Third Degree, we consider you an affiliate. Then, after the Third, everyone has to wait at least two weeks before they can ask to join. After this, they can ask to take the oath, just like Paul did. But *they* have to ask.

We don't ask them. They have to show they really want to join this path and are sure it's the right path for them."

"Then what's next?" asked Serge, who was already eager to show his commitment to the group and move through the ranks quickly. He was usually intense about every activity or person he got involved with and his decision to become an active ODF member and leader was no different.

Pleased with Serge's enthusiasm, Michael went on, though he covered the more advanced degrees quickly, since it would be some time before any of us were ready to go for them.

"Your Fourth involves perfecting the balance between the personal will and the divine, by working with all of the elements. In the Fifth, you have to recognize that the power out there is both male and female, and that you have these male and female energies in yourself. The purpose of this grade is to bring those energies into harmony; you have to recognize that these polarities can become one, both spiritually and physically. Once they do, there's a tremendous amount of energy released, and you experience it as very flowing."

Next Michael talked of the Sixth Degree and described his own experience of creating and going through a Gateway into another dimension where he observed a long black obsidian plane. Then he compared the Sixth to the solo. "But you're taking a solo in a new way. You're not just opening yourself up to whatever comes but you're consciously pushing yourself into a new dimension first, so you experience what comes on another level."

Michael then said he had to stop here, becaue he couldn't talk about the Seventh through Tenth Degrees now. "I've taken an Oath not to reveal them to non-members. But after you take your Oaths, I can then speak of these Levels."

Michael sat down, looking a little drained, and suggested we take a short break. When he returned, he would tell us about the ten principles of action, attitude and belief, which were the keys to success on the shaman warrior's path.

CHAPTER ELEVEN

The Principles of the Shaman Warrior

Michael resumed the class by introducing the ten principles of the warrior's path. He explained that the ODF had adapted them from the ancient Japanese school of bushido to meet the realities of the modern day.

As Michael explained, "The old code called on the samauri to be so honest, that anyone could take advantage of him, such as merchants. Also, the requirement for honor can go too far. For example, under the old codes you might kill yourself for honor on the command of others. So misplaced honor can be impractical, especially in modern American society, where many people have no honor—they'll stab you in the back at the first chance. So unlimited honesty won't work. Thus, the ODF adapted these principles, which are ideal for the warrior, to take account of modern society."

Michael turned to the small blackboard in the front of the room and listed the ten principles: 1) Right Action, 2) Self-Control, 3) Courage, 4) Service, 5) Compassion, 6) Honor, 7) Awareness, 8) Persistence, 9) Purpose, and 10) Patience. We copied the words in our notebooks.

After he finished writing, Michael turned back to us.

"Remember these ten principles. Follow them. Hold them in your heart. They'll help you listen to that little voice, achieve your goals, avoid danger, and work well with others. Now we'll take each one in turn."

Michael raised his staff and pointed to the first principle.

"Right Action. That's determined by your heart. Your key tool for discovering the right action is listening to your little voice. You need to be in rhythm with your intuition, and do whatever it says immediately if you feel it's right, or don't do it at all. By waiting too long you lose the inspiration of the moment, and you'll act out of synch."

"What about ethics when you trust your gut level feelings?" Teri asked. "How can you be sure your actions are ethical?" She described a situation where a friend at work had to go out on an important personal errand and Teri had covered for her when their boss came looking for her. Then when the woman returned, she completed the assignment the boss needed quickly, and Teri felt her assistance avoided a possible confrontation. She believed she did the right thing and kept peace in the office. But was it ethical?

"Normally, you can trust that little voice," Michael replied. "Usually, it will lead you to do what is moral and benevolent, as long as you follow exactly what your heart says to do. Say your first inclination is to get out of a bad situation. Do so. Or if you feel a need to intervene, do. Yet, combine trusting your heart with common sense. Be aware of your feelings, and then act intelligently. For example, suppose you encounter a problem, like a conflict in a relationship. Your heart may say to solve it now. Then, your intellect tells you various ways to do it. So listen and assess what you're hearing, and you'll come up with a response that works in the long run."

"How do you know you're correct?" I asked. "How can you trust your little voice or intuition?"

"There's just a sense of knowing what's true," Michael said. "We can know truth if we can master ourselves and develop an inner silence, so we can listen to our voice. That's why the seeing exercises are so important. They give you the ability to act from that voice, which is like the Zen mind, the intuition, or the warrior's heart. Whatever you call it, the ability to know differentiates the master from the student. In other words, you simply know that you know . . . and you have to leave your rational mind behind to do this."

Michael gave an example. He was on a trip to Death Valley with Paul and Gene, when suddenly, he said, "I had an odd feeling. I sensed there was a blizzard coming. We were going to watch stars, and the night was clear. But I had this sudden feeling it was time to go. So we turned around, due to that feeling alone, and as it turned out, a blizzard did start up about an hour later, and we got through just in time before the blizzard sealed the path. Thus, however you do it, you need to open yourself up, ask questions, listen to the answer, and act in tune with that inner voice."

Michael pointed to the next word on the list, "Self-Control," and continued.

"You need this to help you assess each situation. Besides listening to your heart, you need to use control. So after you get an insight, maybe take a few breaths, or look at what's happening like a drama you and others are in. By using self-control, you can step back and determine the best way to handle something."

Michael gave a few examples. "Say you're having problems at work, and you wonder if you should tell your boss off, which may help you feel good for a brief time, or wait. Usually, it's best to avoid a frontal attack. So your self-control helps you step out of the way and come up with another plan to resolve the problem as you listen to your heart. Or say someone who's very upset wants you to do what they want, though it's not something you want to do. In this case, it might be better to agree provisionally, because they'll calm down, and you can talk about the situation intelligently.

"In other words," Michael emphasized, "you should step back, take control of the situation, and tell the person what he wants to hear, so he relaxes and his negative emotional state loses its momentum. Then, you can deal with the problem rationally.

"Think of it this way. The key that distinguishes the warror from other people is that most people are emotional. They want to think they're logical, but they aren't. Instead, they normally react and let themselves get manipulated by the world, and they're driven from situation to situation. But the warrior can stop and observe the situation to say to himself, 'How should I deal with this?' Thus, you need to have a certain calmness. That way, you can not only assess outside situations objectively, but you can look at yourself and what you're doing and see that that's okay. And that strengthens you to deal with the outside world, since you feel more sure of yourself. You feel in control. You can't continually have doubts about yourself and deal with the outside world, too."

Michael paused and glanced around for questions.

"What if there's a conflict," I asked "between what you have to say to someone to calm him down and what's really true?"

"You have to take it situation by situation. You listen to your inner voice you assess it; and finally, you look at your priorities and what's practical at the time. It may make more sense to compromise with the absolute truth for awhile, if you're dealing with a bad situation and there's no other way. As long as you have a benevolent heart, in the long run, the truth will work out."

Then, Michael pointed to the third word, "Courage."

"This is the ability to recognize that you must move forward and do it. You may often feel skeptical about your ability—and overconfidence is as bad as feeling underconfident. But you need to move forward once you get the sense in your heart you should do it.

"It's like running into anything that you find frightening or scary. You're confronting the dragons in your life—whether they're magical monsters or everyday realities. Ask yourself if you can handle it; then, if you feel you can, go into the fray to get the grail. You'll find that once you take this position, many things will become easy, because you've dealt with worse. Also, you may find that average people are more difficult to deal with than the monsters you encounter in the magical world.

"So the important thing is to focus your attention and devote most of your effort to having courage in the everyday world. Sometimes people who get involved in magic spend so much time being courageous about magical things, that they forget about regular life. So strike a balance, and apply what you learn from expressing courage in any magical battles to what happens to you every day."

The next word was "Service," and here Michael stressed the importance of balancing a desire for developing oneself with offering benevolent, unselfish service to others.

"You see," he stated, "one goal of self-development is giving to others. True service is doing something for others without expecting any reward. It's knowing you did something good for another person. For example, in the ODF, when we go to meetings with other groups, we volunteer to help with set-up, security and first-aid. Likewise, you can provide service in many ways, by finding something you have to offer and giving that.

"Giving is important, and service teaches us something. For you must give as well as get to have balance in your life. Your heart helps you determine the proper balance, and it can help you learn more about yourself and what you can do."

"Service sounds like a good way to create good PR, too," Harvey broke in. "Maybe if I started doing more for people, they'd do more for me, too."

Michael shook his head. "No. Not at all. Service should be done without expecting any reward—as a natural thing you want to do. If you do it expecting something, you're doing it with the wrong reasons and intentions, so it's no longer true service. Rather, it becomes a way of guilt-tripping or manipulating others, by making them think they owe you something or have to do something for you in return."

Michael described an example of what he meant. He was in a bus station in Los Angeles, when he saw a woman of about 70 who appeared very upset. She was trembling nervously, almost on the verge of tears. He sat next to her, and for about the next hour, he listened as she related her problem. She and her boyfriend were living in a convalescent hospital, and she was frightened that she would die there alone. Yet, she was afraid to leave, because she felt she was too old. So, Michael tried to help, telling her that if she truly wanted to leave, she should do so and have the courage to go into the unknown. Her age didn't matter. "If you care about your life," Michael told her, "you'll live it so you feel satisfied whatever you do." He urged her to believe in herself and make the move.

Later the woman sent Michael a letter saying that as a result of their conversation, she and her boyfriend did decide to leave, and they felt confident of their ability to make it successfully. Now they were looking forward to experiencing the rest of their life together for as long as they had. She concluded by asking Michael to write, but he didn't, because he explained, "I didn't want to take advantage of the situation. I felt she got what she needed by my helping when she needed help. After that I didn't want her to feel obligated to me in any way. So I felt it was time to let the situation go. And a lot of life is like that. You see a situation where someone needs help. You give it, and then you move on, not expecting anything for your service."

"What about a situation of danger?" asked Serge. "Should you help then?" He mentioned some of his own experiences in working in the social service field. Sometimes his heart went out to some of the clients he met, and he wanted to go beyond the call of duty to help, say by bringing needed clothes or food to their homes. But then he became afraid. Maybe they would take advantage of his kindness, maybe he might even get attacked or hurt in a bad neighborhood.

"Whether to help or not really depends," said Michael. "You have to listen to your inner voice to know. For example, I don't normally pick up hitchhikers, because of the crime situation. But one time at 2 a.m., I felt I should pick up a young woman who was waiting on the side of the road. As I did, I was passed by a low-rider car, and three guys in it hooted and jeered as they passed. It was apparent they were about to pick her up, and I feel I saved her from a bad situation. Later, she tried to give me her phone number, but I turned it down, because again, I wanted what I did to be its own reward. For a reward for service is really being in harmony with what must be. It doesn't involve expecting anything else or accepting other benefits for the service. The act should be complete in itself. Doing it is the reward.

"In short," Michael concluded, "service is founded on listening to the heart and acting rightly with a selfless act. In turn, when you listen to your heart to do this, this helps you learn about that little voice."

Next Michael discussed "Compassion."

"It's the ability to give someone what they need versus what they think they need or you think they want. Usually, people will see such an act as a benevolent gesture, but sometimes you may appear to be doing something negative, though it turns out to be helpful later. The key is to have a benevolent intent."

Michael gave an example to illustrate. At one time he participated in some Zen training, and during a session of sitting meditation, a woman suddenly became extremely agitated and reported seeing some scary visions which upset her. At this, the Roshi hit her, and she became angry. "It may seem the Roshi did a hurtful thing when he hit her," Michael explained. "But once he he hit her, that made her angry and brought her back to reality. So it was a compassionate, helpful act after all."

In another case, Michael had been in a house where there was a fire, and as he ran out, he encountered a man sobbing loudly on the front lawn. Michael tried to be sympathetic when he asked the man what happened and offered to help him up, but the man continued to cry helplessly. So shifting to a challenging tone, Michael asked the man: "Well, did you do anything bad to anyone lately, like steal from them?" Michael's thought was that perhaps this incident had happened as a kind of divine retribution. Immediately, the man became furious and yelled at Michael. "God, no. No. Of course not. What do you think I am?"

"The point of this story," Michael said, "is that what I did probably did not seem compassionate at the time, but it really was, because I acted to get the man out of his deep pit of sadness and helplessness. I said something outrageous, and he became furious. So at once, he calmed down and this got his feelings of self pity and sorrow out of his system."

"However," Michael paused and looked around thoughtfully, "when you're performing a compassionate act, you need some discernment to choose the appropriate action. There's a difference between performing a right action which is harsh, is based on a benevolent intent, and has a good outcome in the end, and performing an egotistical action which is cruel and really hurts someone. You have to work with your inner voice and your heart to decide what to do."

Next on the list was "Honor," and Michael had a lot to say about this.

"The basis of honor is keeping your promises to yourself. Also, if you're part of a group, you should keep your promises to the members of that group, too. For example, in the ODF, when you make an oath to others, we expect you to be honest and keep it. Of course, before you make any promises to others, be sure first you can trust them. Then, to be honorable, keep your promise."

Michael made a distinction, however, between being honorable with fellow group members and outsiders. "Your honor should be reserved for those you are close to—or for those who are very important to you and you to them. For example, these might be members of your family, your closest friends—and if you've made that commitment, others in the ODF. But . . ." and Michael spoke the words very carefully, to be sure we wouldn't misunderstand, "there's no requirement to be honorable to others. It's generally to your advantage, since it's good for public relations. But you have to be realistic about the outsiders you deal with in everyday life.

"You may have to be ruthless, if necessary. For instance, if you're dealing with a person who has no honor and no integrity, there's no reason to extend honor to them. You'll only get hurt yourself if you leave yourself open to a person who is acting from ill will. Thus, you need to deal with others based on what they give you. Use your own discretion, depending on the circumstances. Be honorable if you can, and you'll find it feels good to do so. But if you can't, don't try. You'll only get taken advantage of if you do."

Michael described a typical situation where it might be advantageous to avoid telling the truth because of the consequences.

"Suppose you're in a basically hostile situation, and someone is confronting you and could be a danger to you if you say what you really think, which might happen in a street situation or a bar. Say some guy asks for your opinion in a challenging way and you know it's different from his. If you speak your mind he might pick a fight, maybe punch you in the mouth. In a case like this, you should ask yourself: 'Will it profit me in the long run to tell the truth or not?' Then, if necessary, let the other person believe his illusions. You've got to be honorable to yourself first.

"It's like an exchange. As long as you feel it's a 50-50 even exchange, proceed with the person honorably. They're meeting you on an equal ground as an equal. So treat them with honor. On the other hand, if someone seems devious or dishonest, the exchange is no longer balanced. So, assuming you have a reason to continue the relationship, you may need to be less than candid to keep the status quo or preserve your own balance in the interchange."

"But what about when you're offering service? You're not expecting the person to treat you back equally then," Serge commented. "I sure don't expect that from my clients, or even from my friends when I help."

"That's different," Michael replied. "When you offer true service, you're giving 100%, and your profit is from the reward of simply giving. But few situations require true service. Mostly, you're involved in a series of exchanges with people. And that's when you should judge whether to act honorably with the person based on whether they are willing to act honorably with you.

"Or look at it this way. Your first promise should be to yourself to see your quest through on the path you have chosen. That's your first honor. Then, your second honor is to those who are trustworthy and to whom you have taken an oath, such as others in the ODF if you have chosen that path. Thirdly, your next commitment is to those who need to be served and to whom you should act with benevolence and compassion. And fourth, there's the rest of the world, and here the key to go by is the spirit of exchange. If it's equal, approach the people in the exchange with honor. And if not, do what you must to preserve a balance."

Next Michael spoke about "Awareness," and he emphasized that "It's vital to pay attention and be alert to both the voice inside and to your outer environment. Most mishaps occur because a person isn't watching or paying attention"

He reminded us of what happened to the man who was shot in a liquor store hold-up. "If you're alert, that sort of thing shouldn't happen. If the man knew better, he would have felt something funny before the incident happened. He might have heard his little voice telling him to go home, because our instinct tells us when danger is coming, if we listen. Or if you work in a situation where you expect problems, knowing about this possibility should make you even more aware."

Michael compared the difference between the aware and unaware person to what happened on the Titanic. "Some people had a premonition and didn't go. So they survived. But other people had a premonition and went anyway. And of course, they didn't make it."

"Sometimes I have premonitions, but they don't happen," Harvey said. "For example, I thought I was going to get a job working with computers, and I didn't get it. And another time I thought a girl I liked would go out with me, but she said no."

Michael glanced at Harvey with a quick grimace of annoyance. "Then you need to be careful in assessing your premonitions," Michael observed. "Of course, not all of them are correct. You have to look for a certain tone or quality to a premonition which suggests that it's true. Then, if it's a potential disaster, you avoid it or head it off. For example, you don't go on the Titanic. Or if you think someone is going to attack you, and it's not appropriate to avoid this, you get prepared so you can defend yourself or strike back. The other strategy is to intensely visualize the situation occurring in your mind to change it, so the difficulty you perceive happening doesn't come to pass.

"It's up to you to decide on the best approach. Though whatever you do, you need to do something when you sense the premonition is real. The feeling of danger is really basic. Our instinct is warning us, and if we're sensitive to it, this helps us survive. Too often, though, many people don't act, because they feel a need to remain in familiar surroundings or stick to familiar actions, and that interferes with what they perceive. But if you are aware and recognize that warning feeling in your gut, you should do something and quick. That's your survival instinct operating, and it's telling you to take some action to survive."

Finally, Michael pointed to the three words "Persistence," "Purpose," and "Patience," which the ODF incorporated into its motto and sometimes included with its lightening bolt through a triangle Fire From Heaven symbol. Michael drew the symbol on the board to illustrate. On top of the triangle, he wrote the word "Silence," along the left side, the word "Purpose," and on the right, the word "Patience."

"We consider mastering these three principles the mark of an ODF knight," Michael said. "These show you have real commitment and mastery of the path—and they enable you to achieve what you want in everyday life."

He pointed his staff at the word "Persistence." This means that no matter how badly things go, you must stay on the path or stick with whatever else you are doing to get through it. It's like you've made a promise to yourself to persist, and so, in keeping with your honor, you must go on. Then, eventually, you'll achieve your goal.

"It's like that with anything. Some people say to themselves, 'I'm too busy to deal with day to day things,' or they don't put the energy they need into achieving a greater goal. So they fail. But to get what you want, you have to see your goal through. Eventually, it will work if you have that commitment and drive. But you have to work on it; you have to persist. The ability to endure counts much more than talent. Determination is the key to success."

Everyone nodded in agreement, and Michael went on to the next word: "Purpose."

"To get where you're going you need a purpose or goal, and you must feel or know it's the right one for you."

He wrote the words, "Personal," "Mutual," and "Societal," on the board and continued.

"There are basically three types of purpose you need to commit yourself to. There's your own *personal* purpose—which is the path you've chosen for yourself—both spiritually and in the everyday world. There's your *mutual* purpose when you interact with the world. This could be a purpose you have with other people to get a project done. Or it could be a purpose you have in performing Magic, where you have to work with nature with a clear goal, and direct everything you do, like a dance, to that end. Finally, there's the *societal* purpose of the world as a whole, as society evolves towards a more advanced state.

"Whatever you do, it's important to keep your purpose in mind. Yet, we believe a warrior should be able to adapt in situations. Whatever happens, you should be flexible in facing it. Your purpose gives you direction. Still, all sorts of things may come up—obstacles to get over, distractions that may divert you from the path. So you have to do what is necessary to deal with them—such as being aware, following premonitions, acting honorably with others, and stepping out of the situation to exercise control. Then you can continue along the path."

Harvey butted in, "But what if there are so many disruptions, you lose sight of the path. That always seems to be happening to me."

"Then maybe you're on the wrong path," Michael snapped at Harvey.

"The point is to combine flexibility with purpose. But you've got to start with that purpose."

Michael glanced back at the blackboard and then went on. "Also, if you do have any problems along the way, be aware that your curiosity can help you override the odds and keep going. If you ask yourself: 'What is going to happen next?' or take whatever comes with the thought: 'Gee, that's interesting,' it helps you want to move on. You approach whatever comes with a feeling of eager anticipation and excitement, and you're ready and prepared. That's because having a purpose gives you a feeling of reassurance. You know what you're doing is right. That way a warrior doesn't need to fear anything, even death. You just look whatever comes in the face and go on. That's the warrior's way."

Finally, Michael spoke about the last word, "Patience." "Patience is difficult to learn, but it involves much more than waiting. It's the ability to kick back, look at the situation, and decide the best way to deal with it. It's the ability to ask: 'What will profit them and me best?' and wait to hear your inner knowing respond. Also, it's the ability to know you must spend time growing, and to accept whatever comes when you do your best.

"It's a little like persistence, in that you have to hang on and continue going, knowing you'll eventually get where you're headed. But patience is the attitude that goes along with persistence, and tells you that everything will work out and things will happen in good time. It involves agreeing with the conditions around you and accepting them, while persistence means pushing on regardless.

"So patience and persistence work hand in hand along with purpose, to keep the warrior on the path. In addition, these principles work with the other seven principles to help the warrior achieve his goals. The key is to choose the right action, be aware of what to do, have the necessary self control and courage to see it through, and work with others in a spirit of service, compassion, and honor."

Michael stepped away from the blackboard and sat down.

"So that's the shaman warrior's way. In short, the ideal warrior follows this philosophy and develops the magical knowledge and skills to back it up. It means becoming a warrior in a true spiritual sense. On the one level, you're able to deal practically and pragmatically with what happens in the everyday world; you're able to handle the down-to-earth issues of survival. At the same time, you're able to use mediation and magical ritual to move to the astral or other-worldly plane, and you know how to protect yourself magically and survive spiritually when you get there.

"In other words, you must learn to balance your spiritual ideals and your efforts to develop personally with the attitude that real life is sometimes difficult or dangerous and must be dealt with. Furthermore, you must be able to deal equally well with any dangers you might encounter on the streets or in the spiritual world, for both are equally real. Sometimes people on a spiritual quest forget this. They think if they are spiritual and positive enough, everything will be glowing and rosy. But you *do* have a body; you *do* suffer or encounter difficulties at times; and these must be dealt with.

"So you have to be able to take care of yourself physically and emotionally to get any spiritual work done. That's why the warrior path stresses achieving a balance between the two. You've got to develop along both tracks—the everyday world and the other world at the same time. As you do, you'll find your development in the one will be reflected in the other.... And, you'll learn more about how to put these principles into practice as you travel along the path."

CHAPTER TWELVE

Death and Practice

The last part of the class on principles dealt with the warrior's appropriate attitude to death.

"You may feel squeamish about discussing this," Michael began, "but it's important to do so, because each person's attitude toward death affects how he or she lives life. It's the most critical event in your life, short of birth. We try to avoid this in everyday life, but you can see the fascination with it everywhere—in the movies, on TV. And that's fine, because to live and experience our lives fully, we must have a sense of our own mortality. Otherwise, if you have no sense of death, you feel you have time to kill and feel no need to strive any further.

"Thus, in a way, strange as it seems, death helps us live. When you realize you will die, you realize time is a-wasting, and you must make the best of the time you have. So you must either accept failure or decide to grow.

"When you decide to try, you have the hope of doing the best you can in getting to your goal. There are no guarantees. But the better you are in your timing, in your balance, and in the other things you learn through magic, the better your chances."

Michael paused and looked around the room. We all sat quietly, reflecting on what Michael had said.

"That's all pretty grim," said Teri. "I think I'd rather not think about this, and just go blithely through life without worrying about the end."

"Oh, thinking realistically about death is not grim at all," Michael replied. "Just true. One way to look at this is to realize that the warrior has two companions on the path—laughter and death. Death shows you the total path—the cycle from birth to death, while laughter makes it bearable. You need that sense of humor, that feeling of okayness to keep you on the path."

Michael gave some examples from his own experience. Every time he went for a grade, for instance, he saw death on his path. And often, he saw death standing there laughing.

"It's like he was there and laughing at times to point up the irony in the constant closeness of life and death. Sure, death can be waiting at the end of the path. But he's ever-present along it, too. For at any time we can step off it into the arms of death. And when we take risks—physical, emotional, spiritual—death can come even closer. Then, as we balance on that edge, we can see the rim between two different worlds, and to some extent we know we have that choice—because we determine where we step. When we choose life, our experience of it, our love of it, our joy in it can be that much more intense. At first I was scared when I kept seeing death along my path, but now I accept it, and use the image as one more way to learn."

To show us how we could learn from this image, too, Michael announced he had a homework assignment for us: to meditate on our own death.

"It'll help you see what has the most meaning for you in life," he said. "So I'd like you to meditate for one full day before our next class. To begin the meditation, imagine that it's your last day on earth—that the next day when class begins your life is over. Then, let yourself feel the presence of death around you. Invoke it. Imagine you can do whatever is necessary in the next 24 hours to get your affairs in order, and live your day as if this is your last. In the process, notice what you value as a priority. What do you choose to do? Suppose you have unfinished business with someone: would you really tell them off or not say anything? Be aware of what happens. Say to yourself: 'I'm going to die in 24 hours,' and take it from there."

Could I really do this with a busy schedule, I wondered. "I'm hosting a big party the night before," I explained. "It's going to be hard for me to concentrate on this then."

"That doesn't matter what you're doing," Michael said. "Your death can happen anytime. So you have to be prepared for it at all times."

Then, getting up, Michael announced that next week we would deal with power objects and psychometry. "So bring along your staffs, any other power objects, and small objects with a history, such as crystals or watches, so you can psychometrize them."

Now, class over, we adjourned to the pizza parlour across the street. The boisterous, laughing people and the aroma of warm, spicy pizza seemed a paradoxical contrast to our talk about death and the principles of the path. Yet a concern with death and the other world still lingered, and after we placed our orders, Harvey commented: "Well, personally I believe in reincarnation and if that's true, there is no death." He stuffed a big slice of pizza in his mouth. "Besides, I'd rather enjoy it all now."

Michael shook his head. "We don't know for sure about reincarnation. We know we can communicate with the other side. We have been in touch with spirits that have come back. And we can explore our own past lives. But in the case of our own particular reincarnation sometime in the future, we really don't know."

"Why not?" Harvey asked between mouthfuls.

"Because," Michael explained, picking up a piece of pizza himself, "there are many probable futures. In one, perhaps you may get reincarnated. In another, you might not. It depends on what happens in the past; what people do in the present; and how people who can envision these probable futures choose to act now. So many outcomes are possible. At the same time, there are multiple realities, which exist simultaneously. We're just finding out about these things."

"Multiple realties?" Harvey said. "I'm having enough trouble with this one." He grinned mishcieviously, like a little kid, and reached across the table for another piece.

Michael leaned back in his chair thoughtfully, and his chair teetered on its back legs, and swayed back and forth.

"Let me give you a few examples to explain," he said. "You may wonder if these stories are just hallucinations or illusions. But I'm convinced they're true. Others saw the same things I did, and I've read of many other such. experiences people have had. For example, one time Gene and I were driving along a road, when suddenly we saw a white car following very close. But when we looked closely, we saw it had no driver. After I notice this, I said to Gene, 'Hey do you see what I see in the car behind us?' and he said, 'Yes, I see it. Or rather I don't see it, because there's nobody driving it. So I'm getting out of here.' And he stepped on the gas.

"Another time, we were both in Westwood near U.C.L.A., and we saw a lone woman walking ahead of us on the street. She passed under two street lights, and at the third, she suddenly vanished. There wasn't a car on the street, and it was 1 a.m., so she couldn't have ducked into a store. Thus, we quickly drove up the street to see what happened, and found there wasn't a place open and there was no one on the street. So there wasn't anywhere she could go. She just disappeared. And we both saw this happen.

"But the most dramatic experience we had of people appearing and disappearing occurred at a vanishing Safeway. Gene and I were driving along the freeway in Southern California, when we noticed a Safeway just off the road in the middle of farm country and we stopped to pick up a soda, since I felt a headache coming on.

"But when we got inside, we felt the atmosphere was very strange. We saw housewives staring ahead with a glassy-eyed expression, and their children had this glassy-eyed look, too. Everyone was moving slowly like robots, and no one said a word. So the whole thing felt very eerie, and we both felt we wanted to get out of there as soon as we could.

"On the way out, I quickly picked up a Dr. Pepper, dropped the correct change on a counter, and we left immediately. Oddly, as we raced back to the car, I felt something was pushing us, as if the energy there wanted us to leave and quick. So we zoomed away. However, after we got a few miles away, we felt better, and wondered what made us feel so strange about the place.

"So we turned the car around and drove back. However, we didn't see the Safeway. There was no exit from the freeway where we had been, just open farmland. So after we drove back a few miles, we turned around, looked again, and circled around five or six times. But we never saw anything, just open farmland with nothing on it for miles around. It was as if the Safeway had suddenly appeared on the farmland from another reality and then got sucked back in again."

"Well, maybe you just missed the turn or didn't drive far enough," I suggested, trying to think of a more everyday explanation.

But Michael quickly rejected my suggestion. "No. No. I'm convinced we stepped into another reality, because we checked the experience out and we know the Safeway was no longer there. We clocked the distance to the Safeway on our odometer. We knew how far we had driven when we turned around, and we even drove off the freeway the last time we stopped to check. And there was nothing, except for a strange, damp coolness in the air. So we felt sure the Safeway had been there. But now it had disappeared."

"That's quite a story," put in Teri. "It's like we think we know what's real. But then we don't. I know I'd like things to be certain. But then I have to accept that they're not."

"That's right," Michael continued. "These kinds of things happen too much to be only hallucinations. Also, these are situations where at least two of us have independently seen the same thing together. So we're certain something unusual has happened, and we're trying to explain it.

"The way we see it is there are parallel realities which exist simultaneously, and sometimes there's an interface. The two realities come together. Or perhaps there's a kind of hiccup or sudden opening in our usually linear reality, so there's a hole for a brief time and the other reality slips in. Then, we can see or interact with people in the other reality. But when that hole closes or that interface disconnects, we're back in our usual linear reality. Another possibility in some cases may be that people from our dimension or the other dimension can visit us through geoteleportation, and we can see them while they're projecting into our reality. However, once they cut that connection, maybe because they see that we can see them, they disappear."

"Could that be why I sometimes experience a former lover with me so intensely that he feels real?" Serge asked. "Mostly, this has happened with someone who's still alive. But a few times I experienced this with someone who had died a few months earlier. It was so real. For a moment, he seemed like he was right in the room, so I could go over and touch him. But then, when I tried, he disappeared."

"Perhaps," Michael said, picking up another slice of pizza. "And these principles seem to apply to the cases I just described. Take the vanishing woman case. Possibly the woman might have been astrally projecting herself into the situation, just as we might project ourselves somewhere else and influence that reality. Or maybe she came through one of these holes in reality and went back in again.

"As for the car case, maybe some unknown energy was following us, like a blob of energy might in the field. Then, perhaps we imagined there was a car following us in order to interpret or structure the unknown. It's a common phenomena. We see some unknown energy, and we perceive it as a familiar form, which often happens in the field. We see the energy of an elemental assume a humanoid shape. Or we see other energy forms appear in the shape of some animal, like a dog or a cat."

"So what happened with the Safeway?" Harvey cut in. "Was that a real Safeway you went into or not?"

"Well, we think that's like the case where people see a city appear, and then it seems to fade away. For instance, a recent local newspaper reported that several people sighted a mysterious medieval-looking city that appeared to come out of the water off the California coast. And then it disappeared, just like the Safeway did. So what may have happened in the few minutes that we saw the Safeway and went in, there was a brief overlapping of realities. So they came together more closely than usual. Then, we were able to get out comfortably because the linkage was still there. But afterwards, the linkage ended, and so we couldn't find the Safeway again."

"Well, what if that link was no longer there while you were still in the store?" Harvey wondered. "I mean, that's what I worry about sometimes when I enter the world of magic. That I'll lose that connection with the here and now."

"Usually you don't," Michael replied. "But you never know. Say in the Safeway case. We might have driven off and found ourselves in the middle of a field. Or maybe we would have been sucked into the other reality and wouldn't be able to leave. Things can get tricky when you enter other realities. You just don't know.

"And it's the same in the field, when we experiment with entering other realities. We have a few theories which others who think about these realities share, too. For example, one theory is that you open up a space when you create a Gateway and can actually step in. Another is that you look through the opening. A third is that the separate realities come together and interface, so you experience them together. Yet, we really don't know."

Harvey looked puzzled. "Well, what about when you seemed to vanish when you did a working on a recent field trip? Could any of these theories explain that?"

Michael nodded. "Perhaps they could."

"On the othere hand," Harvey continued, "did you really vanish? I saw you vanish. But was it due to the darkness or my own perception?"

To answer the question, Michael suggested we return to the apartment to practice the seeing exercises. "The vanishing was real," Michael assured him. "But I want you to have the confirming experience for yourself."

After we got back, Michael set up two chairs facing each other, and he sat down across from Harvey. Serge, Teri and I sat about eight feet away on the couch to watch.

"Now I want you to lift your hand when you see something happen," Michael told Harvey.

Then, Serge dimmed the light and the experiment began for about ten minutes. While it lasted, Harvey slowly lifted his hand a few times, and when Michael called time, we each gave a report.

"I saw you go black briefly," Teri said, "and there were parts of you outlined in bright yellow."

'I saw you fade into the darkness, too," Serge reported.

"I noticed the blackness as well," I said. "And besides this, I saw your face suddenly become masklike, almost like an Aztec mask with splotches of yellow."

"So you see," Michael said, "we all have similar experiences, because something is really happening. One reason you saw me disappear is because I was projecting my consciousness through a black hole. So it's not just your imagination."

"But I wasn't able to actually see through you," Harvey complained. "You didn't really become invisible."

"Don't worry," Michael reassured him. "That takes practice, and you can't expect to have every experience at once."

Harvey fell silent and frowned slightly, as if not fully convinced.

"Anyway, practice your seeing," Michael reminded us, "and remember to imagine your own death. We'll describe our experiences next week. And bring an object you've had for some time, so we can do some experiments on power objects."

As we walked out, Harvey continued to feel perturbed. "But I'm still not sure what I'm really seeing," he said. "I'm still not sure, and I'm not sure I can be sure."

You just have to believe it's true, or you can get stuck in wondering forever," Serge commented. "I know I do believe it."

"And so do I," said Teri. "You have to trust your inner feelings and perceptions. For someone who has been dabbling with magic for so long, you should know that by now."

And on that note we waved goodbye — Serge, the intensely committed believer; Teri, the casual and believing seeker; Harvey, the uncertain explorer who wanted to believe but still had doubts; and me, the uncertain rationalist, seeking for explanations and wanting to understand.

CHAPTER THIRTEEN

Using Power Objects

Our fourth class was on using power objects and power words to communicate with the other world and gain its support for what we wanted. But first Michael wanted to hear about our "last day before death" experience.

It'll make you more aware of how you'll respond to the other world in the field," he said.

Michael described his own day first. "I started by writing my will Friday evening, and that got me thinking about who and what was important to me. In the morning, I went for a long walk in Chinatown and bought some Chinese grave markers. Then, when I walked out of the store, I saw a Chinese funeral. As I watched it go by, I realized I felt very satisfied with my direction in life, and I took stock of what to do next."

Serge reported that he had thought about putting everything he felt he needed in life in a suitcase. "Then I could better see what my life is all about. I feel it's so scattered now. I feel like my emotions are so tied up with so many people. This could give me a chance to sort through all my luggage and decide what I really needed."

Serge also considered what it would be like to have to "walk out the door of life" right away. "I wondered if I would be ready," he said.

"You will be, if you're prepared," Michael said. "And that means being prepared for both life and death. For as we'll see, the lesson of the death experience applies to everyday life and to the warrior's path."

He explained, "The experience teaches another important lesson about adaptability. As a shaman warrior, you must be able to adjust to every situation, and be willing to give up your physical possessions, when it's time

133

to do so, whether you're facing death or going into the field. You need to be able to separate and detach.

"You see, if you can give things away, that shows you're not run by material things; you're not trapped by the consumer society. As a result, you can easily bounce when you need to. Also, when you can get rid of things and simplify your life, that focuses you on the Zen conception of only doing what you must and using only what you need, which tends to produce a very peaceful, calm and centered way of life. You're ready to concentrate on and deal with whatever comes — whether it's life or death. It's a very centered way to live."

It was my turn to describe my experience next. When I explained I hadn't been able to think about my death, since I had been so busy with other things, Michael remarked, "Whatever you do with the experience shows something about how you deal with both life and death. If you're too busy now, that's how you're likely to face death, and it's how you're likely to deal with the spiritual beings in the field. You may not be willing to take the time to truly let them into your life and benefit from what they have to teach."

For Teri, the experience was calming and centering, and Michael observed, "That's probably because you're usually calm and centered. And when people are, most experiences are like this. A person uses the day to take stock of his correct situation, is very calm in doing so, and uses the time well to do what needs to be done, without any big rush. The lesson to learn from all this is you can begin improving yourself immediately, yet feel relaxed about doing it. If nothing remarkable happens, that suggests you're content with your present life, and you've got the stable base you need to build on further."

Harvey, however, found his own day unsettling. "It was so typical. I was expecting something more exciting or unusual, but then as usual, nothing seemed to happen which I wanted. Anyway, I sat around in the morning writing down my ideas, and I was surprised I suddenly didn't care if people accepted me or not. As a result, I didn't try to go to a bar or be the life of the party or chase skirts, which I usually do — though without a whole lot of success. I suddenly felt like it would be easier to live with reality, if I didn't feel like I needed to run after people so much. But then, I felt a feeling of confusion or resistance. Like which is me? Or if I changed from the way I usually am, would I still be me?"

"Well, that's the whole point of being a warrior and on the path," Michael replied. "You want to be open to change. And of course, you're still you, because you're developing yourself to gain more knowledge and power. So your philosophy as a warrior should be to stay flexible. You shouldn't be tied to either ideas or possessions. Thus, if a belief or an object inhibits your purpose, discard it.

"Just think of being on the path as if you're making an investment for tomorrow. The beliefs and concepts you hold now are built on assumptions you have about what will happen in the future. But we can drop or change our ideas whenever we want. And we should as our expectations about the probable future change. It's the same in the field. You have to practice, so you're able to change what you're doing on the spot, as conditions around you change. You've got to be alert, so you can respond and adapt to whatever happens in life."

Michael turned to the wall behind him and pointed at the large poster of a skull and crossbones against a black field.

"Since change is so important, that's why we've chosen the death head as one of the magical symbols we use at times—because the skull stands for transformation. It reminds us that magic forces people to go through transformations as they develop, just like death. Thus, if you make death your friend and adviser, it's impossible to fear it. The whole point of this exercise was to help you realize you can use death as a helpful tool for your own development.

"So capitalize on your own death. Learn from your experience of it coming near, to discover what it tells you about yourself. Also, realize from this experience that you have no reason to fear the unknown. Then, too, be aware that by acknowledging death, the warrior becomes more jealous of life and lives it more fully. The reason is that you realize time is of the essence, and therefore you become more truly present and alive.

"So, as we go out in the field, and as you work on developing magically— take that understanding with you. It'll help you become better warriors, and it'll help you better enjoy your journey and the challenges you encounter along the path."

Everyone now felt complete about our discussion of the exercise, and so Michael turned to the subject for today: using magical words for power. He began by describing the ODF's own magical language, Fermese.

"It's gradually being revealed to us," he said. "So we're gradually discovering words in this language. Later, we'll teach you this language. It was developed for use in ritual like any magical language—to give you a greater sense of power and to emphasize the gravity of the occasion."

'What if I already know a magical tongue?" asked Harvey. "I'm active in several other magical groups, you know." He grinned proudly, as if these links showed he knew a little more than the rest of us in the group.

Michael ignored his posturings and continued. "Use that or ours. Whatever you feel most comfortable with. The point is to use any magical. language in the field to help you converse with any spiritual beings you encounter.

Some groups use languages with a long history, such as the Order of the Golden Dawn which got it's start back in the late 1800's. We could do that, too, but when the ODF was founded, our Founder's allie or spiritual helper started giving us our own language. The Founder went into deep trance, and heard these words. Since then, we've found these words are very powerful for us. Also, some ODF members have gotten their own words through trance, and in some cases other ODFers have started using them, so we've taken them into our language. Our approach is to stay flexible and responsive and use what works."

To illustrate, Michael went over to a large green trunk, rifled through several files, and pulled out a large thick black folder. "We even have our own Fermese dictionary. We've got about 350 words and phrases in it, and we're still working on it. It goes from English to Fermese and Fermese to English."

"Why do you need a special language?" I asked. "Why can't you use English words in a ritual and feel the same sense of power or gravity?"

"It's easier to express certain principles with these words," Michael explained. "They're shorter and more intense to use. Also it's easier to communicate with our allies and the spirits. I don't know why exactly. But it feels more intense, and there seems to be a clearer channel. It's easier to get into another space . . . maybe because the special words add to the impact of the ritual. They make it feel more significant, more out-of-the-ordinary. It's much like wearing costumes or setting up a ritual environment. They help to separate the ritual from what's everyday and mundane.

"Thus, when we use Fermese, we're able to open up another channel for information, just like magicians do with magical words and images in other systems. For example, one group sends out a black ray, which acts like a transmitter and receiver to send out and take in information. Another group uses the Enochian Keys developed by Aleister Crowley to get on a certain communication channel, like turning to a channel on a TV. We experimented with some of these systems in the early ODF days, but found that Fermese seems to be the right channel for us. So we use it in rituals and taking oaths."

As he explained, the group had developed a version of the language called a "low Fermese" for everyday speech. "We use it for internal communication, to speak among ourselves. We can say what we mean quickly, in just a few words, and we can't be understood by others.

"Also we use it when we have to be forceful with some spirits, as in a banishing. For example, once we were at a friend's house, and someone got upset, and we had to get rid of a spirit. So when we did a ritual, we used the Fermese word: 'Acheta!' which means 'Be gone' in speaking to the spirit. And that made it start up, listen, and respond more quickly, because that's a really powerful word—more powerful than saying the same thing in English."

Michael held up a sheet of parchment with several rows of rune-like characters. It looked like an old English manuscript.

"We also have our own alphabet," Michael stated, pointing to the letters. "It's helpful if you want to send information secretly, like a code. Or you can use it if you're carving magical names on objects." Michael held up a staff with a column of rune figures carved along it. "The letters give you more of a magical feeling. And it's more private, too."

After a brief break for coffee, Michael launched into a discussion of power objects. Holding up a long sword and scabbard, he began.

"You can use almost anything as a power object. Swords, staffs, and knives are ideal. They're a way of focusing and extending your power."

He took the sword from its scabbard. "For instance, this is what happens in the Arthurian legend. Arthur's sword is Excalibur, and it's a real practical weapon on the one hand. Yet it also has magical powers. It made Arthur virtually invincible against his enemies. And you'll find lots of other power objects mentioned in myths."

Michael put the sword back in its scabbard and laid it on a table. He glanced at each of us and continued.

"Well, the individual—each one of you—is like that sword. You have both practical and spiritual abilities. And any power object you use is an extension of that. The object is like a channel for your own power. It gets its power through you—or anyone else that charges it with power. It doesn't have any power on its own."

Michael drew two long staffs on the blackboard. One had a fuzzy cloud of energy around it; the second looked like a beam of energy was streaming out of one end and coming to a point, like a knife of light.

"This shows you the difference in what a power object does. The first object is an undisciplined power object. The energy just swirls around the staff, but it doesn't go anywhere. So the staff is no good as a power tool. By contrast, the other one has a single high-power beam of energy, and that's what you need to do anything magically. You have to have some concentrated energy that flows through the object and out into space. You might imagine a laser. Once you have an intense energy beam, you can use it like radar or an antennae for sensing ahead, or as an extension of your will. The key is you need that concentrated energy for the object to work."

As Michael spoke, I recalled my early field experiences, when Michael had taught us to sense with a staff and direct our energy through it to extend power over the surrounding natural and spiritual world. Now he wanted to show us how to make these objects even more powerful energy-focusing devices.

"You need to build and maintain your power object for it to work properly," Michael emphasized. "It's like a car. You've got to keep the battery charged and gas in the car for it to run. And from time to time you need a tune-up. It's a little like that with magical power objects, too. You have to charge them up and keep them charged to keep them running."

So we could do this Michael told us to each get a staff, dagger, sword, or other power object, if we didn't already have one, and spend the following week or two charging and empowering this object.

"You should incorporate this charging process into your regular seeing exercises," Michael said. "When you're looking at something with your usual seeing mode, hold your object, and see the energy coming up through your solar plexus, extending out your arm, and then going into and permeating this object with your energy. Then, if you want, you can channel this energy for a specific intention. For example, if you want to take control over a certain spirit, imagine yourself directing your energy out through your object and getting this being to respond to your will.

"Also, be aware that you can make your object become either more aggressive or receptive than you. You don't always have to use it to exercise more control. You can also use it to receive information and ideas more intensely."

"What about other people?" Teri asked. "I have lots of friends over, and I wonder if they might interfere with the object's magical power. Should we keep out object away from others, so their energy won't disturb it?"

"That's up to you," Michael replied. "Some people or magical groups believe you should. They say you should keep your magical equipment in a special place, so no one can ever see it, much less touch it. But you don't have to do that. When you charge your object, you can build in the idea that you will let people touch it or that you won't. For example . . ." Michael held up his own staff, "I let other people use my power object, and there's no problem with other people's energy, because I have it charged with enough of my own energy. So this overrides any new energy which is added to it. Also, when I use my power object myself, I recharge it again.

"You can visualize your own power acting this way, because the power object is like a battery that can store power and can be recharged at any time."

Michael picked up several objects from a small altar at the side of the room—a round ceramic disc with a five-pointed star; a metal chalice; and a small silver bowl used to burn incense.

"These are all power objects, too," he said holding them up. "In fact, all objects are capable of having energy pumped into them. But these are also ritual objects, used in a ritual in a certain way. Thus, when you charge the pentacle, you should normally visualize it with the spirit of earth; when you charge the chalice, you usually visualize water; and when you charge the incense burner, think fire.

"However, staffs, swords and wands serve a different magical purpose, since they are used as tools and weapons to either banish or evoke spiritual entities from the spirit world. As a result, you use them for much more than for ceremonies—though, of course, they can be used for that, too."

Michael picked up the staff again.

"In any case, as you visualize energy on a successive basis in an object, a charge builds up. It becomes more powerful."

He paused and gazed at his staff thoughtfully.

"In fact, it's good to take a newly acquired power object to bed with you, so you begin to dream with the object."

He told us to try this for the next two weeks. "Start with the seeing exercises to pump energy into your object; then go to sleep with it."

At the word "sleep," Harvey reddened slightly and tittered softly to himself. "I've slept with stranger things," he commented as an aside.

Michael glared at him. "Now, this is serious. I really want you to do this. It's not a joke."

After Harvey nodded his assent, Michael continued, "Now once you start sleeping with this object, notice any changes in your dreams or see if you have more dreams than usual. You may find some changes, because you're dreaming your object into being by sleeping beside it, and doing this physically helps to charge your object more than if you were only doing this mentally while you're awake. This is because your object travels with you in your dreams, and it gets empowered by the dreaming process.

"This kind of charging should last up to two weeks. Don't do it any longer, because after the object reaches the peak of its charge, you'll get drained if you try to charge it any longer, and the object will gradually lose its charge, too."

Then, once our power object was "pumped up," Michael told us to give it a name. "You're dealing with a living spirit now," he explained. "You have been pumping in living energy, so your object has acquired a life force or spirit. You'll be able to feel this out in the field in the way your object reacts. For example, you may think someone is okay, but then you realize you're wrong because you feel your power object resist, since it's acquired a life of its own."

Michael also encouraged us to start using this object actively after we finished charging it. We should take it on field trips. And if we were doing something important, we should take it along, too.

"The more you exercise it, the more you give it life. And the more you practice with it, the better you'll get. You'll find as you discipline yourself, your will becomes more focused, and you'll have more power.

"In fact, you'll find that these fully charged power objects are extremely powerful in the field, especially for banishing potentially dangerous beings, because the charge you've built up has created a strong beam of energy. As a result, you're presenting any entities you encounter with a column of living fire, which can cut them in half."

He described how this happened when he, Gene, and Paul were exploring a cemetery. "We encountered a group of teenagers who told us they saw little gnome-like beings near some grave stones, and then they ran away, because they were scared. We decided to check it out, and we went after these beings with out power objects, ready to do whatever was necessary. At first, we didn't see anything. But after a few minutes, we saw some small dark forms flitting around between the trees, and we headed for them. Some of them broke away for the open ground, but we got up to a group of them, and I shot my wand at one of them. I saw the energy pouring through, and he ducked and ran. He could see the fire coming out from the end of the staff and he retreated."

Michael claimed he had done a similar banishing on another field trip with 30 students. The students were meditating in the field, when Michael saw a white humanoid-like form walking towards them. He zoomed out to protect them, and when the being turned and headed toward Michael, he pointed his staff at it. "And that zapped it," he said. "There was a purple haze for a moment after I shot it, and then nothing. Some of the students saw this happen, too."

"How does the process work?" I asked. "Are you imagining that these beings are gone, and then you don't see them anymore? Or are you referring to the real physical events?"

"Oh, what's happening is very real," Michael reassured me. "It's the same kind of damage that would occur if a physical being was hit by a physical object. The energy charge you send out operates like a laser or a bullet. It blows up the beings.

"You see, these beings are really forms of life, though at a different level. There's no imagination involved. They're real. Some are physical, some semi-physical, some non-physical—but they're all real. It's because we're all energy, and these beings are, too. So if you interrupt that energy by sending out a blast of your own energy, it's the same as what happens when someone interrupts the energy in your own body by striking you in any way."

"When do you have to start worrying about these things and do something to stop them?" Serge wondered. "With my luck, they'd probably jump me before I could do anything."

You only have to get concerned about them bothering you if they get too close," Michael said. "I'm generally comfortable as long as they stay about 30 feet or more away, unless I've already gotten control of a being. But if something starts coming at me, and I don't have this control yet, I just vaporize it. These things move fast. Some of them can go up to 90 miles an hour or faster. So you've got to pay attention and be alert."

Michael picked up his staff again and waved it in front of him a few times.

"Thus," he said, summing up, "you use your object to banish and command the elements, to invoke things, and cut Gateways. You can do these actions without an object. But the object helps you focus your concentration, and it boosts whatever you're doing, since you tap into its power as a reserve of additional energy. That's why when you charge it up, your object has even more energy to offer. You've built up that charge like a battery—and when you call on that energy, it's like turning on a flashlight. The object sends out its beam directly into both the natural and spiritual world, and you can use that beam to do what you want."

"What about using it in other situations when you're not in the field?" Teri wanted to know. "Say I'm in the office and someone or something is bugging me?"

"Sure, use it. Your power object is also good in practical situations," Michael said, "because other people can feel the energy in these objects. They might not be able to understand exactly what they're experiencing or why—but they sense something powerful is affecting them. Thus, if that's what you want them to do, they'll pull back."

Michael described an encounter with a California Highway Patrol Officer to explain. "Gene and I were going a little fast, when this officer pulled us over. He warned us about driving too fast, and then said he wanted to search the car, because he noticed these strange objects on the back seat, which were basically our power objects and some ritual gear. We had some staffs, swords, chalices. However, when he opened the back door and reached over to them, he suddenly stiffened and snapped back his hand, as if it had been burned by the heat or spirit of fire residing in these objects. And really, he had, because you can feel the energy coming out of the tip of a power object. Anyway, after that, the officer became disoriented, shut the door, and told us to go. He didn't even write the ticket. I don't think he really knew what hit him. It was just too weird for him, and he let us go."

"How far does this power extend?" Serge asked. "Say I'm home and my roommate has been giving me a hard time, like happened yesterday. I really felt like telling him to move out, he was complaining so much. And he was in the other room when I thought that."

"The level of power is different, depending on how you charge your object and what you're using it for. Usually, when you're at rest with your object and are not trying to do anything with it, you can see a semi-transparent beam of energy about six inches long. But this beam can become very intense when you're working with the object. Usually, the beam will go out about six feet from the tip, when you're working on passing a grade or doing any action that requires some intensity like an invocation or a banishing. But the beam can go even further, say up to a mile or so, when you're really working hard, such as when you're trying to sense if someone is on the other side of a hill, or you want to influence someone who's off in the distance. Or in your case, you could use it to influence your roommate to leave.

"So, your staff is an extremely adaptable little tool, and that's why we use it as the main power object in the ODF. But it's not the only power object you can use, for you can build others."

Michael went over to the alter and picked up a few small objects. He held up a small grayish stone.

"This is an example of another kind of power object—a talisman. That's something you build up by charging it with power with a specific purpose in mind. For example, maybe you might use this for good luck or to ward off something."

"Like my roommate?" Serge commented.

Michael nodded and glanced back at the alter. "Possibly you could. You see, having a variety of objects in a temple or at an altar gives you flexibility. You can have objects for different purposes; and perhaps even have a specific object representing a certain person, say for banishing."

"Like voodoo dolls?" Harvey asked.

"Well, that's one kind of talisman," Michael acknowledged. "Though I'm not advocating sticking pins in people to harm them. Basically, I'm saying that any object can become a power object or talisman if you charge it. For example, you could charge a penny and give it to a person, and it has an effect."

"Does the person need to know you charged it for it to work?" I asked. "Is it the recipient's awareness that gives the power object its effect?"

"No," Michael stated firmly. "The effect isn't due to the person's imagination alone. It's real energy. It assumes a physical form. Sure, you've built up that energy by clearly visualizing it; by using your imagination, combined with your will, to direct your own force into it. And you can keep your object recharged in the same way. But that energy you direct into it becomes real. You can see it and feel it. And other people can, too. However, if you leave a power object alone for awhile, it will gradually lose its energy, just like a battery loses its charge. Thus, when you use a power object, you might think of it as functioning on some wave length, depending on how much energy you have given it. It's a little like a firecracker and a grenade.

You can make your object as strong as you like; but no matter how strong, over time, that energy will wear down. So to keep that energy up, you've got to charge your object again."

"However..." Michael paused and rummaged through the small pile of objects in his lap. Then pulling out a pebble, he went on:" ...there are also one shots—power objects you charge for the moment and use just once."

As an example, Michael described an incident that happened to him in the woods a few years before when several people were following him. He was walking along a narrow isolated path by a creek, and he felt nervous about the other hikers. "So," he explained, "I picked up a pebble and charged it. Then, I tossed it back at them, and they walked around the pebble by going into the woods and about 10 feet further, they returned to the main path. So that slowed them down and I felt like I diffused any problems, if they had intended any harm. A little later, when I was returning home on the trail, I saw the same pebble on the ground—but now it was just an ordinary pebble."

Michael then suggested a few more techniques for charging objects, stressing the need for good visualization.

"When you charge anything, you can use your breathing, words, chants, incantations. Whatever you want. But it's also crucial to visualize your energy pouring into the object, and you should see this as a clear direct beam, which is carrying your intention about what you want the object to do."

Michael passed around his collection of pebbles and asked us each to take one for an experiment. I picked out a small brown stone with white streaks and held it tightly, as Michael explained what to do.

"Now, I'd like you to handle the object, hold it tightly, and visualize your energy going through it and out into space. You want to mix your energy with whatever is there and send your intention into the object. Your intention is the key. For example, you could create one object to attract; another to repel; one to invoke; another to banish. Or you can create an object you use for a number of things, although a single purpose object can be especially powerful for that purpose."

As Michael instructed, we each concentrated on our object for a few minutes, until he told us:

"Now, release the energy. You want to let the energy go if you're not going to use something again after you're finished with it. . . . So just visualize the energy dissipating and break your connection with that object."

When we were done, we passed the objects back to Michael.

"I felt a real surge of power," said Serge.

"I could feel my object getting much warmer as I charged it," said Teri. "And it wasn't only because it was in my hand. I could feel it radiating real heat."

Michael nodded. "That's right. You can often expect that feeling of radiation, because we're dealing with real energy. And when you create that energy, you can not only see it, but you can feel it is there."

Michael put the objects back on the altar, returning to the center of the room.

"In fact," he continued, smiling broadly, as he often did before making an especially important, yet unexpected announcement, "you don't need to have a physical power object at all, though it helps. For you can create your own power objects, just by visualizing them and charging them with energy. For example, when you create a pentagram with your staff in the field, you're building a power object. And it's not just a visualization. It's real, because you can see the sparkles or energy trails in the air, and you will often experience a change in temperature. Then, when you draw a circle around the pentagram, that helps you focus your energy in it. Also, the circle acts like a shield to protect the power object you have just created."

"Does that mean," I asked, "that you could imagine you have a knife, staff, or any other power object, rather than using something physical?"

"Of course," Michael said, "you certainly can. But having the real physical object helps. It gives you a focus. It helps to set the mood, to get you in a magical space. The idea is to use what's appropriate for the occasion and what you feel comfortable using. So if you don't have a power object with you—sure, use your imagination to create what you need. After all, the power comes from you; the power objects are merely used to help you generate and focus that power. . . . In fact, the symbolic value of the objects you use can be a source for creating power, too."

Michael held up a small disc with the image of a pentagram on it as an example. "You see, the pentagram represents the four elements. So when you work with the elements and make a pentagram, the image helps to reinforce your work. That's why we use the clockwise pentagram for invoking, and a reverse or counter-clockwise pentagram for banishing. After all, it makes more sense to use a forward movement to bring something forth and a backward movement to send something back."

Michael passed the pentagram disc around the room and asked us to hold it and see if we could feel anything. "Notice any energy, any vibrations coming from it," he said.

As we passed it around, he continued. "You see, the symbols you use resonate and interact with the environment. So when you use a symbol that reinforces what you're doing, you strengthen that action. It's one more way to intensify the focus you want—so you have all your energy and everything around you all working to the same end. Then, you're more effective in getting what you want."

Finally, Michael cautioned us against letting others handle these objects, unless we took the necessary precautions.

"Normally, you don't want others handling your power objects, because others can pollute it. They can contaminate it with their energy, unless you do something to counteract that. For example, I use my power objects in classes and let my students use them. But I prepare for that in advance. When I charge each object, I tell it to suck up any other person's energy and to use that energy as long as it is positive. But if the person's energy is negative, I instruct the object to recycle it to make it positive, so no one can put any energy into the object to use against me. Thus, no matter who touches the object, I can use it without any problems. If you want to allow others to handle your objects, you should use this kind of a protective charge, though whether you let others touch them is completely up to you."

After a brief break, we returned to the final lesson of the evening—on psychometry, which Michael described as "the reverse of building up a power object. You use it to get a feeling of the energy of the object, and then you can pull out information and images from that energy."

To illustrate, Michael asked Serge to hand him the staff Serge had adopted as his power object. Michael held the staff in front of him and concentrated on it, as he continued to talk.

"You want to let the power circulate through your object as you hold it, and then concentrate on being totally receptive to this power. So let the energy flow from the object into your mind, and open yourself up to the essence of that object flooding in. Soon, you should start getting pictures or feelings that represent the energy impressed in the object. It's like your object has become a camera taking photographs, except that you're taking a picture of the energy structure that's in there. You can do this because when the energy is put into an object, an impression or an image stays with it, even though the energy itself may have dissipated. You can't always tell why a particular image is so important. But even so, you should let the images come through and be open to them, whatever they are. Later you can try to interpret them, or maybe get some feedback from the owner of the object on what they might mean. And the more you do this, the better you'll get at seeing images and interpreting them."

Michael closed his eyes for a few moments to concentrate on the impressions he was getting from Serge's cane. Then, he spoke softly, slowly, as the images came to him.

"Okay . . . I'm seeing an image of a hand. Now, I see something red. It's a car. . . . And now a street."

He shook his head and opened his eyes.

"Do those images mean anything to you?" he asked Serge.

"Yes," Serge nodded, and he explained he recently had to defend himself with the cane against a gang of toughs. He got out of his parked car in a rundown city neighborhood, when three men approached him, asked for money, and began beating him. He struck back with his cane, and they finally fled, leaving him a little bloody and bruised.

"Then, it's probably those images I'm picking up," Michael observed. "They got impressed in the cane when you had that experience, and now, since I'm being receptive to your cane, I'm seeing those impressions."

Michael handed the cane back to Serge.

"So, you all should do a little detective work when you do psychometry. Ask some questions and see what images come to you. The key questions to ask are: 'Who had the object?' 'Where was it?' and 'What was it used for?'

"Then, listen to whatever comes. You need to trust your ability to feel the object, sense its essence, and get important accurate images. As you practice and learn to be more receptive and trust yourself more, your ability will improve, and you'll gain more confidence in yourself. You may still have a lot of unanswered questions from your experience. But even so, you must still believe you're getting something of validity—and increasingly, you will."

"When should one use this technique?" I asked.

"To get information whenever you want," said Michael. "It's extremely valuable for telling you things you can't learn about otherwise. You can also use it to do detective work."

Michael described how he did this during Samantha's solo, when he approached her on recovery. He found her hat a few yards away from her and psychometrized it, so it would tell him what was happening and whether it was safe to approach Samantha.

"And I learned it was safe," he related, "when I picked up a sense of neutrality from her hat, so I was able to step forward and feel everything was okay. Otherwise, I would have been less certain about what to do, since I felt all these strange energies in the air, which I later learned had tried to lure Samantha over a cliff. So the hat gave me the information I needed to feel it was safe to go in.

"A warrior needs this kind of information," Michael added, "since a warrior should always be skeptical and cautious. You've got to test the waters first, before you rush in. The psychometry technique is a tool to help you find out about and read people, whether you know them or you happen to see them on the street."

As Michael explained: "Say you want to read someone. Send your energy through as if you're doing a healing. Then, feel around the person's body to see if anything is wrong or pick up any thoughts. Another way to pick up information is to extend your aura out until you feel their aura. Then, mingle your own aura with the person's, and with your eyes still open, allow yourself to pick up any images you experience."

Michael suggested we try this with objects and people we saw far away. "Cars and people are especially good for this. Just sense where they're coming from. Even if you're far away, that doesn't matter. The key is to contact and interact with their energy. Then, check yourself later to see if the information you got was correct. That feedback will help you get better and better at doing this."

Michael gave an illustration from his own experiments in L.A. He was driving through Death Valley, when he saw a car several miles away, and he projected his energy to the car. "I picked up the image of a lady by herself," he commented. "Then, when the car caught up with us, I saw I was correct. There was a single lady driver."

Michael went over to the trunk again, rummaged around in it and returned to the middle of the room with a road map atlas. He flipped through a few pages and held the book open to California.

"You can psychometrize any object," he continued. "It doesn't matter if the owner is there or not. For instance, you can take a book or a map of a local place or even a whole country, put your hand over the picture, and pick up what's going on. Even though the object is only a piece of paper, you can do this. This works too, because even a picture or a map will contain an impression of the energy it has accumulated over the years."

Now Michael asked us to take out the objects we had brought, so we could test our abilities to psychometrize for ourselves. "The way to do this test," he explained, "is to gather several objects with a history which you don't know about, but someone else does. Then, focus on each object, touch it if you can, perhaps hold it in your hand, and see what images come up. Afterwards, ask the owner of the object to respond to what you describe and see if you are correct."

To do the test, Michael asked us to pair up.

"You'll take turns reading each other's object. Just let your mind relax, like you're doing a seeing exercise. Then, once you feel fully relaxed and receptive, experience the images that come."

We settled down around the room, each facing a partner. I first sat across from Harvey and handed my watch to him. He scooped it up in his hands, made a fist, and concentrated on it with his eyes closed.

"I see a desk. I see the watch laying there when you aren't wearing it.... And nearby a clothes closet.... There are many clothes there.... It's in the corner of the room."

Meanwhile, as Harvey spoke in a low monotone, Michael moved around the room, listening first to us and then to Serge and Teri. After awhile, he stopped by us again, and when Harvey fell silent for a few moments, Michael interjected:

"Try a tighter focus on what you get. Don't just report on the general environment. Get more focused and directed."

After several minutes, we shifted around, and I sat opposite Serge. This time, I handed over my keys, and like Harvey, Serge held them tightly as he concentrated on the images and sensations they suggested.

"I see a roundish structure with columns. . . . You're on a trail by the ocean. . . . You're going up a hill, then looking down on a grove of palm trees. . . . Now you're looking over the coast line. It's much greener than in California. . . . I see you alone with a man, someone you are close to. . . . Now, I am seeing the inside wall of a cabin, and there's a lake near it. . . . It's like in the Midwest. . . . Now I see rubber boots walking through a grassy area. It's full of rain. It's soft and wet . . . "

Just then, Michael passed by.

"Good . . . good," he commented. "Nice and specific. . . . Now, after you get all those images, you can interpret them."

"Who should do the interpreting?" I asked.

"Either one of you. If the images have some meaning for you, you might comment on them. Or maybe Serge might say what they mean to him. These images will mean different things to different people. They may be literal—or maybe only symbolic of something else. So the first step is to let them come through and get whatever comes. Then, you can think about what they mean afterwards."

"Well, they don't mean very much to me," I stated.

"There's also the possibility they may have some meaning in the future. For example, maybe something will happen that will show the images are predictive. So keep track of these experiences, and check them out in the future. If they don't have meaning for either of you about the past or present, they could be significant about a future time. Or maybe since you're both learning, regard this as an experiment, and pay attention to what feels accurate and what doesn't. Then, notice what happens when you feel you're right, so you can be more confident when you pick up images in the future to know when you're right on."

We experimented a little longer, and when we finished, Michael explained another form of psychometry with images alone.

"You use the same mental faculties, as if you're psychometrizing an object. The difference is that you're focusing on a mental image or symbol. For example, suppose you're trying to come up with a symbol for a new group or organization. You might already have a few possible images in mind. With this technique, you focus on each one in turn, and see what sort of images and associations come up. Then, that can help you decide if something is a good image to use. Or it can tell you about the person who uses that image as a personal symbol."

To illustrate, Michael asked us to imagine what various ODF members might be like who wore different patches on their shirts. He described one emblem as a thunderbird, another as a firebird, a third as a rearing horse.

"Now what do you see for each person?"

We closed our eyes, concentrated, and stated whatever came to mind.

"The person with the thunderbird looks like a boy scout. . . . He seems to be powerful, maybe progressing rapidly. . . . The person with the firebird seems outwardly ordinary, but he is very disciplined, too. . . . He's warm, friendly, humorous. . . . The man with the horse has a backpack, and he's walking through a green meadow with pine trees around it. . . . He has companions nearby. . . . He seems to be an authority, with command over his companions and himself . . . "

"You see. It works. The person with the thunderbird is Carl, and he's like that. Gene is the firebird, and he has those qualities. And Brad wears the horse. . . . So you see, you can tune into people with images and symbols. Just like people choose these symbols to represent themselves, you can use them to see who they are."

Now the class ended and Michael urged us to spend the week practicing with our power objects and to experiment with reading objects and images. Then, next week, we would finally have a session with his allie or spiritual helper, and we could ask for her advice and help.

CHAPTER FOURTEEN

Session With The Allie

When I arrived for our fifth class, Serge, Teri and Harvey were already there. As I joined them in the living room, Serge was telling Teri about his latest blow-up with his roommate. "I'm concentrating on getting him to move," he said, "and I think he's starting to pick up on that. He talked about how maybe he might be better off somewhere else. Now I'm going to concentrate on his looking for something."

Meanwhile, Harvey, looking cheerier than usual, told me how he was already starting to use some of his psychometry techniques to help him be more successful with women.

"I've asked a few women I recently met to give me a watch or piece of jewelry to hold for awhile."

"And did that work?" I asked.

"Well, I haven't learned how to pick up much psychic information," he said. "But it does get a conversation started."

After a few minutes, Michael appeared and sat down in a straight backed chair he had placed facing us in the center of the room. At once, everyone became silent and somber, knowing that soon Michael would have a session with his allie. He had described this session very generally as a very deep trance experience, in which he would let his spiritual helper speak through him. Now, he wanted to explain in more detail what would happen.

"I'll be doing a concentrated channeling in a few minutes to contact my allie," he began. "Once I bring her through, you can talk to her and ask her questions. When this happens and you hear her speak, you may wonder whether she is inside or outside of me. You may ask is this an outside spirit coming through, or am I calling on an inner being or part of me for help? But it doesn't matter. The allie is a being both within and outside of each of us, and she or he is capable of both external and internal actions. There's a real intelligence involved that's separate from us, and if we listen, our allie can guide us through some tight and difficult situations."

"How does that happen?" I asked.

"You have to have enough knowledge to ask the right questions. Then, after you ask, you'll get back answers, and it's a process of working with what you've got."

"Do we all have allies?" Serge wondered.

"Of course," Michael replied. "But it takes time to develop a good and strong connection with your allie, so your allie is readily available to give you information and advice. Right now, for example, we do a lot of work with my own allie. She's the main one we call on in our L.A. group. But there are many allies we work with. For example, Gene and Paul have a very strong connection with their allies. And other ODFers are working on developing a close connection with theirs."

"What's the allie like?" I asked. "How is an allie different from other spirit beings?"

"Essentially, she or he is like a personal guide or friend. The spiritual essence is the same for everyone, but the personality, the traits are different for everyone, since every spirit being has his or her own essence. But your allie is never in conflict with you. He or she always speaks the truth, as long as you listen carefully. However, your allie can still be playful with you at times, and sometimes humorous and joking. You can tell, though, when your allie is being serious and has important information to tell you, or when he is being a big tease. So the way to tell is to flow with it, whatever is happening. Just trust your allie, and you'll find the answers and experiences come when you need them."

"What's your allie's name?" Harvey asked. "And what does she look like?"

"I can't say her name," Michael said. "That's because some magical names can't be spoken aloud or told to others or they lose their power. Also I have never been able to see her form. When I asked once what she looked like, she exploded into a brilliant white light. But that's typical. An allie doesn't want to be seen or pinned down. But when I need her, she'll be there. I just have to use the trance to open up the door to communicate with her.

"For that's how it is with most allies. When you try to get answers about who they are, you tend to get ambiguous answers. So simply think of your allie as an intelligent and benevolent being with whom you can develop a close relationship. Then, to do that, you have to go through a process of interaction, a little like a training process, where you learn to get better and better at how you communicate."

"How does she communicate with you?" Teri asked. "And can I communicate with my allie that way once I meet her?"

"And how do you know if the information is correct?" Harvey put in. "With my luck, I might get all the wrong information from my allie and never know it."

Ignoring Harvey's comment, Michael continued his explanation. "Well, the information seems to come across as it suits the listener best. Also, allies seem to be both good and evil. Much like most people, they seem to have two sides to their nature. For example, some things they say can be very benevolent and helpful. But they can put you through some tough tests, too, some of which really test your personal power. If you fail, that can take your life. But when you come through it, you go on to higher and higher peaks. It's like the allie can push you into doing things correctly or else."

"What kind of challenges?" I queried.

"Well, say you're on the street in a dangerous situation. Say someone's threatening you. The allie might come to you with some advice on how to stand up to this person. However, if you don't use this information correctly, you've put yourself at risk. For instance, if you don't know what you're doing in a street encounter, the guy can turn on you. But if you do have the right knowledge, you can conquer the situation."

Michael explained that his own allie had appeared to him a number of times on field trips, sometimes to give a warning about potential dangers; other times, just to talk.

"It's really unpredictable when she appears. However, generally we have found that these allies show up when you need them. Sometimes it can be a long time between contacting them. But when they're there, you can reach very deep levels of communications with them. It's like having an angel around you, who can give you a feeling of being overseen at all times, so you feel protected. Yet, at the same time, it's like having a two-edged sword, since your allie can set up potentially dangerous challenges and tests for you—especially in the beginning, until you prove yourself worthy. But other times, you'll find your allie can be very gentle and benign."

Michael gave an example of a challenge he had experienced. He was on a field trip, when he saw the image of a wolf turn into a woman. "I saw that change as a sign that I should be alert to potential dangers, both in the field and on the street. You have to be sure when to trust what you see, because things may not be what they seem. For example, the outward appearance may be of a woman. But there may be some evil creature lurking underneath. So you have to be prepared to deal with it. In this case, I felt my allie was giving me that information, so I would be alert and ready to deal with a dangerous situation later."

"Where do these allies come from?" Teri asked. "How do they learn what they know?"

"We think it's a process of evolution," Michael replied. "These beings once existed on earth, and then they evolved spiritually to a higher plane. For the most part, these beings leave us on our own and don't interfere. But when something critical comes up for us, they intervene. They're a little like a tough parent who turns a kid out of the house when it's time to grow up. They help us when we need them—but when they think we're ready, they give us new lessons so we can move on and grow."

Michael paused and looked at us intensely, as if ready to make an important point. He continued.

"Perhaps the easiest way to see this being is as a separate spirit guide that communicates with us, but isn't oriented to any particular religion. However, it can link up with any religious system you believe in. For example, the allie might be like the Holy Guardian Angel in Christianity, or an aspect of the Goddess, if you have that belief. In any case, it's a privilege to establish contact with your allie, and once you do, a deeper realm of experience and communication becomes possible. Also, whenever something comes up that you lack knowledge about, you have a source that can provide you with the answers every time. Additionally, you can use this source to test whether what you're doing is valid. For instance, when we had to make some decisions about ODF policies, we asked our allies, and they helped us decide what's best for the group."

"Does this knowledge come from inside you or outside you?" Serge wondered.

"We're not really sure whether that knowledge is from a deeper part of oneself or from an external source. Where it comes from is not that important. What is important is that we have this source to turn to when we need it, and the answers we get are always the truth."

Now, having concluded his explanation, Michael was ready to demonstrate how he communicated with his allie—or as he termed it, he was about to have "a session with his allie." Briefly, he described the process.

"I don't need any special preparation to meet my allie. Mainly, I need to be centered, clear, and honest when I deal with her."

Michael sat forward on the chair and placed his palms on his legs. He shifted around until he felt comfortable and planted his feet firmly on the floor.

"Essentially, what will happen now," he continued, "is I will go into a trance state. Then sometimes while I'm in that state, the phenomena produced will become visible, and you can use your seeing to observe it. When I first started channeling, I didn't remember what happened in this state, but now I can."

"What does it feel like when you're in touch with her?" Serge asked.

"I get a sensation of moving back in space when she enters. I feel like I'm floating backward, and after awhile I can look out into space, where I see people as points of light. Then, it feels like I'm having a very rapid conversation, even two at once; but soon, the conversation drifts over to the most important topic. It focuses on the subject that needs the most attention.

"Then, the answers seem to come freely. It's as if there's a force there that knows these answers, whatever you say. And when I'm in trance, I become a channel for that force.

"You'll also notice that the aura of the room changes when the allie is present. The shift will be very quick, but you may be able to sense it. It's like a heaviness—a fullness. It's hard to explain. But when you pay attention, you can feel another force or presence there."

Michael added that he preferred to speak to his allie in Fermese, the ODF's magical tongue, because that created a clearer channel of communication. "Fermese is the way they normally talk to us; so that smooths the way." However, as Michael assured us, "I'll report what was said to you in English, so you'll easily understand what she said."

"What about coming back?" I asked. "When the session is over, how do you come back?"

"It takes time to return and get control. But gradually, I feel her leaving me, and then I'm back."

We had no more questions, and so Michael got ready to begin the session. Though he often contacted his allie by merely concentrating on relaxing his body and going into trance, this time, he began by performing a short ritual to consecrate a circle.

"You need to set up a proper working situation to contact the allie most of the time," Michael explained. "When I'm alone, I usually just go into a quiet meditative state. But since you are present, I felt I needed some extra ritual preparation to open up the door to that connection and help her come through clearly and correctly."

To start the ritual, Michael went over to his altar near the window where he had set up some ritual objects—a cup, pentagram, incense, several candles, and a knife. He put on his black ritual robe, and held up the cup representing water, then the pentagram for earth, and lastly the incense burner for fire to salute the four directions. Then, using his knife he drew a series of pentagrams in circles in each direction plus one above and below himself to make an opening into the other world and create a chamber of protection for the ritual area. Finally, after scattering water from the cup and shaking the incense burner at the four directions, Michael sat down on the chair in the center of of the circle and began to meditate quietly.

In a few moments, the four of us noticed that the room felt colder, as Michael claimed usually occurred when he did a working. Soon we all noticed a shimmery white aura around him, and Serge and Teri saw a shadowy image or "double" behind him.

"Good evening," Michael said suddenly in a small faraway voice, which indicated that the allie had taken over his persona and was now speaking through him.

Serge, as arranged in advance with Michael, now began to question the allie. Each time Michael replied, Serge posed another question.

"Are you aware of our presence?"

"Yes."

"How many of us are here now?"

"There are four of you. . . . And two others seem to surround yourself." Michael gazed directly at Serge.

"Who are the two?" Serge continued.

"Both are males. One is light haired and younger. The older is dark haired. He's more agitated, less in control. The younger seems more familiar with you."

"What are their names?"

"I do not know. They tend to hold back. I gather that the one with the dark hair has had some dealings with you that still causes you to need to finish the matter. But the younger one seems content."

After Serge asked several more questions, Michael, still speaking as the allie began describing some relationships Serge had with these two men, which Michael, in his waking state, didn't know about. He described one as a lover, the other as a friend.

"It seems you have been having some difficulties with this situation. I can feel a pull. Maybe the sensation of a continuing loss is difficult to deal with."

"Are they the same beings who visited me in a vision a few weeks ago?" Serge asked.

"The younger one is. The older one . . . it's difficult to say for sure. It seems he hasn't found peace yet."

Serge responded as if he knew exactly what Michael was talking about.

"I thought he might be suffering when we parted. It happened so unexpectedly, and so many things were left unfinished and unsaid. How can I assist him?"

"Perhaps inquire about what needs your attention, and let him know you will take care of it. Thus, he doesn't need to concern himself with any of that."

Serge then asked about his own allie. Was Michael aware of him? What was his allie like? Did he have a male or a female identity?

Michael responded cryptically. "You perceive it that way . . . as a male. But in whatever form it appears, the force exists for you. . .it may be related to that dark haired person. Perhaps some incident ties them both together.... In any case, you have left behind you a great darkness out of which the lighter side of you has traveled.... Now there's a great choice for you in the future. Maybe lighter times lie ahead. You can make a decision to stay where you are or move on. That choice rests with you.... Neither of the men really hold you, though you seem to have been stuck and are holding back. But now, it's your choice—to stay or move on."

Michael fell silent and gazed at the floor, having finished with his comments to Serge.

After several moments, Teri spoke up. "Is there anything you wish to say to me?"

Michael began hesitantly. "This is somewhat new to me, talking to you, since you are not familiar.... Yet I feel obliged to tell you what I think. You seem hesitant, cautious. I wouldn't be afraid to give. I wouldn't be so reluctant. Perhaps certain painful things have happened in the past, yet you must take certain risks. I don't know if you'll take them. There is some doubt. Yet, it seems the wisest choice for future goals is to take risk.... Little can hurt you. You have found strength through hardship.... So now you must know this path you are on better.... Your experience is already great. . . . Yet, you can look more deeply and challenge yourself. . . . You can increase your ability to receive. . . . But you must become more aware of your own space to do so."

Teri nodded with comprehension. She had been exploring a number of religious paths in the last few years, and Michael's message seemed to zero in directly on her feelings of uncertainty about how far to go along the ODF's path. Michael hadn't mentioned being aware of her feelings before; but now, in this trance-like state, he, speaking as the allie, seemed to tune right in on them.

Meanwhile, as Michael spoke, Serge walked over to him and began walking in a circle around him, while moving his hands up and down to feel Michael's aura. After several passes, Serge sat back down again on the couch.

"What advice do you have for me then?" Teri persisted.

"I would say what you find of value is the key. Take it and use it. Do so with whatever gratitude you see fit.... And don't be concerned about any complications that may arise as you proceed. The key question to answer is what are your priorities. Decide on these and then go on."

"Thank you." Teri leaned back on the couch, thoughtfully contemplating the message.

Then Serge had a few more questions. "Do you have any advice on how I can strengthen my communication with my allie?"

"The bond is something you must seek," Michael cautioned. "Yet it arises at its own time. You allie is aware and does want to communicate with you. So seek him out. Yet be aware of the power around you. . . . You're still feeling some conflict over a past relationship. So a direct contact might be devastating now. . . . Better to act through your allie. He can help you by broadening and strengthening you, so you're better able to cope. . . . It's difficult to say exactly what events will arise demanding your allie's immediate presence. Yet, there will be some, considering the possible mischief you like to get involved in. So seek out your allie; then wait. It won't be long, and he will contact you."

Finally, Michael had some observations about Serge's relationships, which were an important part of his life.

"I see there will be a number of lovers. But how well things will work out remains to be seen. Anyone you draw close can be a challenge to you. So in dealing with lovers, you will often find the time comes when you both realize you have separate paths to follow, and that may end things. But keep going along the path, and there will be more."

At last it was my turn to ask questions.

"What do you see for me?" I asked.

"You take excellent notes."

"What else?" I asked, concerned that my note-taking might block Michael, as the allie, from seeing anything more. But Michael went on.

"Well, I see you faced with a challenge. You're not completely aware of what you have involved yourself with. The challenge ahead may prove difficult. . . . You can remain as you are. And it may be wise to take this course. But if you want to go further, you have the opportunity, though you place yourself at risk . . . "

As Michael spoke, I wondered what challenges and risks. Was he suggesting that I needed to let go and respond more intuitively rather than seeking to analyze everything? Was he suggesting that I might find it difficult to do this or face some dangers if I did?

He continued. "You desire power, as do we all. . . . And certain things ring true about this path for you. Yet a change in affairs comes with difficulty. . . . Things become different, and that represents a world change to you . . . one that's hard to conceive. . . . You have touched this new world to a degree. It can proceed much further. . . . Certainly, it would be well if we could remain as we are. But we do not. Therefore, I warn you of what lies ahead. . . . Circumstances may become so altered, you may have to learn to see things in a fashion you have yet to understand."

I nodded, recognizing Michael's message, even though he spoke in an indirect, round-about fashion, alluding vaguely to events and feelings, rather than offering specifics. Yet the sentiments certainly rang true, for I knew the basic conflict. My rational mind wanted to know rationally what it could not; I wanted logical proofs for things not subject to rational proof. And these demands of reason held me back from fully entering this other world. I knew I had to let go and be more open to my intuition to do this. Yet could I, I wondered. Could I let the rational go?

Michael interrupted my thoughts with a final warning to me. "So you run the greatest risk of everyone here. . .Through habit you can react to this other world, like other things, in your usual way. Or you have the option to change. So consider each step along your path very carefully. Think about your thoughts and intentions. How do you motivate yourself? And what do you really want?

"At this stage, perhaps you have simple curiosity. . .But to go further, it's best to give up any idea of success. Then, you might well succeed--in life generally, as well as the path, as they are one in the same. . .Then, you'll find that everything can change. Your body. Your spirit. Everything is part of a solid whole. And when one change occurs, it can alter everything else. . .So seek what you will, but ask about your motivations, and be prepared for change."

Again, Michael fell silent, signalling that he was finished answering my questions. Now Serge had a few last questions about a recently ended relationship.

"Why is the person who used to be in my dwelling no longer there?"

"The problem is anger. Anger at the circumstance. . .You can only attempt to help or try to touch. But if this isn't possible, there's nothing you can do. To suffer needlessly, when you have done what you could, is pointless. . .This person who has left is angry at *things* rather than at *you*."

Serge seemed satisfied by this answer and wondered if the allie had any advice on his path as a healer.

"Learn to love your fellow beings. And before you reach out, ask and understand. . .Also, consider whether your love exists for people generally or not. . .This becomes more important as your ability to heal improves. The key in healing is not how the symptom is healed, but how the person is. You are healing the person and not the symptom. . .You ask whether the power to heal is in you? It requires a complete commitment. . .What you can offer is great. But first you must heal yourself."

Finally, Serge had one last question about a close friend who had died, but still seemed very close.

"What do you think of our present and future relationship?" He asked.

"Concern yourself more with the future than the past. You will probably find at times your continuing friendship is of great value. . .Your friend will try to help. Maybe he will come to you with a need, perhaps to be healed. We must be ready to give help as well . . . . Your friendship, though distant will probably remain genuine. Life is hard for him where he is. And he may have needs in the next year, the year after. So as you help him, he will help you."

Finally, the allie speaking through Michael had some observations about the whole group.

"This weyr now represents a potential. It's just becoming a cohesive unit. And there's a potential for things to arise in some of you. . . . You have an opportunity to explore interesting roads and experiments. You can use your imagination and seek possible opportunities that sound right.

"Now many paths stretch ahead. Any can be taken. . . . In time, others may want to join the group, too. If they are interested, invite them. They will react as they do. It's the same as with a love. Some are more likely candidates than others. . . .

"This is a time of preparation. Yet there will be a time when preparations come to an end, and you will find yourselves in a situation where effort is needed. Then, you'll find these preparations have been well laid and will bear fruit."

As the allie finished speaking, Michael leaned back in his chair, and his arms dropped to his side. His breathing came more heavily, and his eyes misted over with a faraway look. The allie spoke softly, slowly: "I would leave you now. Perhaps we can arrange for another time when I will try to be present. . . . At several future times, the opportunity may arise."

Michael fell silent for about a minute, then shook himself and opened his eyes. He rubbed his neck and said it was stiff due to the high level of energy involved in letting the allie speak through him. He explained he needed to relax for a few minutes, to allow his normal consciousness to return.

"But it won't take long. It comes back more quickly now than in the past. Just a few minutes."

We waited quietly while Michael focused on being back in the present. After a few minutes, he stood up and opened the circle by drawing four reverse pentagrams.

Then, back in normal time, Michael took off his robe and sat down on the chair in the center of the room. We had many questions about what the experience was like.

Slowly, thoughtfully, Michael described it.

"Well, the session with my allie begins when I relax and close my eyes. Then, I reach out and can feel her in the distance. In a few moments, I feel the sensation of something coming in, like a presence moving inside me. It feels like my whole body is spinning inside. It's as if I have the same arms, the same head, the same leg length. But there's a distinct feeling of a separate body within me.

"Yet, it's a much gentler feeling now than it used to be. I used to feel a great unpleasant rushing experience when she entered. But now it's like taking a breath and I feel an infusion of energy. I also used to feel weak for a few days after each session, since the experience took so much out of me. But not anymore. She comes in more easily, and I feel I'm working closer to her vibration generally. So she gives me more energy now, rather than taking it away.

"Also, it seems like the more I do this, the better I get in the field, and the better I get in the field, the better I do this. So there seems to be a reciprocal process at work. As you get better contacting and communicating with the energies out there, you get better in contacting and communicating with your allie, too, and vice versa."

"What else did you experience when she was there?" Serge wondered.

"Well, mostly a feeling of withdrawal," Michael replied. "I had a sense of floating in the chair. I wasn't certain what level of reality I was on, and at times the room seemed tilted, and I felt drawn to the left. But then, she has a tendency to move into me from the left and leave that way."

"You know, when I felt your aura and she was there, it felt much denser and more intense," Serge observed.

Michael nodded. "I know. It should be heavier, When she's here, I feel a sudden intensity. It's like two people are inside me, or maybe something is in there filling in the spaces. So I get a feeling of heaviness."

"Your aura also seemed further out than usual," said Serge. "It felt a little like furry tendrils of energy streaming out."

Again Michael nodded. "Yes, that's what having her there is like. It's like having a radar inside me and getting intensely into my senses. Also, I feel like I'm looking out on a yellowish world where people are easier to sense than usual. I can send out that radar beam and easily pick up anything."

Michael found the sensations hard to describe in words, but he kept groping for ways to explain the experience of being in touch with his allie, and what we might experience when we contacted our own allies.

"I feel like I'm going into a deeper level of consciousness just before she appears, and then this other presence glides in. So your perception becomes much more intense than usual, and you gain new abilities you can use in seeing. Also, you can understand the relationship of things better."

"I noticed some personality changes, too," Teri observed.

Michael nodded. "A lot of traits do change. I talk slower when I'm in contact with her, since things are dictated. If I miss something or feel uncomfortable saying something, she'll repeat it again. So normally I just let her speak. Then, too, sometimes the ideas come to me so slowly, I don't know what the end of the sentence will be. Another characteristic is she tends to talk very generally about things. So it's hard to ask her about specific things, though sometimes she may focus in on something. For example, I've gotten her to give me specific details when I've asked about myself.

"Then, too," Michael grinned slightly, "I always feel a certain sense of mischieviousness when she's around. Like she wants to tease . . . or sometimes she tends to come on like a sledgehammer and says exactly what she thinks."

The conversation then turned to the accuracy of the allie's comments and our perceptions of the changes in the room. Serge, Teri and Harvey wanted to confirm that something out of the ordinary had happened with another presence; that it wasn't just Michael talking to us; and they soon concluded this was so.

"You didn't know some of the questions I asked about my former roommate," Serge told Michael. "But the allie verified the hunches I already had about the answer. Also, she seemed to understand when I asked about another relationship.

"She seemed to recognize just what I was searching for, too," Teri observed.

"I also saw some unusual changes while you were in trance," Serge reported. "Almost immediately, I saw a whitish glow, and then your face and eyes came close in together, and I saw her face around yours in your aura. Then, for a moment, your face looked like a gauze-like curtain between the two faces, and there was a brilliant white light before your face. After that the light faded and I saw your aura around you as usual again."

"I saw a different smile on your face than usual. It looked almost wicked and challenging," said Harvey. "Also, your body appeared illuminated. Your face seemed to glow in the darkness."

"Good, I'm pleased your comments reflect my own experiences as a channel for the allie," Michael stated. "That shows what we're doing here is something real."

Then he had some suggestions on how we could find our own allies.

"Try to seek your allie in dreams or use geoteleportation. Just get relaxed, go into trance, and leave yourself open for your allie to enter. We'll have a session to help you do that later, but meanwhile, realize the experience is much like dreaming, or even being on a tranquilizer. However, you feel an awareness or a pressure of a presence in your body.

"Some people see the allie as the higher self or as a Holy Guardian Angel. There's also a big debate whether this is an external being who enters or an internal presence you summon up from within. But it's really both. It's both internal and separate. It's part of you. Yet it comes in from outside you. You have to learn to be open to it, and it will come in."

I had one last question. "Do you normally have to do a ritual or set up special conditions for your allie to come in?"

"No, not at all. I've had sessions with my allie everywhere. I had one in the middle of a river in a meadow. I sat in the bright moonlight and meditated, and she came in. But usually I prefer to do these sessions inside. In the field, you can disturb the beings who are already there. They feel it's their territory, and they see the allie as an alien presence. So it can get weird. You feel this hostility around you, and it can be a little disturbing. But otherwise, you can call on your allie at any time, whenever you feel a need for help."

The session over, we got up to leave and arranged to meet for a weekend camp-out the next Saturday. Michael said he thought Teri and Harvey were ready to go for the second degree, and Serge could try for his third.

As we left, he cautioned them, "So think about what you want to do for your grade. You want to show you can control the elements whatever you do."

CHAPTER FIFTEEN

Making the Grade at a Magical Camp-Out

As arranged, we met at Michael's on a crisp and sunny Saturday in November to leave for the camp-out. Harvey and Serge were already there when I arrived and Sharon, a friend of Michael's came along, too. In her 20's, Sharon had been exploring magic and witchcraft on her own for about five years, and now had become an ODF affiliate or supporter, though she planned to stay on her own path.

"I'm just along for moral support, and I'm interested in what you're doing," she said.

We assembled our gear in the middle of the room, and while we waited for Teri, Michael went over the requirements for the Second and Third Degree to help Harvey and Serge get prepared.

"The Second Degree is an act of self-expression. Basically, you open yourself up and are receptive. Then, you act as you're inspired to act. For example, the act may begin with your moving an arm, and perhaps using that to raise or direct energy. Or maybe think of what you're doing as a dance with nature. You want to feel the presence of nature and show you're part of nature, too. Then, since you're part of nature, you want to show you can get it to respond to you."

Harvey nodded. "Sure. That sounds easy," he commented with an arrogant smirk. "I made Sixth degree in a little over a year in another magical order. So this should be a snap."

Michael cringed slightly at Harvey's overconfidence and arrogance, but said nothing. Instead, he launched on a review of the Third Degree for Serge.

"It's a willed act of magic. In this case, you decide in advance on something you want to do, such as invoke an earth elemental and take charge of it.

165

Then, you go and do it. You may not have the skills yet to do so, but that doesn't matter. It's like in the Second. You trust that you'll have the information you need when the time comes to do what you want to do."

We checked over the food we each brought to make sure we had enough, and Michael reminded us, "Dress warmly, because it will be cold." He also urged us to hurry up and get packed, because, "We have to get there by five o'clock, at sunset, or they close the park. Then we can't leave until eight in the morning."

Harvey and I announced we were ready, and Michael and Serge led us downstairs to the cars. Just as we reached the lobby, Teri rushed in, apologized for being late, and explained she had come from seeing the minister of a spiritual religion she was studying.

"She just gave me a 'weather report' about what we might expect on the trip. She says the trip should be successful. But she cautioned me to protect myself and warn others about the possible dangers ahead. She says there are some heavy dark spirits on the mountain where we're going, and she gave me some protective ash we can use."

Teri held up a small jar with a layer of soft gray ashes.

"She suggests that we put it on our faces, head and body. Also she had one more warning. She says to 'keep your hats on' for protection from the spirits."

Though the idea of a spiritual weather report seemed unusual to me, Michael responded as though this was a usual occurrence.

"Well, it's good to know about what we might encounter," he said, explaining that on some previous trips, he and other ODFers had received reports about possible difficult conditions. "It never kept us from having a trip. But knowing what was ahead helped us to handle it."

We loaded the three cars we were taking—mine, Serge's and Harvey's—and Serge scribbled out directions for me and Harvey.

"We'll meet at the gate," he said. "Once we're all together, we'll continue to the top."

When I arrived with Teri about sunset, Michael, Serge and Sharon were waiting at the park gate, but Harvey hadn't arrived. Then, just as the ranger was ready to leave, and we were about to write Harvey a note to meet us up the hill, he drove through the gate.

"I got lost," he said breathlessly.

Michael scowled slightly, then motioned for Harvey to follow our caravan to the campsite. As we drove off, the ranger locked the gate, closing us in until morning.

"We'll have to be especially careful now," Teri said as we drove up the mountain. "We'll really need to pay attention to that weather report, and there's no going back."

When we arrived at camp, about a mile up a steep windy road, the last light was fast disappearing, and we quickly set up camp. Michael urged us to hurry, since we had a lot of work to do that night, for Teri, Harvey and Serge were all going for grades.

Teri quickly set up her dome-shaped three-person tent in the middle of camp. Then, after a brief snack of trail mix and coffee, we stored the supplies in Teri's tent to protect them from raccoons and set off up the mountain.

We began hiking up a steep trail which Michael had previously explored. It led to a high plateau overlooking the valley, and Michael planned to have Serge, Teri and Harvey work on their degrees once we got there. With Michael in the lead, we walked quietly along the edge of the woods at the base of the hill and gradually worked our way up.

"Pay particular atention to the shadowy forms that flit about near the trees," Michael advised us as we walked. "It should be an active night. A lot is happening even now."

As we climbed above the tree line, the valley below appeared like a big black slab with a myriad of glittering lights. Meanwhile, ahead, the high grass of the hilly meadow glistened like a living glowing carpet in the moonlight. We walked in silence for several minutes, just experiencing the sights, sounds and feeling of the night.

However, about half-way up, Harvey suddenly began to pant and heave. "I've got to stop. I can't go on," he sputtered, collapsing in a heap on the meadow.

We stopped and waited several minutes for him to catch his breath. When Michael asked if he was ready to continue, Harvey lumbered up. But after a few more yards, Harvey collapsed again.

"No . . . no. I can't do it. I can feel my heart beating like it's ready to burst. It's too much. I can't make it."

He lay back on the hill breathing heavily. Michael and Serge conferred briefly about what to do, and finally announced they would help carry him back, while the rest of us waited on the slope. Harvey could do his Second Degree near the camp after we finished our work on the hill. They helped Harvey up, and holding him between their shoulders, his arms clinging tightly around their necks, they guided him down the hill.

Meanwhile, Teri, Sharon and I waited quietly on the hillside for Michael and Serge to return. As we did, I noticed several large gray-black forms moving along the edge of the woods. Would Michael describe these as real elementals or beings, I wondered. Or were they merely shifts in the movement of shadows with the wind.

When Michael and Serge returned a half-hour later, we continued up. It was a steep climb for another half-mile or so, and finally we arrived at a narrow plateau. It had an eerie golden glow from the light of a nearly full moon.

Since the plateau extended in two directions, we briefly discussed which way to go.

"See which way feels right to you," Michael suggested.

Serge held his staff out and drew a circle; then he pointed towards a narow promontory, about ten yards across, overlooking the valley.

"That way," he said. The rest of us agreed and we headed to the plateau.

The area was barren, windy and cold, with several projections of jagged rocks—suggesting an ideal site for a raw confrontation with the elements. At the end of the plateau, Michael stopped and asked Serge if he wanted to try for his Third Degree here. Serge nodded.

"Then first you should try to calm down the wind spirits, so you can do your work," Michael said.

Serge stepped forward, ready to begin. He held his staff ahead of him and walked towards the edge of the plateau, while the rest of us squatted or stood about ten feet away watching. Serge then made a circle around himself with his staff and projected energy from his belly to try to calm the area down. Meanwhile, the wind continued to whip around us like a gale.

Finally, in frustration, Serge banished his circle with a flick of his staff and walked back towards us.

"The winds are too much to control," he said.

"Let's try together," Michael offered, and they headed back to the edge of the plateau.

Again, both of them raised their staffs and projected energy to get the elements to calm down. For a moment, there was a brief lull in the wind, and a brief rumble of excitement coursed through our group. But, a few seconds later, the winds started up again as strong as ever.

After a few more minutes, Michael and Serge walked back to the group.

"We better move to a quieter place," Michael said. "The elements are proving to be too distracting to do good work. And even if we can calm them, it'll be more productive to find a more sheltered area, where we can concentrate on what we're here to do."

Michael led us back towards the base of the plateau, and near the bottom, we came to a small grove of trees that seemed protected. The area was brighter than the areas the ODF usually worked in because of the moon, but Michael thought it ideal for our purposes because of the grove of trees.

"Are you ready?" he asked Serge.

Serge nodded and stepped out in the center of the plateau, while the rest of us sat watching from the shelter of the trees. As he stood there silently meditating to get in the right mood for the working, Michael explained that Serge planned to evoke the spirit of an earth elemental from a rock and direct it to do his bidding.

When he finished meditating, Serge began his working by drawing the four pentagrams in the air and charging them with his staff for protection. Then, he concentrated on sending projections of energy from his body to bring up an earth elemental. In a few minutes, he saw and felt the presence of some being, and beckoned it to come towards him. Once it did, he began moving his staff to direct this shadowy form to advance or go back.

Meanwhile, as he worked, I noticed that his body seemed to be surrounded by an aura of light, and I observed a few flashes of light in the air.

At first, Michael hovered nearby to make sure Serge's ritual was going smoothly and provide any necessary back-up. But soon, once he felt Serge was in control of things, he moved over to where Teri, Sharon and I were sitting and began to point out things we should pay attention to.

"You'll notice some reddish sparks shooting out of that rock."

I looked where he was pointing and saw a few brief flashes of light and nearby a shadowy, catlike-mass. Sharon and Teri reported seeing a hulking sort of form, too.

"That's the being just starting to show himself," Michael remarked, and later, Serge explained that he had projected his energy at a rock to get the being to emerge.

A few moments later, this form seemed to dissipate, and Michael asked us to look carefully again.

"You'll see a big concentration of energy about nine feet high about 30 feet ahead of Serge on the trail. Notice how it has the shape of a humanoid being."

However, since Serge, still concentrating on the rock, wasn't aware of this, Michael went over to him to point it out. Serge apologized for not seeing the being and now sought to draw it to come towards him and then stand still about 30 feet away. He extended his staff, directed a stream of energy at the being, and motioned it forward.

Meanwhile, Michael returned to our group.

"Now, watch," he told us pointing his staff at the being. "It's staying there on the path. Serge is managing to hold it there."

I looked carefully but could see nothing, though Sharon claimed to see a big grayish shape, and Teri saw flickers of energy.

Michael went back to Serge.

"Okay," he said. "You can let the being go and banish it back to where it was living."

Serge complied with a few flicks of his staff, closed his circle, and returned to our group with Michael.

Beaming broadly, Michael patted Serge on the back and told him, "You passed. Good work. You made the grade."

Then, Michael explained that Serge had passed because he not only raised the energy from the rock as he intended, but he was able to control the elemental that appeared by making it stop for about a minute. "It would have been better if he was aware he called the being up without my having to tell him. But the important thing is that once he was aware of it, he did control it. Also, some other phenomena occurred while he worked. For example, the wind died down."

Now we discussed what we wanted to do next, and Michael said he wanted to do some work with the wind.

"I call it the Eagle Dance," he stated, "and it's a way of playing with nature." As Michael described, he would move around like a bird in this dance and work on getting the wind to respond to his movements.

"You'll find that the wind elements are usually the easiest to work with. You should watch for synchronicities as I work. For example, when I raise my staff, the wind should go up, and when I lower it, the wind should die down."

Michael moved his staff up and down a few times to demonstrate. "Or if I direct my energy to the right or left, you should notice the wind start to shift in that direction, too." Again Michael waved his staff. "You should also look for flashes or swirls of light around me, and other phenomena. This can occur because they're produced by the energy raised in working with elementals."

Michael chose a high rocky promontory to do his ritual, because he felt this was more dramatic, and he asked us to stand about 20 feet away.

After beginning with the usual circle and pentagrams, he made a series of passes through the air with his staff. Repeatedly he raised and lowered it, then made sweeping motions to the left and right. As he did, the wind seemed to rise up and quiet down a few times, though I couldn't perceive any directional movements.

Next Michael imagined opening up a Gateway of energy above the valley, and he concentrated on directing the wind to sweep through it and blow over the valley. While he did, I noticed a pale whitish cone of light rise overhead, and saw a dark shape in the air which looked somewhat like a bird. At the time, we didn't know what Michael was trying to do, and I wondered if there was any connection between this imagery and what Michael was doing.

Meanwhile, as Michael was creating this Gateway, Serge heard a strange rustling sound in the bushes about ten feet away to our left, and he rushed over to check out what it was and provide some protection if necessary. As he approached, he explained later, he saw a cat-like creature emerge and he projected energy at it to stop, so it wouldn't interfere with Michael's working. After a few moments, it dissipated back into the bushes, and Serge returned to our group.

"Everything's okay now," he said.

Then, Michael returned to our group wanting to know what we experienced to see if our observations tallied with what he had been doing.

Serge told him about the cat.

"Oh, yes," Michael replied, "that's probably one of the spirits Teri's minister warned us about. You did well to check it out and banish it."

I mentioned the cone of light and the bird-like shape I had seen.

"That checks out, too," Michael said. "You may have seen the cone of light, because I directed the spirits of the wind to go up towards the nearly full moon. And then the bird form would certainly be appropriate, since I was doing the Dance of the Eagle."

However, Sharon and Teri said they didn't see anything.

"I think it was too cold," Teri said. "I couldn't really concentrate on anything."

"I had a lot on my mind from today. So I let my mind wander," Sharon said.

"That's okay," Michael commented. "You can't expect to be up all the time."

Michael then pointed out that we might each have different ways of perceiving the energy around us, and that was fine.

"For example," he told me, "when I pointed out the reddish sparks coming from the rock where Serge was working, you saw a cat-like form. That's your way of seeing the phenomena. We each perceive things differently. The main point is to pick up something, and you did."

Now since everyone was quite cold and the high wind was still blowing strongly, Michael decided we should head back to camp. Teri could do her Second Degree there, rather than on the mountain. As we started down, Michael added, "When we get back, we'll wake up Harvey, so he can do his Second Degree, too."

After we returned to camp, Teri organized a cooking detail for dinner, and I wandered to a nearby grove of trees to experiment with some of the techniques Michael had taught us. So far, everything unusual I had experienced had occurred when I was with the group, and I wondered if I might experience some of the same phenomena when I was alone. Or did I need the suggestions of Michael or the others to perceive what I did?

I stood in front of a large shadowy tree and held out my staff. Then, as Michael had taught us, I directed my energy out through my hand, into the staff, and out into the tree. As I did, I projected the thought that any elemental in the tree should come out and reveal itself to me. "Come forth, come forth, let me see something," I repeated silently to myself. Yet, even as I did, I felt a little peculiar doing so, since this seemed like such a strange thing to be doing. After all, most people don't talk to trees expecting spirits to come out of them. Still, I kept saying the words, wondering what would happen and hoping that something would.

Then, gradually, I saw small white beam of light extend slowly out from my staff, until it was about a foot long. I felt like I could draw with the beam, and I began to move my staff about, as if the air was my canvas. As I did, I noticed that the beam continued to extend even further and for a few moments, a faint outline of what I had drawn seemed to hang in the air. Then suddenly it faded and I wondered: Was I imagining these images? Or were they real?

I focused on the tree a few more times, thinking if maybe I concentrated enough, some shadowy form would finally emerge from the darkness—even if my own imagination created it—but after several minutes, nothing. I concentrated a little longer, hoping that even if I created the vision, I would at least see something that matched the reports of other ODFers about the appearance of strange humanoid-like beings. But again, nothing.

Finally, hearing people bustling around the fire to make dinner, I suddenly felt self-conscious about doing a working on my own and returned to camp. As I approached, Teri was dishing out a vegetable stew, while some sausages sizzled in a pan over a blazing fire.

After dinner, as everyone put away their dishes and prepared to hike to a nearby meadow, I asked Michael what I should do on this trip, since I wasn't going to work towards a degree myself.

Michael had several suggestions. "After you pass the Second—or any degree for that matter—work on perfecting it. And that's especially important for you, since you barely made your Second when you tried for it. So practice doing additional self-less acts, either by yourself or in front of the group. Just let yourself be inspired to do something and do it. This will help you feel more secure with the grade you just passed, so you can come to feel really comfortable with it. When you do, you're ready to go on for the next degree."

I observed that Serge had called forth an earth elemental when he went for his Third.

"Should I expect to do that, too?" I asked.

"Oh, no," Michael replied. "You can work with any element. Many people start with earth, since that's one of the easiest elements to work with. These earth elementals are all around us on these trips, so they're fairly easy to evoke. And perhaps, since I've always had a special affinity for the earth myself, that's what most of my students have chosen to work with first."

I noticed the last flickers of light in the barbecue pit and commented that I had long been fascinated by fire. So perhaps it might be good to do my Third Degree with that.

Michael immediately cautioned me. "Fire's the hardest element to work with and control. The flames seem to have a will of their own, and I find they often try to play with me. But if you want to, go ahead. Or perhaps before you formally go for your degree, try experimenting with some fire first."

"How?" I asked.

"Try looking at some candles and getting the flames to move. That'll help you prepare before you try for the Third Degree," he advised.

Michael returned to his tent to get ready for the hike, and I observed that the fire in the barbecue now appeared out. I hadn't seen any hint of flames for the last several minutes while we spoke, and I wondered, based on Michael's comments, whether I could revive the fire and make it rise up by concentrating on it. I didn't seriously expect to do anything; yet I was curious if I could; and so I started concentrating. I focused my eyes directly on the small box of coals in the barbecue, and as I gazed at it, I imagined my energy going out in a beam from my eyes directly at the fire.

Then, suddenly, as I gazed ahead, I saw a glow of red light flare up for a few seconds and die down again. Did that really happen, I wondered. Wanting further confirmation, I concentrated again. If it really happened once, could I do it again? I gazed at the dark coal box for a few minutes more, and just as I was about to give up and turn away, I noticed a brief flash of white.

I glanced around to see if anyone else was near enough to notice and saw Michael a few feet away at the picnic table. He said he hadn't seen anything, and I asked, "Do you think it's coincidence that the fire flared up twice as I looked at it?"

"Were you sending energy to it?" he asked.

"Yes," I replied.

"Then take credit for it. That's very good."

Just then, everyone else appeared around the picnic table ready to hike toward the meadow. After a few minutes, we arrived at the meadow about 100 yards from camp. It was a small open space perhaps 50 feet across, which was surrounded by trees and bushes on three sides. To the south, it opened up onto a longer grassy meadow.

As we gathered at the entrance, Michael asked Teri and Harvey who wanted to go first.

"I'd rather go second," Teri said. "It'll give me more time to get in tune with the energy and vibration of the meadow."

"Then you're up first," Michael told Harvey, and led him to the center of the meadow, about 30 feet from the group.

Michael spent a few minutes giving Harvey the usual guidelines for the Second Degree ("Just open yourself up to the experience. . . . Do what you feel. . . . Let your inspiration be your guide. . . ."). Then he returned to where Serge, Teri, Sharon and I were standing at the edge of the meadow.

For a few moments Harvey stood silently meditating. Then, as if a vast dam of energy had suddenly opened, he began whipping his staff through the air and thrashing his left arm up and down wildly, while calling out to the spirits of the directions in a loud commanding voice. His words were hard to understand, since he mixed English and some strange magical language, and alternately announced orders and chanted, so his monologue sounded something like this:

"Hail ye spirts of the East . . . Amenee, shamoney, alouehe . . . I command you, come into the circle and do my bidding. . . . Now ye spirits of the South . . . Amoney, hamoney, arovey . . . I demand you, harken to my bidding. . . . Be here now. Make your presence known for this ritual. . . . ."

As he chanted, breathing heavily, he made pentagrams in the air around him with his sword, and he finished each one by stabbing his sword through it, as if he was ripping a hole through the air.

"Know that I come among you as a mighty magician. . . . Feel my power. . . . Know that I am here to command you. . . . You must obey. . . . Now I am summoning you . . . Amenee, shamoney. . . . Come, appear among me. . . . Immediately. . . . I demand it now."

Meanwhile, as Harvey thrashed about, crying out loudly, and occasionally uttering curses at the spirits of nature and calling for demons, including Lucifer and Beezlebub, to come to his aid, Michael became noticeably disturbed.

"Jeez," he said under his breath. "What's this guy doing out there? What's he raising up?"

To protect our group from anything evil that Harvey might be calling forth, Michael walked in front of us and drew a circle of protection on the ground with his staff. Then, he watched warily as Harvey continued.

Unfortunately, Harvey was having difficulty getting the spirits to respond, and he bellowed out several additional commands more loudly and with more force of will.

"You must approach. . . . Alouee, amaney. . . . I demand you approach. . . . You must realize I have the more powerful will. . . . So you must obey."

Finally, Michael could bear the process no longer, and he walked towards Harvey to stop him. As Michael later explained, "I felt I had to do something, since Harvey was calling in some demonic spirits and upsetting the other spirits in the area." Though Michael thought Harvey had gotten the wind to rise up slightly and had persuaded a few masses of energy to start forward from the woods, Michael felt the elements were generally resisting coming out to avoid being controlled and directed by Harvey.

As Michael advanced towards Harvey, Serge followed a few yards behind, sending healing energy ahead to strengthen Michael and being ready to assist as needed.

When Michael came near, Harvey suddenly fell silent. He held his staff aloft, glared at Michael, and looked as if he was about to hit Michael for interrupting. For a few moments, they stood eyeing each other like two animals in a power struggle for dominance.

Finally, quietly, steadily, Michael told Harvey, "Put the staff down." He motioned for Harvey to follow him, saying, "We better discuss this. Come back to the group."

Silently, sullenly, Harvey followed him, and as we clustered around, Michael explained what was wrong. He spoke gently to calm Harvey down, soothe his feelings, and help him understand what was wrong.

"The basic problem is you were being too arrogant out there," Michael began. "Your chant was fine, if we were doing ceremonial magic. But that's not what the Second Degree is about. You're not out there commanding the elements like a ceremonial magician. Instead, you're being open and receptive like you're doing a dance with nature. Also, you were bringing forth some very heavy entities, some demonic forces, which are more than someone at the Second Degree can handle. And as you can see, the forces were resisting you. You were ordering them around; you were trying to force them to do things, you weren't treating them with respect."

At first, Harvey protested, "But I was open. You said to listen to my inspiration. And I did. I was inspired to chant what I did. I didn't try to direct anything. It just happened that way."

"Well, you let your previous programming as a ceremonial magician take over. But we're not ceremonial magicians. We respect nature. We work with it on its own terms. We don't threaten and terrorize it. We're the ODF."

Almost at once, Harvey crumbled as if he suddenly realized what he had done, and now he became very contrite.

"Yes. Yes. You're right," he said, nearly sobbing. "I was arrogant. I was obnoxious and overbearing. Just as I started the ritual, I had a brief impulse to humble myself to nature, but I ignored it. And, then, you're right. I let my past magical training take over. So now I feel like I made a fool of myself out there. No wonder the spirits didn't want to do anything for me. I offended them. I tried to take them over, rather than trying to get to know them and treat them respectfully. So do you think the nature spirits will forgive me? I'm really sorry. I really am."

Harvey looked at everyone with a genuinely pained expression. "I truly hope they forgive me. I really want to make amends."

Michael tried to console him. "Sure, if you're genuinely sorry, the spirits will accept your apologies. So if you want a second shot at the Second Degree, go ahead."

But first, Michael wanted to clean up some of the negative energy left over from Harvey's ritual and show Harvey how to do a self-less act correctly. He told Harvey, "I want you to watch closely while I'm out there to get a sense of how it should be done."

Michael walked out to the meadow where Harvey had been and drew a series of clockwise crosses symbolizing healing in the air to send healing energy to the forces of nature in the area. He felt this energy would calm them down and show them he meant no harm. As he circled about, he raised and lowered his hand several times, asking the spirits to feel soothed and healed. He wanted them to realize he regretted that they were offended and violated, and he wanted to reassure them this wouldn't happen again. After a few minutes, Michael felt the spirits were calmed, returned to our group, and told Harvey he could try again.

This time Harvey acted with a kind of frenzied humility. He made a quick circle with his staff. Then moving rapidly, almost frantically, from one part of the far meadow to another, he repeatedly begged the spirits of nature to forgive him, and he assured them that he would not approach them with arrogance again. From time to time, he threw himself on the griound to show his humility and deep sorrow over what had happened.

Yet, when he returned to our group to find out how he had done, looking like a woebegone begging dog, Michael was not convinced Harvey had been effective. He felt Harvey's actions, while humbling, had been too desperate, too intense. Also, he noticed a strange glazed look of perhaps confusion, terror or almost being at the edge—Michael couldn't tell exactly what—in Harvey's eyes. Then, too, Harvey still clung to his knife in an odd clutching way, as if he was holding it tightly for reassurance, rather than putting it away as was normal at the end of a ritual, and Michael felt concerned about the behavior.

"Did I do all right this time?" Harvey asked plaintively, almost pleading with Michael for acceptance.

Michael looked at Harvey guardedly. "Yes . . . yes. You did okay." He paused. "Now, just put down the knife. . . ."

"Oh, yeah . . . yeah. . . ." Harvey suddenly became aware he was still clutching the knife and gazed at it.

"Just put it away," Michael repeated.

"Yeah. Sure. Sure." Awkwardly, Harvey jabbed the knife into the sheath on his belt.

Then, the potential for danger gone, Michael told Harvey his reactions to Harvey's second try.

"You did the proper thing when you returned to the circle. You were responding to the appropriateness of the moment with the right response. The spirits of nature needed healing, and that's what you did. But . . ."

Michael paused and gazed steadily at Harvey. "I think you should continue to work with this feeling of healing. Keep trying to feel that sense of attunement with nature, rather than trying to set yourself apart. You'll have a chance to try for the Second again. And now that you've seen several examples of people doing it, you should be better able to succeed next time."

Harvey backed away a few paces, looking dejected. Then, he walked towards a large tree about ten feet away from the group and stood there silently for a few minutes like a hurt dog licking its wounds.

Michael took me aside for a moment and said softly, "This is the first time this has ever happened. In the eight years I've been with the ODF, no one has ever failed the Second. And I've seen dozens of people go through it. But Harvey was too arrogant. He didn't understand what we were about. And even after he tried again, he still seemed upset and confused. So I couldn't let him go on."

We returned to the group, and Michael told Teri, who was lying on the ground to experience the earth more closely, that it was time for her to try. She continued to lie there quietly, and so to rouse her, Michael directed some energy at her head. Meanwhile Serge, closely behind him, concentrated on sending some healing energy towards her head, too.

After a few minutes, Terri roused herself, looked up, and commented, "I really wanted to feel what the earth is like at night, which I never did before."

Michael told her it was time to do her Second. "Are you ready to try for it?" he asked.

"As ready as I'm ever going to be, I guess," she replied, getting up. "Give me about 20 minutes on the meadow, and I'll see what I can do."

Michael asked if she wanted to use the same area as Harvey, assuring her that the spot was now completely cleaned up from Harvey's ritual, but Teri preferred the large adjacent meadow. So we followed her to the edge of this meadow to watch. Harvey, feeling recovered from his earler humiliation, joined us, though he hovered a few feet away.

At first, Teri stood in the center of the meadow and gazed at the moon, which was peering out slightly from the clouds. Then, fueled by the moon, she began to whirl around the area, doing a frenetic dance. Around and around she went, moving faster and faster, until suddenly, the energy peaked, and she threw herself to the ground. Slowly, she unfurled herself, like a large flower.

Next, thrusting herself back down on the ground, she curled up, with her knees tightly under herself, like a rock. After a few minutes, she removed her socks and gloves to blend in more closely with the earth and remained motionless for several minutes. The, rising, she took off her hat to let her hair flow free, and now pranced about like an animal, with graceful and pouncing cat-like motions.

Meanwhile, as we watched Michael commented that "She seems to be shape shifting as she assumes each position," meaning that she was not merely acting like these objects, animals, and plants, but actually becoming them.

"Some ODFers like to experiment with this shape shifting," he added, "and she seems to be especially good at this."

I remarked that I usually saw a whitish aura around her just as I observed when others did rituals in the field. "But when she curled down as a rock, I didn't see anything," I said.

"That's because a rock is a dead thing," Michael commented. "So, of course, you wouldn't see anything."

Then, after lurking in the grass like a panther, Teri suddenly perched on her knees and stared rigidly ahead. As she did, the moon appeared from behind the clouds and illuminated the meadow with a bright silver glow, so it looked like dawn. A moment later, Teri cried out with a loud cackle-like laugh and a sharp gust of wind hit the group. As it did, my hat blew off, and Harvey was blown off his feet, rolled a few feet across the grass, and crashed into a bush.

Michael immediately felt something special was happening and spun into action. He darted to the front of our group and told us urgently, "Come on. Move together. It feels like Teri is bringing out the crone, and I'm not sure what will happen." He was referring to the older woman aspect of the Goddess, which is sometimes associated with the spirit of night and darkness, and is commonly reflected in the symbol of the evil Witch.

However, a few seconds after she finished laughing, Teri got up, picked up her gloves and socks, and in her normal gait, walked over to us. She felt her Second Degree experience was over.

"Well, did I do enough to pass?" she asked.

Michael nodded vigorously. "Yes. We were definitely impressed."

Then he explained what she had done. He mentioned that the moon had suddenly appeared while she was working and that we had seen a lot of shape-shifting. Also, he was impressed by the wind that had blown up.

"You even knocked poor Harvey away."

We then compared our impressions with what Teri had been doing. "I saw you emerge like a plant at one point," I said, and Teri said she had been imagining herself as a lily pad at the time. Michael noted that "Momentarily, you looked like a large black crouching panther," and Teri said, yes, she had experienced herself as a cat. Serge commented that, "Everything felt so dead when you were a rock." Again, Teri agreed she had experienced a similar deadness.

"You might want to explore shape-shifting more when you go for your Third Degree," Michael commented, and Teri agreed that she would explore this.

Finally, Michael observed that her work seemed to alter the usual pattern of the wind. "The wind seemed to hit you first, before you gave your laugh, and then it came to us, rather than hitting all of us at the same time. So you really seemed to work up a lot of power out there."

Afterwards, we returned to camp, and as we sat in Teri's tent sharing a bottle of Polish vodka, Michael talked about how working on these degrees and taking ODF classes was merely the first step.

"After you've gotten the basics, we can go on to do research in hundreds of areas. There's so much to do . . . in geoteleportation, in working with the allie. We can experiment with shape shifting. Whatever we want."

People in other ODF groups were already experimenting with different things, he explained, and he was anxious to go on.

"This encampment has given us a chance to see how we work together. We're just starting to become a team. And as we contiue to do magic together, there's so much more to learn."

CHAPTER SIXTEEN

Learning Psychic Defense

Our next lesson, at Michael's, was on "Psychic Defense," since Michael felt we had been opened up magically, over the last few weeks. As a result, we now needed techniques to protect ourselves from others who might use magical techniques against us.

Serge agreed. He was feeling more worn down than ever in his ongoing battle with his roommate, and felt perhaps his growing sensitivity was the reason. Teri complained about the growing pressures of work, and thought anything she could do magically to protect herself against stress might help. Meanwhile, Harvey sat quietly in an armchair in a corner, lookng unusually cowed because of his humiliating experience of the weekend.

Michael began by contrasting the ODF system of magic with that of other groups. He used Harvey's misadventure as a kind of counterpoint to show what not to do.

"The problem with ceremonial magic is these magicians start out by trying to command things without understanding what they are dealing with. But as you saw last week, you need to develop a rapport with nature first. Only then can you seek control."

He thought that the ceremony and words could be good for focusing one's energy. But, he explained, "You can get too restricted by the ceremony, if you have to handle something different than you originally planned to work with. To do good magic, you have to be able to move and adapt. And that's the ODF way. We emphasize flexibility, and we want to work hand and hand with nature. We respect it and convince it to do our will. At the same time, we're ready to respond and move, and that includes having psychic defense skills."

As Michael explained, we needed these skills in order to quickly define what was happening. Then, we could use this information, if necessary, to be ready to defend ourselves psychically.

In turn, this defense was part of the natural balance of things. In nature, the forces we deal with magically, are both positive and negative. Thus, we must deal with them in a balanced fashion, which includes protecting ourselves when we experience the negative energies coming in.

"It's only natural for those negative forces to be there. There's nothing wrong about them. They're part of nature and human experience. In fact, when something negative happens, it's usually a challenge to help you learn something; or it's a test to show you you are ready. For example, that happened last week on the field trip, when I was doing my Eagle Dance and Serge saw a cat—like shape in the darkness and banished it. He acted quickly and was ready to act, so there was no problem. He confronted the situation when necessary, and that way, he was able to overcome and resolve anything that could be potentially difficult.

"Yet, at the same time, he acknowledged the presence's right to be there. He respected its being and then banished it. And that's an important key. It's like saying, okay, you exist, we take note of you, we respect you, we honor your power; yet, we don't need you here now, because you're in our way. So now, zap, you're gone."

Michael also felt psychic defense techniques were crucial when a person felt threatened and needed to be strong and stand up to obstacles in the path. It was like having the necessary arsenal to win a battle; the necessary knowledge to pass a test. As Michael observed: "If you look through the history of other magical systems, you'll see many examples of spiritual warriors, shamans, and magicians being confronted by tests they must pass. They had to show they were worthy and could put aside their fears and go on. For instance, in ancient China, the Taoists set up stone dragons, and the potential initiate was told these beings might come to life and attack him if he wasn't worthy. If the person proceeded anyway and passed this test, he would be inducted into the order. Otherwise, he would return to regular life.

"It's like that in the ODF. In the field, in everyday life, you may encounter various tests, and you must be strong—whether that involves simply standing up to someone or taking the offensive and going in for the attack."

Michael gave a few examples. "The need for psychic defense can start on your solo. Suppose a few strange beings dive over your circle. Even though they may not be pleasant, the event is positive, since it shows the elements are making a response to you. Also, the encounter is a test. It's an opportunity to assert yourself even more to emphasize it's your right to be where you are. . . . So that's where your psychic self-defense starts—within you. You need to be aware that you have the necessary power to confront any challenges you may face, and then you need to take the appropriate action to overcome that challenge, learn from it, and go on.

"In fact," Michael went on, "wherever you are—in the field, in daily life, negative beings or negative incidents can occur as part of a screening process to make sure you are truly worthy of the magical or shamanic path.

"Think of it this way," Michael explained. "Sometimes you'll encounter a negative being who's the guardian of a threshhold or door you want to pass through. The being may seem like a block, but that's only because this is a new level of experience for you. But then, if you take on the challenge, work hard to meet it, and pass the test, that being may have a secret or ability to help you. For example, on one of our trips, some spirits that took the form of wolves tried to block our way at first, and when we turned around, they tried to attack us by charging at us. But once we decided we had no reason to run, had a right to be there, and stood our ground, they stopped. Then, when we started walking back calmly, they offered to help us and ran ahead of us as our guides through the woods."

"How does all this relate to real life?" I asked.

"Well, what happens in the field is really a metaphor for what you experience every day. It's more intense. You're dealing with the unknown out there. But the same kinds of things happen. It's like a parallel but different universe, at a higher level to what we experience every day, but with similar laws. For instance, if you confront negative people in everyday life and stand up to them, they'll see you in a new way. They'll treat you with respect. In turn, dealing with spiritual beings in the field can help prepare you for that. You see, life is all of one piece and what happens in the field parallels what happens in everyday life. But it can help you to deal with the everyday world even better, because experiences in the field are more intense."

"Like a spiritual testing ground?" Serge wondered.

"Yes, exactly that," Michael said. "So the lesson is, whenever you deal with anything that appears hostile to you, recognize and respect it. It may be alien, but it has validity. So stand up and face it on its own terms. . . .

"Then, gradually, as you keep doing this, you'll learn how to face more and more challenges and become even stronger. For example, some nights in the field, we may face nothing but negativity when the spirits are hostile and uncooperative. So we'll experience things like high winds we can't control. But other times, things may be completely serene. Thus, you need to be able to adjust, take what comes, and appreciate what you're dealing with. Then you should try to get on an equal footing with it. Or if that doesn't work, prepare to be humble to it. The idea is to listen to your heart—to that little inner voice which will tell you what to do.

"That's why, whenever I encounter anything that appears hostile or dangerous I assess it, whether it's in the field or in everyday life. Then, if it's bigger than me, I accept that. And whatever it is, I try to handle it as best I can by listening to my heart."

"But that's what sometimes gets me in trouble—listening to my heart," moaned Serge.

"That's your emotions," Michael explained. "You need to distinguish the voice inside and listen to that. Then, when you pick up important insights and information, you need to have quick reactions and be in a state of psychological readiness to react.

"That's because things can happen very quickly on a psychic level, wherever you are—in the field or in daily life. So as soon as your voice says, 'danger,' you have to be ready to respond. For example, when we're in the field, these dangerous beings can travel at great speeds—perhaps 65 to 90 miles an hour—and they're usually about 30 to 60 feet away. So they get across the area very fast. Thus, you have to react immediately, say by assuming a defensive position and using a quick banishing motion. . . .

"And even if you can't see any danger, you have to be able to sense it and be ready to react, since it can come in an unseen form. For example, these spiritual beings can sometimes use a cloaking device to become invisible. So one second you might see a solid apparition, and a moment later it's gone, or it appears as only a ripple in the air. That's why you need to stay really in tune with your inner voice and listen to any warnings."

"How can you notice or verify these things if they're so slight?" Teri asked. "For example, at work I had a feeling that a woman could not complete a project. There was no rational reason I should feel this way because the person had always come through before. But something told me it wouldn't happen. Yet, I gave her the project to do anyway. Then, it dragged on for several weeks with unexpected mistakes, like one night a printer broke down, and then, when the project was just about completed, the woman literally disappeared. She went to a meeting and no one heard from her after that."

"Yes, such things happen. But you can generally pick up these beings if you're using your seeing," Michael explained. "That's why it's so important to keep up with your exercises. Say something vanishes on you in the field. The easiest way to pick it up is to focus your seeing on the middle of the area where it vanished. Then, you may notice a ripple coming at you through the air. Or if you don't see anything, rely on what your heart tells you is there and listen to your heart when you get those little feelings that something is wrong in everyday life, and focus on them to check them out.

"At the same time, stay alert to the possibilities of sudden dangers or attacks. For example, sometimes when one of these beings starts attacking in the field, it'll firm up, and suddenly you'll see a humanoid shape or maybe an arm or leg coming at you. . . . But often these beings tend to blend into the scenery. Or they may jump into something to hide, like a boulder. And then they may pop out again. Likewise, at work, with others you know, someone might decide to hurt you. For example, maybe you're standing in the way of their promotion."

"So how do you protect yourself?" Teri asked. "I know people at work who might be like that."

"That's one good reason for making a magical circle or a zone of protection for yourself. If you do this, they'll generally stay out—though they may get close."

Michael described a few experiences in the field to illustrate. "One time when we were working, a full humanlike figure suddenly became a cloud. Then, after I banished it, it disappeared into a shadow by a tree and tried to loop around and return. You have to realize such transformations are possible, since these spiritual beings transcend the boundaries of physical matter. And sometimes people you know in everyday life can transform themselves from an apparent friend to a dangerous foe."

"Yes, office politics, as usual," Teri agreed.

"However, your preparation in the field can make you more sensitive to what's going on and to what to do to protect yourself."

"It sounds like things can get pretty dangerous out there," Harvey commented nervously. "Like when I was out there last week."

"Yes and no," Michael replied. "Essentially, you're going out into the unknown, and sometimes things can be friendly. Other times they aren't. It's just like it is on the streets, or even in an office. You want to be prepared, yet you don't want to let paranoia take over, because that opens you up to all sorts of hostile beings that might not bother you otherwise. . . .

"Also, your fear acts as a real magnet to draw other beings around. In some cases, you'll see familiar beings or ones you feel comfortable with. Then, there's nothing to worry about. But if you don't know what something is, it's best to keep a safe distance of about 30 feet. Or if you pick up that something strange is going on with people around you, hold them off for awhile. Don't make any hasty decisions or commitments. That way you have time to react and find out what you're dealing with. In short, it's best to be cautious—but don't let your fears get to you."

"What happens if something comes at you and you don't stop it?" Serge asked. "Like that could have happened to me when I was doing my solo."

"It depends. Generally the being will go over you or through you. If your circle's in place, you may feel its passing is like a breeze. Or if it goes through you, you may fall sick, maybe faint, or maybe nothing will happen. It depends on the being and how strong you are."

"And if this happens in an office?" Teri asked.

"Well, then you might feel a rising sense of frustration or being caught in a vise, until you release yourself from this situation or person."

"What else can you do for protection, besides creating a circle?" I asked.

"Well, you have a certain focusing ability these beings don't have, since you're working on the physical plane," Michael said. "It's like having more batteries. So, if you can concentrate your force of will, you can shoot out your energy at them to make them go away or dissipate.

"Also," he continued, "these beings generally don't have allies like we do. So they're alone when they come at you. But you can call on your own allies or on the elementals to help you, and they will."

"Can familiars help?" Teri wanted to know, referring to the physical or spiritual creatures that often accompany a person involved in magic, much like a pet might in everyday life.

"Sure," Michael said. "That'll work. It's a good idea if you can attract one or a few of these familiars. Then, you can have them around to help for awhile. Or maybe after they've done what you wanted, you can release them."

To illustrate, Michael gave an example of one of his own familiars, pointing out that these familiars could be either real creatures, like dogs and cats, or spiritual beings that might take many forms. "One of my familiars," Michael reported, "looked like a six foot white gorilla with insect-like antennaes on his head. I initially called him up when I was doing some workings in L.A. and I wanted to see what was out there. I did an invocation and this odd looking creature appeared. Then, it developed some affection for me and hung around. . . . Anyway, as you start working with familiars, you'll find they become easier and easier to attract and you can call on them in the field or in daily life, too."

"In the office, too?" said Teri. "But what if others are around?"

"You can always go off in a quiet place by yourself or close your own office door. Besides," Michael grinned, "other people generally don't see the spiritual beings around you, anyway. They haven't been trained to see them like you. Or they might think something is an ordinary cat or a dog."

Michael drew a quick sketch of his large gorilla familiar on the blackboard to illustrate. Then, he continued, "You should find out the source of any problem after dealing with it. You have to take care of the situation first, but after you've handled the problem, find out where it came from. It could be a part of the environment you're in. Or possibly someone who doesn't like you could be sending some negative energy your way."

"What's the difference?" Serge asked.

"Well, generally, a magical attack on you by someone else takes a more pedestrian form, such as encountering a spell of bad luck, experiencing poor health for awhile, or losing a job."

"But that can happen anyway," I observed. "People have those kinds of problems all the time."

"Sure. That's why you check with your inner voice to find out the source of your problems—natural or magical. Even if someone is out to get you magically, usually it'll be something pretty routine."

"Why is that?" Teri wondered.

"Because it's hard to call in a lot of spiritual beings or negative forces to affect you. The person needs to see where you are and direct them to do something extremely unusual. So mostly, people can't or don't do this. They just send you a general run of bad luck or misfortune."

"That sounds familiar," Harvey commented. "With all the magical groups I belong to and all the people I may have rubbed the wrong way, maybe that's why things seem so screwed up for me sometimes."

"Could be," Michael nodded. "You'd have to check it out further to be sure."

"Well, suppose I do, and decide I want to go after someone, which might be only fair, under the circumstances," Harvey asked. "What would I do?"

Michael replied slowly, cautiously. "If you're working with an elemental, you might direct it to affect the person at his house, or several people there at the same time. Then, whoever is affected might experience bad luck or possibly some things in the house might fall apart.

"But generally, it's not a good idea to do this sort of thing. First, on ethical grounds, unless someone has done something really bad to deserve this, you don't want to go around hurting people spiritually. Also, when you send out something negative, there's a risk it might come back at you, since it can be difficult to maintain a screen of protection around yourself for a long enough time. Then, too, your protective circle might not be as secure as you think, since these circles often have chinks or unexpected openings in them, and that can let the negative stuff back in, too. Thus, it's best to stay away from launching any psychic attacks and stick to defensive measures."

Harvey curled down even further in his corner, looking chastened at having been squelched again, and Michael continued. "Another strategy to protect yourself if you think something is wrong is to go into a selfless mode and let whatever is out there go through you. When you go into this mode, you become nothing, and whatever is attacking goes right through you. It's like letting someone's anger or threats slide off your back, without your getting upset or bothered in any way. And that's why working with the Second Degree is so valuable—it helps you learn to flow with things, so you can be receptive and adapt.

"By contrast, if you resist hard, whatever is attacking sticks with you. That's why protective shields are of limited usefulness. When you set them up, you put up something that someone else can hit. And even if your shield is very strong, it can be overcome if someone throws a lot of things at it. It's like being hit repeatedly by a battering ram. Eventually, something will get through. By contrast, when you become like nothing, you make yourself invisible, and your attacker doesn't know where to hit. Then, after you have foiled the person's blow, you can reappear and respond."

Michael gave an example from a field trip. One man began arguing with him, and when the man threatened to hit him, Michael immediately focused on disappearing. As a result, when the man swung at him, he missed. Then, in moments, Michael said: "I was back in action, ready to respond, and I stared at the man forcefully, until he backed down."

Michael went on to the next defensive strategy.

"It's important to size people up, too, when you meet them. Again, listen with your heart. Get a feeling of how much these people put out positively and negatively.... Even in the friendliest situation I do it. You never know how things will change.... So ask yourself: 'Suppose there are problems? Suppose this person is put under pressure? What is this person capable of?' Again the key to defense is be prepared and don't let yourself be victimized."

"But isn't that a pretty dark way to look at things?" Teri asked. "I'd like to think most people are well-meaning."

Michael replied, "Well, people may want to be. But people are under great pressures today. The world has become very complex and difficult. So things can get very dark at times out there. It would be nice if everything could be all sweetness and light. And it can be with people you have learned to trust and with people who have come to respect you. But otherwise, you have to be ready. That's the way of the warrior. Being well prepared is the key to self-defense."

I mentioned I had previously researched a group that used black magic techniques, including destruction rituals, as a form of self-defense. "Are you recommending something like that," I asked.

"No. No. Not at all," Michael stated vehemently. "When you're involved in black magic, you're giving the negative powers in yourself more leeway, and they're able to come back at you. In psychic self-defense, you're only doing as much as is necessary to protect yourself. You're not trying to damage the other guy vindictively."

Serge wondered: "How can you tell if you are under psychic attack? Are there any visible physical signs, apart from intuition or that little voice? What should I look for?"

"Oh yes, there are signs," Michael replied. "You might get a headache unexpectedly. You might suddenly come down sick for no apparent reason. Or you might experience unusual manifestations. For instance, in L.A. I found a voodoo doll someone left at my door one morning, and when I got dressed, I noticed strange scratches on my body just under the skin."

"Is it usually physical like that?" Serge asked.

"No," Michael replied. "Someone could project a feeling of hopelessness around you, and then you might feel discouraged and don't know why. Or maybe when everything seems to be going well, you suddenly feel depressed."

"So what can you do to defend yourself?" Serge asked.

"You've got to keep assessing your situation on an ongoing basis. Then act accordingly to get rid of the problem."

Michael gave an example of how he combatted some vague feelings of depression he felt were due to a psychic attack. "Nothing was wrong, and I asked myself why I felt this way. Then, I got a sense that the problem was focused in this mask." He pointed to a large papier-mache dog's head hanging on the wall. "So I did a ritual and got rid of whatever spirit or concentration of negative energy was in there.

"In short," Michael concluded, "ask yourself why you feel the way you do, and if it doesn't make sense to have those feelings, ask some more questions to check out the possibility of a psychic attack. For instance, ask: 'Why should I be morose?' Then, solve the problem. Get your inner detectives out and deal with whatever's wrong. Most people feel things must be so when they're hit with different feelings. But that's the road to resignation and destruction. You've got to know you can make things change and act accordingly."

"Are there other signs to look for besides your feelings?" Teri inquired.

"A number of them. It might become clear to you that you've got a problem when you go out in the field. Or an unexpected difficulty or series of difficulties might occur in daily life, like everything going wrong with that project you mentioned. In either situation, you might experience the energy as being strange or off. Or maybe someone else may pick up that things seem weird. You may seem different, maybe a little spaced out or off center. And you could have trouble with your magic, too."

"What kind of trouble?" Teri asked.

"Maybe you're less aware; maybe less focused. Or perhaps you may attract some strange being to you which your partner spots. For example, once when I was in the field, a friend saw an odd thing sucking on my neck. I suddenly felt it when he pointed it out. So I did a ritual and that banished it."

Harvey suddenly stirred in the corner: "But suppose you're not sure about your own perceptions about the problem?" he asked. "Suppose you feel confused or the situation seems confused."

"Then, get some feedback from someone else. Most of the time, psychic attacks are expressed through bad fortune and negative events which are unexpected. For instance, a slow lingering illness or an unusually bad experience could be a sign. And most of the time, you can pick up these signs if you keep in touch with your own inner radar. But if you feel this isn't working right, I'd recommend checking with your close companions; and your allie is good for spot checking on this situation, too.

"Thus, if the situation seems weird or if you feel uneasy about things where you are, get out, but also investigate. Is it the place? The environment? Or is someone else trying to do something to you psychically?

Michael also recommended overcoming problems by clearly seeing the situation, letting go of it, and focusing on new things. "Use your seeing or dreaming abilities to see what the problem really is. Then, you can mentally disassociate yourself from the event or anything that may have led to it happening. Finally, use a meditation to concentrate on replacing the old with something new. This way you can get away from the situation and let go of any misfortune you're experiencing. This works because once you can step back and observe the situation, you can banish it. You're no longer part of what's happening; it's now an object that's separate from you, so you can treat it like other objects. Keep it if you want it, or get rid of it if you don't.

"In short," Michael concluded, "the key to dealing with any problem is to be good with your timing, stay flexible, listen to your heart, be ready to be receptive and respond, and act properly, so you can quickly resolve the problem. At the same time, have the ability to zero out and detach yourself. Because if you're too solid, something is sure to hit you.... Yet, you still need to stay focused and controlled."

"That's a big order," said Teri.

"Well, it takes work. But you can use some of your magical tools to help you. For example, when you make a circle or invoke some assistance, that saves some of your own power in self-defense. You can also use power objects. Or perhaps visualize or draw with your eyes to imagine the objects and helpers you need, though that takes a little more effort than if you have the objects themselves."

Michael paused and spun around in a small circle, while moving his left hand to the right, "You see, as I just did, sometimes I may push the energy out with my hand to create a circle if I don't have a power object. Or..." he pointed to his waist, "I may extend fibers out from my stomach and send them around my body. And the advantage of these techniques is you can use them not only for protection, but for interacting with the forces of nature, so it's a double defense."

"How do you know you're acting properly?" Serge queried.

"The world will confirm that repeatedly with good omens," Michael replied.

"But how do you decide when you need protection and when you don't?" Harvey asked nervously. "How do you know? Like the other night—maybe I should have asked for protection."

"Again, it's that little voice and the situation. For example, when Teri did her Second Degree, she didn't set up her circle or use any protection. But in that sort of situation, that's okay. You're opening yourself up to the universe, saying, 'Here I am.' And you're appealing to the deity to protect you, even if you don't specifically say that. However, it's different when you encounter elementals in the field, or when you're in a tough situation in real life. You need protection then."

"How good is your protection? Say a circle. . . . Can you count on it?" Harvey asked.

"You don't normally have to worry about things getting into your personal circle unless they're invited. As long as you put up a circle around yourself, it's like a wall of protection, and it keeps things out."

Michael picked up a small round stone from the altar, and suggested that objects could be used to create protective walls, too.

"You can take an object, like a pebble, and charge it to represent a physical wall against an opponent or someone who wants to hurt you. Or you can project a charge or image of a wall into something you pass on the street, like a pole, as a way to slow people up."

Michael described how he did this once in Los Angeles, when he was in a run-down neighborhood and a group of toughs appeared to be following him. He mentally drew a banishing pentagram in the air and sent a bolt of energy at the group. "And that slowed them up for a few seconds," he said. "One of them felt the bolt coming and suddenly turned around for a moment. Then, when I reinforced the action by tracing a banishing pentagram with my hand to create an even stronger image, the group broke up and the four men walked off."

Michael also recommended we visualize Gateways as a protection at times. "Just imagine the Gateway is next to you, and then any negative energy goes in and disappears, instead of hitting you. This happens whether this energy is emotional, psychic, or physical, since the Gateway attracts energy more easily than you."

"How long should you hold this image?" Teri asked.

"Just long enough to swallow up the energy. Then you can let it go. Or use the technique of grounding energy. Experience the energy passing through a large portion of your body and let it disperse into the ground."

Then after a break for coffee, Michael said he was ready to explain a very special technique to us which was known only to a small select number of people. He called it "hunting" and cautioned us that he could only make the basic version of it public. "It's the most powerful technique we konw. So we want to reserve it for ODF members only as a kind of 'ultimate weapon.' We have something extra powerful we can use if we need to."

There was a sudden hush in the room and a sense of breathless anticipation, as everyone waited for Michael to reveal at least part of this special secret. He continued softly: "The way hunting works is you have an ability to exude a wave of will which touches the person's spirit. It's like sending a wave of energy into their core. For example, consider what happens when you stare at someone. They'll feel it, turn around, and look at you. Well, hunting's like that.

"Sometimes members of the police force use this when they're confronting a suspect to get him to comply or back down. This technique has a powerful effect, because when someone uses it on you, the wave of energy that person sends out hits your body and goes through any psychic shields you have up into your core. As a result, you feel uneasy. Well, the way to deal with this attack, when you realize what the person is doing, is to zero out, so the negative energy goes through you. Then send it back."

"What happens if you send the energy to someone and they're psychically shielded, too?" Teri asked. "Wouldn't the energy come back at you?"

"If that's the case, perhaps visualize yourself going through their shield like a blade. Shields can work in some cases. But you can often cut through them if you know how. Besides, if the energy should come back at you, you've got your own defenses to diffuse it—such as creating a Gateway, zeroing out, grounding the energy, or any of the techniques we discussed."

"But what if someone starts hunting you?" Harvey queried worriedly.

"The only way to deal with that is to zero out, because hunting will penetrate anything solid. That's why shielding yourself is no good at that time."

"How do you decide which technique to use?" Serge asked.

"You'll find some are more compatible with your own personal style. As you start using them regularly, those techniques you use, like hunting, will eventually become automatic. It's like a muscle that automatically contracts and relaxes. You'll find these defenses will start to operate without your thinking about them after you practice them for awhile."

"But what about the morality of these techniques," Serge suddenly asked with concern. "When is it appropriate to use them if you can hurt someone psychically?"

Michael replied thoughtfully. "The ODF has considered those issues carefully, since these kinds of questions have come up before. They're hard questions to answer, but our view is that you may not be able to have all the answers you need to fully justify acting, because you may have to act quickly, and there's lots you don't know. But if you feel you're being victimized in any way, it's always appropriate to defend yourself."

The class was almost about to end, and I had one last question. What about the dangers of paranoia? Could thinking about all these possible psychic dangers make one paranoid? I hadn't even thought before about the types of dangers Michael mentioned, much less the defenses for them.

Michael nodded when I finished sharing my concern. "Sure, there is that possibility of paranoia," he agreed. "If you lose control of things, that could happen. You could become paranoid. But, on the other hand, if you're aware of the dangers that exist, that can make you more sensitive and more aggressive in reacting so you respond more appropriately. For example, kids who grow up in the slums or a barrio are like that. They're tough and they're quick to react.

"Well, that's the goal of the shaman warrior path. You want to work on getting very sensitive, so you know how to deal with whatever comes up. But becoming paranoid—no. You don't want that. Balance your sensitivity with good sense and control. It's the same ideal in the martial arts. Combine your aggressiveness with a psychic, receptive aura, so you're always ready to react, though with moderation and judgment. That's the warrior's way."

The class over, Michael recommended that we practice the hunting technique. "Try it in a crowd to check people out, and you'll see that people start looking at you. That's because you're projecting your aura out at them when you hunt. It's a forward thrust that goes out in a wave, and they can feel it. So they'll look around to see where it's coming from.

"Also, if you want, send a thought along this beam and see if you can get someone to do something. For instance, if a person is holding an object, concentrate on him putting it down."

Michael led us across the street to the pizza parlour to experiment. We sat down at a long table near several tables of students, and Michael suggested we each pick out someone different to focus on.

"Think about what you would like the person to do, and then send out an energy beam to that person. See if he responds and how long it takes. And don't pick something too far out for the person to do. Just choose something that's relatively possible, though someone might not do it without your urging. For instance, concentrate on having someone put down his glass to his right, or maybe have someone suddenly reach up and scratch his nose. Make it something specific enough so you can tell if the person did it, and unlikely enough, that the person probably didn't do it by chance."

Michael told us to start now, and for a few minutes, each of us picked a student to gaze at.

When Serge's student suddenly rubbed his ear, Serge leaned across the table and whispered to Michael: "I've got one."

"Fine," said Michael. "Pick another person and try again."

However, when Harvey's student picked up another slice of pizza, Harvey wasn't sure whether he had caused the action or if the person would have done it anyway. "How do you know if you caused it?" Harvey whined.

"That's why you have to pick something that isn't very likely, so you have something to verify," Michael admonished him. "Choose something else."

Harvey turned back to the student to try again. Meanwhile, my own student suddenly moved her chair and got up, something I hadn't willed her to do.

"What if they do something unexpected?" I asked.

"Don't worry if the hunting technique doesn't work all the time," Michael said. "Unplanned things can happen. You may not always have control. Like everything magical, it takes practice to become comfortable and good at this technique."

Thus, he urged us to practice during the week. Then, next week, we would experiment with trancework and past lives. "A trance is good for contacting your allie," Michael stated, "and it's the door to learning about your past lives."

CHAPTER SEVENTEEN

Going Into Trance

$\mathbf{M}$ichael began our next class by describing how the ODF used trance and past-lives techniques. He had only a few dim lights on to set the mood and everyone seemed unusually subdued, especially Harvey who had seemed increasingly distant since his failed Second Degree attempt on the mountain.

Michael began by pointing out that: "The trance state is very different from the dreaming and geoteleportation techniques we learned about earlier, because these two methods required only a light shift in consciousness. But a trance goes far deeper.

"Deep trance work requires you to get very relaxed, and you can use it to go deep within your consciousness. Then, in trance, you can do things like contact your allie, do past life recall, or project yourself into the future to do a future survey. It's semi-astral, for in trance you're actually projecting your astral body which surrounds your real body to another plane of consciousness. You're not just projecting your thoughts, as in geoteleportation."

Michael described the trance technique he would use with us.

"You'll shut down portions of your body in turn as you try to achieve total relaxation. As you do, your respiration, blood pressure, EKG, everything, will go down; but you'll remain conscious, since you're directing this. It's a simple technique. We start from the feet up, and in turn, you start relaxing everything, from your feet to your kneecaps to your hips to your abdomen to your chest. Then, the throat, mouth and forehead. Also, you'll relax your arms, hands, and shoulder blades, and if you feel an area of tension, we'll focus on relaxing that, too."

Serge broke in to say he felt especially tense tonight, because his roommate had finally left after a few hours of shouting, arguing back and forth, and slamming doors. He felt relieved he was finally gone, but otherwise, totally on edge.

"Then you'll be a good candidate to show how completely this trance technique can relax you," said Michael.

Then Michael described the light switch technique he used to create this state of total relaxation: "You'll visualize a light switch in each of these areas of your body and imagine yourself switching it off. You'll do that from your feet all the way up. Then, when you come back, you'll visualize turning each switch back on in the opposite direction. Just be sure you don't shut off anything vital as you turn yourself off."

Michael also described the elevator technique he would use to take us into a past life.

"We use the elevator because it's an excellent technique for going deeper. You see yourself in an elevator, press a button, and up you go. When the door opens, you're in a hallway with many doorways. If you're doing past life work, you pick a doorway to enter and walk through it into a past life. Or if you're working with your allie, you open the door and step into a room where you see your allie. You can also use this technique to learn about other people. You simply see the person's name on a door and walk in.

"Then when you're good enough, you don't need an elevator to get where you're going. You can pick out where you want to go in your mind's eye and go there. But this process helps you focus on where you are going in a methodical way. You do one thing at a time, and go deeper and deeper into relaxation as you go."

"Can we do this on our own, once we learn it?" Teri asked.

"Sure," said Michael. "That's possible if you guide yourself in. But it's better to have another person there to direct you, ask questions, find out what's happening, keep a record, and drag you out of trance if necessary. That's what I'll be doing tonight."

To demonstrate, Michael motioned Serge into the center of the room.

"Now you'll have your chance to really relax and put aside what happened today." As Michael instructed, Serge lay down on the rug, and Michael dimmed the lights even more. Then, as Teri, Harvey and I watched, Michael began to speak softly, slowly, almost in a monotone, to guide Serge into trance.

"Now put your attention on feeling your entire body.... Envision a light switch with an on and off position on your left foot, and imagine yourself switching this to "off". . .Now do this for the right foot. . .If you feel any tension in your calves, do the same for them both.... Now as you move to your left kneecap, switch this off. Then, over to the right. . . . There's another switch on your hip. First turn off the left. Now the right.... Does that area feel fully relaxed? If not, go back and shut off any areas that aren't.

"Now, we'll move to your abdomen. See the switch there and shut it off."

Similarly, Michael moved on to the chest, the base of the spine, the upper arms, forearms, and hands. He continued on to the throat.

"Switch it off, too, but you must remain talking. Just relax the muscles and structures in the area."

Then, moving up to the forehead, he asked Serge to turn off his third eye, and finally told him: "Now, lastly, turn off the top of your head and sink into that relaxed feeling. Luxuriate in your body being totally relaxed. And when you feel ready to go on, let me know."

After a few moments, Serge raised a few fingers slightly, indicating he was ready to continue.

"Okay, then, I'd like you to picture yourself in an elevator. The doors are closed. Pay special attention to the panel of buttons on your left. Can you see any numbers on the panel? Does any number stand out?"

After Serge nodded and whispered a number, Michael continued: "Then press the button for that floor. Now visualize the elevator rising. See the numbers flashing by. And tell me when you arrive at the fourth floor."

Again, Serge signalled he was ready.

"Now imagine the door opening, and you're stepping out into a plain hallway. There's a white carpet and white floors and doors . . . "

Michael paused to let Serge move along the hallway; then he continued. "Now, ask your intuition which door seems to beckon to you. Which seems like the right one to open onto a past life . . . "

"The third," Serge whispered.

"Then proceed to that door. Grasp the knob, turn it, and pull or push it to open, and say what you see on the other side. But don't step over the threshold yet."

Michael included this caution so Serge would have a chance to know what was on the other side before he proceeded. This way, if he didn't like what was there, he had the option to close the door and go somewhere else. But if Serge charged in, Michael explained later, it would be more difficult, perhaps impossible to go back.

After a long silence, Serge commented: "It's pitch black inside."

"It's common to see this," Michael said. "Now you can walk across the threshold into your past life. Walk into the blackness and see what you see when the blackness clears."

For the next few minutes, Serge explored what he perceived to be a previous existence in Tibet, while Michael asked him questions about this to find out what he was experiencing and guide him on to see more: "Where are you now?" "What kind of people do you see around you?" "What are you wearing?" "What's happening here?"

After 10 minutes or so, Serge reported that the experience was fading. "Then return to the door in the corridor," Michael told him. Next, reversing his earlier directions, Michael told Serge to get back in the elevator, return to the ground floor, and experience himself back in his body. Finally, Michael instructed Serge: "Now go through your body and turn each of the switches you turned off back on again. Turn them on in that same order you turned them off, until everything is on again."

When Serge signaled that all was on, Michael told him:

"Now, experience yourself back in the room and open your eyes."

After waiting a few minutes for Serge to readjust, Michael turned up the lights and continued: "You've just experienced what's called a full moment, and that can open the door to a past-life experience. Essentially, a full moment is a significant point in time which represents a turning point or a time when we are experiencing things to the fullest. It's a time when our experiences are more intense. They are more significant and important. Thus, when you went into your experience, that's what you were doing — surveying your past life full moment by full moment. And since these moments are times when our experiences are their richest and fullest, these occasions tend to be highly emotionally charged, even traumatic events, such as a marriage, love affair, death, or rape.

"You can experience a repeated series of these moments to find out more about yourself in the past. . . . Or you can jump forward into the future to learn about your probable future, which means you can experience an event that's likely to happen, given what's happening in your life or on the planet now. But the event is only likely, since change is always possible. It's just a probable future based on the situation now."

Michael stopped to ask for questions, and I cut in: "How can you tell these past experiences are not just your imagination? How do you know you're not creating an imaginary past life?"

"You know by the intensity of the experience, by the feeling of immediacy and reality, by your inner voice."

"Do you need a guide to do this?" Teri asked. "I don't always have someone around who could guide me."

"No, you can seek these full moments yourself," Michael replied. "But you need to keep certain ground rules in mind. One is staying out of unpleasant situations. If something seems like it might be unpleasant, only go in far enough to get the information and get out. If you feel you are experienced or can handle things, you can go a little further into something that feels difficult. But if the event is something traumatic, like being in a battle with fur trappers and Indians, get through it quickly and move on. Sometimes it's hard to pull out of something that's negative. It can be very enticing. But leave if the experience is getting heavy for you. It's not wise to go on, since you can get upset.

"Also, as you go deeper, ask yourself questions about where you are and what's happening, because that's how you'll experience the full moment of the past more fully. In fact, you can get some practice with this in real life by playing the following game. Say you're walking down the street. For a moment, just imagine you don't know where you are. Perhaps pretend you were suddenly put here by a flying saucer, and assume you know nothing— not even what your sex is, your race, or anything. Then, the idea is to find out a piece of information at a time just like some alien visitor might. For instance, when you look at a newspaper, that will tell you the date and will give you some idea of the city you are in. . . . However, be sure to look for this information in a safe place, since not knowing where you are can be disorienting, and you want to feel comfortable while you're finding out. It's not something to do in a critical situation, like when you have an appointment to get to. And don't do it in an unstable area such as the tough part of town. You want a place where you can feel in control."

"Like my own room?" Harvey commented.

"I suppose," Michael responded, "if you can imagine knowing nothing there."

"Well, that should be easy for Harvey anywhere," Teri jibed.

Michael glared at them both. And when everyone settled down again, he continued.

"You can also use the door technique to contact your allie. You don't need to use the elevator or hallway to make contact, though it helps to use a dark space as a meeting ground. But feel free to choose another site that feels comfortable. For example, one of my favorite places to meet my allie is a place between two galaxies. I see it as a gray-greenish area with little white lights, and I just project myself there and we meet and talk.

"However," he cautioned us, "wherever you go in a past-life experience or to meet your allie, be very clear and specific in your commands, and check out where you're going before you go very far to make sure it's safe and you want to be there. That's why when you go to that door in the hall, you don't step over the threshold right away. Because, sometimes, when you open the door, you don't want to go in or stay there, since things seem too weird. Thus, wherever you go, the key is to stop and survey, stop and survey, until finally, you feel whatever you are investigating has a comfortable flow to it, and you can experience it safely. . . . And, of course, you have to remember to come back.

"Can you get to these places directly, just by deciding to go?" asked Teri.

"Certainly. You don't need a reference point like the elevator or the door.

You can jump right in after you're experienced. The value of the elevator or door technique in the beginning is it creates an access point to a time period you want to enter or to a meeting with your allie. At first, when I started using these techniques, I went into a lot of detail about the elevator and the door. I spent a lot of time with each one. But now I know where to find my allie and how to get to the past or future quickly, so I jump into it. In turn, getting there quickly saves time and energy, so you can spend more time experiencing the trip more thoroughly."

"Do you usually find out what you ask?" Harvey asked. "I know I sometimes ask questions, but then I don't understand the answers, or they're wrong."

Michael replied, "Well, generally, you'll find the universe pretty open and receptive, though sometimes you'll hit a block. For instance, you may try to go back to a past life, and you find there's nothing there. You keep going deeper into the blackness, but nothing happens. Maybe that's because there's no life in the area yet; you're there too early. Or maybe a guardian there shuts you off, since it's better for you not to know about this past experience yet. Maybe it would be too difficult for you to handle, and since your inner self knows better than you, it shuts you off.

"Think of it this way," Michael explained. "It's like we have an oversoul within us, and we experience present time with one part of ourselves, and other times, with another part of ourselves. Also, we have the possibility of alternative futures and pasts, plus the present, all existing simultaneously, and we can shuttle between each one to discover the history of the soul going from some point in the past to the future. So time is relative. We can jump all over the place, and current time is where we are at a particular point in the flow of time. When we jump, we do so because that's what's significant and needed for us at that time."

"I'm confused," said Harvey, so Michael explained further.

"It's like you're a package of data, and you move from life to life, from experience to experience, gathering data. Then, as that particular life comes to an end, you are like a data package which is shot out into space, where you wait for a short gestation period, before you progress on to your next life.

"That's why, when you're in the present, you may sometimes suddenly get a flash which lets you know you've been someplace or done something before. Or if you're especially good at knowing or doing certain things, you may find if you look back far enough, that you've done that before. In other words, you're picking up on old skills in the present, and as a result, you can move along faster. You've already done a lot of the work in the past, so now you are better able to go on to something new."

Michael noted that this experience had happened in his own life. For example, sometimes, when he went out into the field and made a Gateway into the other world, he felt what he was seeing was very familiar.

"It was like realizing, 'I've been there before,' when I saw the Gateway," Michael said. "Then, after I recovered enough information about me from the past by going through the Gateway, I felt ready to move on. I felt like I had learned all I needed to know, so now I felt ready to ask: 'What new work should I do now? Where am I going next?'"

"Are you talking about deja vu?" Teri asked.

"In a sense, since deja vu involves experiencing something in the present that we've imagined in the past, so there's a collapsing of time between past and present. However, in our case, we're using the Gateway to link up the present, past and future. Since something feels so familiar, we feel we must have imagined or experienced it before, for the mind knows no difference between visualization and experiencing something. So when we feel that familiarity, it's like we're catching up with our vision of the future. And that means, there's no true linear progress, for time itself can shift around, and we can jump around in time.

"Then, too," Michael continued, "our insights from the past in the present can shape our future. For example, I have acquired enough pictures of the future from previously received information to know what to look for when I arrive in the future. Then, because I have this information about what this probable future may be like, I can knowledgeably act on that future image to change it.

"Thus, there's progress, but no linear progression, since events in time bounce around. Or maybe think of your progress through life this way. When you express something in your life fully enough, when you have enough similar experiences, you learn an important lesson. That's a different concept of life than the idea that you pass through a number of stages along a single highway. Our own life and existence is more organic than that. Instead, we feel a kind of beingness and knowledge all at once."

"Shamans know this, and they also talk about our lives existing in different time frames at the same time. For example, Castaneda says the sorcerers told him that when we live our lives here and now, we also live our lives in immediately adjacent and alternate times. As a result, a magician can create events in alternate times to influence a student working with him.

"The student may experience this influence as an event which occurred in his memory. Then, when he does something in the future that brings back this memory, he thinks he has really done this before. And, in effect, he has—in the past and in his mind. In turn, since our thoughts create our reality, thinking about it brings it into the present. Thus, in effect, the magician's intervention creates the student's experience of having done something in present time and space. But while this experience exists in present time, the cause of the experience—the magician's intervention—exists separate and apart."

We looked confused and Michael used an experience of Castaneda's to illustrate.

"Don Juan pushed Castaneda to remember things at the same time that he was talking to Don Juan in the desert. Then, as Castaneda talked to people and did things, he realized that he was both present and elsewhere at exactly the same time."

"So . . . " Michael stood up with an air of finality, "the whole point of this work with trance and past lives is to tap into these other spaces, because we get valuable information that may help us make more progress now. It's important to be clear about what we experienced in the past or in other areas, even when we're working with our guides here and now. For if we can get in touch with the work and the progress we have accomplished before, we won't have to do it again. We can use what we already know to move on that much faster.

"You see, what has happened before is part of an ongoing, dynamic process which is continuing now and will continue in the future. To be part of this process, every shaman warrior should get fully in touch with his own past, present, and future lives. For as a warrior, you need to make real shifts in your focus on reality from time to time; even stop your world to explore it some more. Also, you should become more aware about the other parts of yourself and be able to draw from the others you meet, not only in the present, but in the future and the past."

And on that note, the session ended. Michael urged us to experiment as much as possible with these trance techniques for discovering a different reality and collapsing time. Then, next week, we would learn the shaman view of power, the core of the shaman's way to self-discovery and development.

CHAPTER EIGHTEEN

Understanding Power

We were coming to the end of the ODF formal training program, and Michael was ready to tell us about the shaman's use of power. He had invited his two L.A. associates, Paul and Gene, to lead the session, and Teri, Serge and I sat in a semi-circle around them, as they talked about the meaning of power for a shaman warrior and how to use it. I noticed that Harvey was absent, and when I glanced at his usual corner chair, I noticed that Michael had placed a pile of power tools—swords, staffs and small objects—there as if Harvey was not to be expected.

Paul, a powerfully built man in his 20's, who looked like a stevedore, which he was at times, began. "Don Juan once said that each warrior expresses power through a feeling he is comfortable with, and this is what we believe in the ODF. A person perceives or taps into this power of the universe, when he is in a particular feeling mode and then channels it through himself to get the greatest impact."

Gene, a more slightly built man, who worked with computers, continued. "That's true. Each of us has our individual expression or way to go about magic. So it's important to flow with your own emotions, and let those emotions carry over into your worldly reactions, so you express your own magic. Magic really is a discovery of who you are and where you're coming from. Then, this self-discovery enables you to manipulate and be manipulated by power. It's as if you're tuning into a certain frequency flowing through yourself, and by doing so, you have access to a stream of power, which you can use and direct, if you know what you are doing. . . ."

"Or it can direct you," Paul added. "So the key is knowing which feeling will work best for you, then going with that feeling to direct the power you tap into."

Paul went on: "You might ask, 'How do I get power?' You should use your own feelings to help you hunt for power. It doesn't just come to you. Then, by seeking it, you interact with it and cross its path more than you would by chance. For example, use your hunting technique or your powers of suggestion when you encounter others everyday to affirm your power. Also, accept signs of power or signs you are experiencing a full moment when that happens. Say you see a bird fly by and you feel there is something significant about it. So grab that moment and take that power. Then, hold it within you, and know that you can use it when you need it."

Gene had another suggestion, "Think of it this way. Imagine you are like gun powder on a piece of rock, and a match strikes against the flint. Then there's a spark and a reaction. Well, it's like that in yourself. The moment something makes an impression in you, it's as if spontaneous combustion occurs which sets up a series of other reactions. Well, that's what it's like to suddenly come into contact with a full moment and realize you have the power to choose what happens next. It's like you can shift into another gear and make something happen. So you have to be sure you're going into the right gear. For the more power you have, the more chance you have of either winning the race or going out of control and cracking up. Thus, it's crucial to be aware and fully awake, so you can respond appropriately and quickly when you have to."

Paul had some cautions for us about using power. "Also be aware of the effect of your power on others. People can either help you or hinder you or destroy you at any moment. And the more power you hold in yourself, the greater the potential for that power to help or harm you. Yet, you need to hold onto that power to release the energy at the proper time. Meanwhile, that power will continue to exist in whatever form you hold it, since power endures. It won't destroy itself. It just shifts into other forms and will dissipate when you let go of it, or it will coalesce as you hold it inside. In turn, by holding it in you, you become a vehicle for that power. You channel it through you in the name of the ultimate power, and using your will, you can intervene to direct that power in either positive or negative directions.

"Yet, with knowledge, you'll choose the positive path, for those who truly know how to use power know they can't misuse it. Sure, many people attempt to gather up power and try to do something they shouldn't, but when they do, things happen to them. They make a mistake, and the power turns on them. So a true magician will strive to know power to its fullest extent and will respect that power. Thus, he won't misuse it. He realizes the risks and the dangers if he does."

Finally, Michael had a few last points about the value of gaining self-knowledge and striking a balance between the good and evil in the world.

"When you work with power," he observed, "it's good to have knowledge about yourself, so you know your own capacities and how far you can go. Be aware of both your good and your bad side. Often, we don't explore our limits, so we don't know them, except in stressful situations, when we discover how much we really can do when we draw on our full capacities. But it's better to know ourselves as best we can in advance, so we are better prepared when a stressful situation arises. If you know your own capacities, you can use them as the situation warrants, and you needn't wonder if you can do it and be afraid maybe you can't. You've already explored your abilities and you know!

"Then, too, as a magician, you're always in the middle of the good and the bad. You can't avoid the bad by merely thinking it away or imagining you don't have to use your power to deal with it. Instead, you have to work with both good and bad; so it's valuable to master both sides. You have to be balanced in the way you use power, and you can only know that by dealing with both the positive and the negative in the most appropriate way for each."

When Michael finished, he, Gene and Paul had some questions for us. Why, they asked, did Serge, Teri and myself want to use the power of the shaman warrior? As we each replied, they came back with suggestions about how to achieve our goals.

Serge began. "I want to be more aware of my purpose in the universe— how I fit in. I sometimes feel I'm drifting throiugh life, though I feel I have much to give, especially as a healer and helper."

"Your power can help you find out," Paul observed. "When you look inside yourself, you can do something about achieving your purpose. Use your visions and your experiences with power for clues to help you find out."

"Also, your willingness to see phenomena and to experience acts of power make it easier for you to discover this knowledge about yourself," Gene added.

Then, Michael spoke of the need for flexibility and immediate action. "You should keep your ultimate goals open and be ready to change, too. That's why the ODF grade system is open ended, so as people develop further, we can add more grades. This is necessary, because as you work with power, you may achieve your goals before you expect, since you move ahead faster.

For instance, about a year ago one of my goals was to step through into another dimension and see what was there. I thought it would take several years before I was ready to do that. But suddenly, I found I could do it. I still had the same everyday issues to deal with. However, accomplishing that spiritual goal and knowing I could do this made it easier to deal with those daily concerns. And the reason it becomes easier is because when you experience all the power you have in the spiritual world, that carries over into what you can do everyday."

"Also," Gene noted, "as you go on, your ultimate goal will continually change anyway. So accept that and flow with it. Otherwise you can get stuck with something that has become wrong for you."

"You see," Michael interjected, "the dynamics of what you're doing in the field and power are intermeshed. You're opening spiritual gateways and doors that will open still other gateways and doors—on a physical, emotional and spiritual basis. Thus, be prepared for change. Be prepared to go through those gates when they open. Just say to yourself at any point in time, 'This is the goal I'd like to achieve.' Then when you achieve it or it seems appropriate to choose something else to do, set another personal goal and move on."

Gene had one last suggestion. "While you're looking toward the future, also be aware of what you know now. Knowing can help you find your direction. Suddenly, all of the pieces of the puzzle go click, and you know. When that happens, go with it, since you've found your center of power. You've found your core or heart."

Then, it was Teri's turn to describe what she wanted to do with power. "I'd like to understand many things that have happened in the past and things I see that others don't. I'd like to be able to confront things, see things face to face, not hide from anything. . . . I'd like to be able to tell people off when I think they deserve it, like at work. In short, I want to have the power to understand something, confront it and banish it when I want."

"That's fine," said Gene. "Working with power will give you that power. It'll help you feel centered; it'll make things click for you, so you have that power of knowing; and you'll be better able to stand your ground. You'll have that inner knowing. Then, using magic, you can concentrate on discovering what's you and what's not you, and that knowing gives you strength."

Paul urged, "Also, when you meditate, go with the first thing that comes to mind. That gives you insight into what you really want. In addition, concentrate on trying to distinguish between what's coming from inside you and what's outside. That way, you can choose and do what's true for you, and operate from your own personal power. A true magician can do that. He has the ability to manage these sensations and feelings and select the appropriate action. He doesn't run after just any feeling that comes up, because that can be coming from outside himself. Instead, the good magician is able to sort out the different options and decide what he personally prefers to do. Then, because of his personal involvement and commitment, he can perform a really solid magical act. You'll experience that power based on commitment when you go into the field, and it carries over into everyday life."

Gene agreed. "Everything's so interconnected. Just by moving ahead and achieving your key goal, you should be able to do other things you want. When you get power in one sphere, you get it in others. You become a better channel for power, so you can better use it in whatever way you want."

Finally, it was my turn to state my goals. "I'd like to become more aware and understand things better," I said.

"And you can," Gene replied. "Many people miss out because they limit themselves, and that shuts down their power, and therefore their awareness and understanding. But when you take the view that there is an open universe and that power makes all sorts of things possible, you realize it's crazy to limit yourself. Instead, you have the power within yourself to open up your world.

"In many ways, the universe may seem very chaotic. But after awhile, you start realizing there are certain recurring movements and patterns that give it order. In turn, you can tap into those movements and patterns to help you decide which directions are right for you.

"You may not know where a pattern is going when you first see it. But if you keep looking, you'll see the lines underlying the pattern, and then, if you work with these lines, not against them, you'll enhance your power. It's like tuning into some universal pattern or flow. When you're in touch with this energy, you can draw on it to empower yourself. Then you can see more, understand more. And when you act from understanding, you are better able to act in an appropriate, direct and meaningful way. So the result is more success, and you'll get further ahead in achieving your goals."

"You make it sound so easy," I observed.

"But it can be!" Michael stressed. "Having power doesn't mean the warrior path is easy. It can be very difficult along the way. But as you learn to use power and control it, things become easier. You're stronger, more powerful yourself; though, of course, you must use any power appropriately, or it can come back on you.

"You see, you're really tapping into something bigger than yourself, when you work with magic. So you've got to learn to use that power responsibly and know what you're doing. Then, in time, you'll get to the point where you're not only using this power to work for you, but you've become that power; you've made it a part of you."

And on that note, the class ended. As we prepared to leave to go on the

field demonstration of power following class, I asked Michael why Harvey wasn't there. Slowly, painfully, with a touch of sadness in his voice, Michael replied, "It's unfortunate, but Harvey is no longer part of the group. We believe in giving everyone a chance, and we really tried. Again and again, I hoped he would listen and change. He never seemed to understand that you have to be a learner first and be receptive to have power and grow. He was always trying to grab for power now, before he was ready because he was so insecure in himself. So he was unable to work with and understand the ODF way of working with power.

"So his style of working with magical power just didn't fit. During his Second Degree, he was trying to command the elementals, rather than acknowledge and respect them, and he was arrogant, rather than being humble. He also drew out all sorts of negative forces, without understanding what he was bringing forth. By contrast when we go out in the field, we believe in communicating quietly with nature and the powers out there, not thrashing about. In the last few weeks, I tried to get him to understand this, but he resisted this, and I finally realized that he doesn't and won't let himself understand. So I told him he had to leave.

"You see, the shaman warrior path involves a special way of working with power. You need to open yourself up to it, trust it, let it flow through you. You need to become part of it and act from the knowledge that you hold that power within your heart. But Harvey continued to see himself directing and controlling the powers outside himself. He saw himself standing apart. And that won't work. It's a basic attitude difference, and his approach blocks the energy. For example, no one saw any energy around Harvey when he was doing his ritual, because he wasn't putting out any energy. There was an energy block.

"And that's what happens when you don't open yourself up as a channel for power; when you think the power inside yourself is separate from what's outside. You block yourself off, and you can't do effective work.

"Instead, you've got to be one with the source of universal power. You've got to let it run through you and use it. It's like a car. You're the engine, and power is your fuel. Cut yourself off and the fuel dries up; open yourself up as a channel and you've got an endless supply.... In fact, you'll see that later tonight on our field trip, when Gene and Paul show how to be receptive to that power, so you can get it and use it for what you want."

CHAPTER NINETEEN

A Demonstration of Power

After class, we prepared for the field trip, where Gene and Paul would demonstrate their power techniques. We put on our dress blacks, if we weren't already wearing them, and gathered our equipment and magical tools.

As we prepared, I noticed that Serge now sported two stripes on one shirt sleeve and several colored badges above one pocket, and I asked Michael "What are they for?"

"Serge has been promoted to Assistant Weyr Leader," he told me, pointing to the stripes, "and one medal is for hazardous duty in the field. That happened when he helped me take Harvey down the hill the night Harvey went for his Second Degree."

Around 10 p.m. we were ready, and we drove to a nearby state park. Then, we hiked up a hillside to a large open meadow. Though the night was crisp and clear, the ground was still muddy from last night's storm and there was a feeling of moistness in the air.

Even so, Michael announced, "Don't worry. It won't rain. We have work to do tonight. On previous field trips when rain was predicted, we similarly avoided a storm. That's because of weather magic, and it usually works to make things clear up in time for a trip."

After we climbed about 100 yards up a wooded trail, we came to a clearing which opened onto the meadow. It was a large grassy area, and along one side a few log fences surrounded what looked like a small corral for horses.

Michael led us over to the logs, and while we rested against them, he explained what would happen. He planned to work for few minutes to see what was there and get things started. Then, Paul and Gene would each do a demonstration. "The idea is to show you how to take the power we've been talking about for the past few weeks and use it to mold and shape your reality."

His explanation finished, Michael walked towards the center of the meadow and stopped about 50 feet away from us. For a few moments, he seemed to blend almost completely into the blackness, on this dark moonless night. But then I saw the familiar whitish aura around him that separated him from the blackness.

As we watched, Michael began his dance with the elements by spiralling around in one spot as he moved his arms up and down to shift the energy about. Then, suddenly, he darted to the right for about 20 yards towards a dark grove of trees.

As he moved, I noticed a swirl of sparks of light above him and a grayish mist just ahead of him, which created a double image effect. Also, I saw a pale white column of energy which seemed to be following him, even pushing him, and later, when we shared our reactions to the experience, the others reported similar observations. "You see," Michael later explained, "you all saw my double, which is a fairly common phenomena when you're doing a working. You're putting out so much energy yourself, it creates a trail of energy or double of yourself behind you."

Now, as we continued watching, Michael stopped in front of a small rise in the meadow, which appeared to be separated from the hulking grove in the distance by a long triangular cleft that slashed across the meadow. It was much darker there, and I could barely see what Michael was doing—just occasional flashes of motion, as he began to call forth several earth elementals and direct them around. Later he described these beings as "large hulking masses of grayish energy."

According to Michael, five or six beings appeared, and he began communicating with them. "I told them I brought our group to the meadow to demonstrate ways to use power, and I asked them to move around as I instructed—first to the right, then to the left, then back, and then a few feet forward. Also, I assured them I meant no harm and wanted only a peaceful relationship with the elements."

Later, as Michael reported, all sorts of forms appeared in the distance to watch. "It's typical they gather like that when someone mobilizes a lot of power in a working," he explained. "It happens, because when you go out there and start to do something, you're the most interesting thing out there. You're affecting the whole universe around you by your presence and your actions. So, of course, any beings out there are going to come out to watch."

At the time, though, I saw nothing—just inky blackness, occasional pulses of light, and from time to time, Michael seemed to blend into the dark cleft along the hillside. Meanwhile, as he worked, it felt chillingly cold, and a brisk wind whipped through the meadow, making it even colder.

After about ten minutes, Michael closed his circle and returned to the group to find out what we experienced and to explain what he had done. Everyone indicated seeing an aura around him, and Serge and Teri reported an energy double to his right. Paul and Gene saw the elementals Michael worked with as dense grayish forms.

Then, as Michael probed for more observations, Serge claimed, "I saw a bluish light near you too."

Teri said, "I saw the clouds move quickly across the sky and flecks of gold."

When I told Michael that, "You seemed to disappear into the dark cleft in the hill."

"I saw you become invisible too," Serge said.

When I wondered, "Why did some of our observations differ so dramatically, Michael explained that such differences were to be expected and were quite common.

"People have different ways of perceiving and interpreting what they are perceiving, though they generally agree on seeing something in the same place. For example, several of you reported seeing a whitish form or some other energy mass to my right. In some cases, people see these energy masses take human forms; others see them with colors. But what counts is you're all seeing something in a similar place."

Then, since Serge, Teri and I hadn't seen the elementals, Michael suggested we do an exercise to help see them.

"First, look at the dark trees in the distance. You'll see that the elementals who had come out to watch him and are still there." As we looked, Teri reported, "I see some whitish and grayish clumps of light."

"They seem to hover about in the darkness," said Serge. And I reported seeing some smokey-looking forms too.

Michael smiled. "That's exactly right, what you all saw. That's how the elementals often look, though they frequently take on a humanoid form, too. For example, once when I walked through a wooded area, I saw some earth elementals appear like small gnome-like beings with cords attached to trees. Then, as I walked by and directed my energy to banish them, they were literally sucked back into the trees. Other times, the elementals have appeared like huge hulking forms. So they have that power to take on various shapes. Or perhaps you may just perceive them that way."

Next, Gene stepped into the center of the meadow to show how he worked with power. He concentrated on creating a cone of energy around him that came to a point several feet above his head and directed that energy to pour down around him in two arcs. Meanwhile, Michael came over to me and Teri to point out some things we should look for.

"You'll notice a purplish form about ten feet away off to Gene's left," he whispered. "Also, you'll see a small dog-like shape running in a circle around Gene's feet."

As Michael spoke, I noticed two hazy patches of mist hanging in the air to either side of Gene and a small cat-like mass near his feet. Were they really there, I wondered? Or was I seeing them because of Michael's suggestions. However, when Gene returned to our group after his working, the others who hadn't heard Michael's comments saw similar effects. For example, Serge and Paul saw the purplish haze and sensed the energy swirling down around Gene, and they noticed the whitish form to his right.

Then Serge reported. "It became so cold, I had to get a scarf and wrap it around myself," which Michael considered a sign of success, too. "Whenever the temprature drops, that's a sign something is happening. Especially when you notice a marked drop."

Finally, Paul stepped forward to do his working. He asked us to gather around him in a semi-circle and explained, "Now I'm going to start the ritual by giving you a gift of energy that was given to me. I got the gift by storing up energy for about two weeks to prepare for this event. And I got this energy by taking some extra energy for myself whenever something unique happened. For instance, when a cat unexpectedly walked by my window, I took energy from that. Another time a bird flew by. I just looked for chance happenings that had a lot of energy and borrowed some for myself."

To perform the working, Paul planned to send the healing energy he had stored up to us.

"After you get this blast of healing energy," Paul continued, "I want you to concentrate on taking all of your negative energy and direct it towards the Gateway I create into another dimension. Imagine this negativity in the form of a bad experience or quality of yourself you want to get rid of. Then, project it at the Gateway. As it arrives, I'll be coalescing this energy together in order to control it, scatter it, or get rid of it by throwing it into the Gateway so it's gone. Then I'll end the exercise by closing the Gateway."

However, Paul cautioned, there could be some severe risks in doing this, since we were drawing together all this negative energy in one place.

"It's not totally certain what will happen," Paul said. "Ideally, I'll confront the energy and send it away or make it dissipate. But, since this energy has its own will or force, there's always the possiblity it can turn on me; or maybe it might even get back out through the Gateway and go back at the group. Then you'll get back not only the negative energy you're each putting out, but the combined negative energy of the group as a whole."

"We'll be prepared for whatever occurs," said Michael firmly.

"Good. Then you're ready," Paul nodded, and he asked us to sit close together on one of the log railings as we watched him work. "That way it's easier to give all of you the energy."

Paul turned and walked about 20 feet away, spun around again, held his hands towards us, and focused on sending some healing energy to us. This stage was crucial to all that was to come, he explained later, because he would use this energy to create a calm space in which he could work and raise the positive energy in himself he needed to confront and destroy any negative energy he encountered.

As Paul concentrated, I felt a sense of peace and calm surround us, and Gene and Serge later reported that they saw sparks of warm bright energy surge out of Paul's hands.

Paul returned briefly to hear our reactions to this experience, and then walked back to the same spot. However, now, he stood with his back towards us, as he meditated on creating the Gateway. As he did so, Michael signalled for us to stand and stretch out our hands, palms out, and send our negative energy towards Paul. Quickly, we stood up, then concentrated. I visualized any feelings of self-criticism and lack of assurance going outward towards Paul. Meanwhile, others focused on sending him their hostility, fears and anger.

As they later told me, Serge sent forth his angry feelings about his roommate and a former lover who left him. Teri sent her jealousy over a co-worker who got promoted instead of herself.

Soon Serge and Gene noticed a pale whitish form in the air sevral feet above Paul's shoulder, and it seemed to hang there for several minutes while he worked.

"It has some vaguely human features," Serge whispered. "Maybe it's the monster Paul talked about creating."

"And it feels really cold again," Teri said.

Now Paul focused on directing energy out from his belly to the mass of negative energy he had created from the group. His purpose was to exorcise and dissipate the group's negative energy, and he visualized the particles of energy gradually pulling apart. Then they scattered and were swept away by the wind.

When he saw that the negative energy ball was all gone, he concluded the working and returned to the group to hear our experiences. Afterwards, he emphasized that this had been a "truly difficult experiment," with the potential to leave him physically exhausted.

"Normally, if I had simply gone out without any special preparation to do what I just did, I could have been wiped out by the experience. It takes an incredible amount of energy and power to work with a ball of negative energy like that and get rid of it. So normally, it might take someone a day or two to get back up to speed. But since I've been storing up energy for two weeks, it only took me about a half-hour to come back."

"Why does it take so much energy?" I asked.

"Because, so many things can happen when negative energy is created. So you have to be really intense when you do this kind of a working. You have to be completely alert and ready to respond in an instant, since the energy that appears could be anything. It could be emotional, psychic, spiritual or physical, and it could be hostile, neutral or cooperative. I couldn't be sure what sort of energy I would be dealing with until I did it, and that's what makes this experiment so difficult. Thus, I had to be ready to use all my resources to handle the energy, once I confronted it."

Michael cut in, "But then Paul did what he wanted with this energy. He got the energy from you to form into a massive ball of powerful negative energy, which looked like a monster to some of you. And he stayed in complete control. He stood up to it, used a banishing technique, and got it to dissipate harmlessly in the air.

"And that's the sign of a true magician. The real magician knows what he's going to do. He is able to stand up to danger and mobilize his own powers to eliminate it. And he does so in a controlled, self-assured way. Further, the true magician has the power to enter and leave the other world at will through a bridge or Gateway. So he is the master of both worlds."

The demonstration over, Michael led us back to the cars, and as we drove back, Michael congratulated Paul and Gene for showing a mastery of the Sixth degree, which requires the ability to control power in both the physial and the spiritual world. He explained that Paul showed this ability by confronting and overcoming negative power when he sent the negative energy ball through a Gateway. Also, Gene had shown this mastery when he brought down a cone of power from the other world and brought through a small spiritual creature—the cat or dog-like figure we all reportedly saw.

"So congratulations," Michael told them. "You've proven yourselves tonight. You've shown your mastery of power." Then to Serge, Teri and I, he added, "So, now you've seen what is possible for a powerful magician to do. He can cross over into that other world and work with beings on both sides, so he is truly a master in both worlds. And when you master both worlds, that shows your mastery of yourself as well, since what we do in the physical world has a counterpart inside ourselves. Thus, as you progress in the field, you progress internally, too.

"Everyone has that potential for power and mastery. With training, you all can do it. It'll take work and practice. But everyone has that ability. It's a matter of commmitment, work and will."

We drove on in silence until we were back at Michael's apartment and the ordinary everyday world. Michael announced there would be one more class to bring together all of the ODF's basic teachings. After that, if Michael felt we were ready, Teri and I would go for our Third Degree.

CHAPTER TWENTY

Contacting Our Own Allies

As our last class began, Michael announced that tonight we would learn how to contact our own allie, using the trance technique we had learned earlier. Then, we could gain the kind of insights Michael had gotten for us at an earlier meeting by contacting his own allie. However, now, we could obtain such insights directly.

But first he wanted to answer any questions we might have from previous classes or field trips, so he could wind up basic training with everyone feeling complete.

Teri aired her problem with seeing first. "I don't always see everything everyone else does. Like on our last field trip. Most people saw the dog Gene created, some people saw Paul's red monster. But I didn't see anything."

Michael tried to reassure her. "Well, some trips are better than others for seeing, and some people see better than others. I don't see everything myself. Typically, many things are very vague, so most people just see misty shapes, things look fluid and amorphous. That's why you need to develop an ability to translate them into other things. Also, some evenings are very misty, so it's hard to see. Then, too, it may be better for you to tune into your feelings and sensations. That may be your own style of perceiving things. But try to see what you can."

"What if I tried rituals for improving my ability to see?" Teri continued. "Do you think they might work?"

"It depends. Such rituals can help you focus and concentrate sometimes. But the problem with ritual is sometimes you can get so focused on the ritual process that your seeing ability drops off. You think about whether you're doing the ritual right, and you concentrate on that, rather than on seeing."

"What if I paused occasionally during the ritual to experience perceptions and insights?" Teri asked.

Again, Michael turned down the idea. "You don't need to break the rhythm of a ritual. That can be disruptive. Instead, it's better you learn how to develop a split concentration. For example . . ." Michael picked up his staff and pointed it towards the ceiling, ". . . did you notice that grayish shadow on the ceiling that just moved by?" He put down the staff.

"You see, I've been talking to you, but part of me is still active and alert. So you can still talk to people and do other things, while you're doing a working. Part of you is focused intensely on your experiences and perceptions; you're very alert. But the other part of you is actively involved in whatever you are doing. It could be a ritual or maybe something else you do every day.

"And that's one of the values of this training. You can use it whenever and wherever you want to see. You don't have to wait for a special time and place where you do a magical ritual. However, when you do perform a ritual or are involved in any other group activity, your ability to see can enhance that.

"That's why I prefer to do a ritual or go out in the field with someone who can already see to some degree. They can monitor what's happening around them better. And there's much faster, more immediate communication, which can be crucial when you need a quick response in the field. Normally, there's a delay between the moment I experience something and tell others, which can slow things down. But if someone can see well, they can pick up what I'm sending and respond instantly, and it may be necessary to have the group respond in a hurry."

As an example, Michael described an L.A. ritual he attended. "A strong wind came up and the people didn't respond quickly enough. They were knocked down, instead of having time to steady themselves or get out of the way.

"Then too," Michael added, "when you know how to see, you can use seeing to track someone else who's doing a ritual. For example, when any of you have done a working, you've seen me moving around you. That's to keep an eye on what you're doing and to observe any response you get. You may not be aware something is happening yet, since you're new at this, but I'm there to check things out and make sure everything is going along okay. If not, I'm ready to help out, stop things, or do anything else necessary in the situation."

As an example, Michael described how a group of earth spirits had appeared to watch when a former student did a ritual. "But she wasn't aware of them and didn't know how to banish them, so I had to step in, calling her attention to them and then helping to banish these spirits.

"So you see, it's really important to observe each other in the field. In a formal ritual, you can designate a person to watch out for unexpected spiritual or other things that pop up, and he can make sure the ritual is going on course. But in the field, the roles shift so frequently as to who's doing a working. That's why you need to be able to switch roles, so one person can watch what's happening for a time, and then another can take over. And that's why you need to get your seeing skills up to par so you have them when you need them."

"What about balance in a ritual?" Serge asked. "I sometimes feel like the energy is moving too fast or in the wrong direction. Or it's moving too slow."

In response, Michael stood up with his feet slightly apart and brushed his left hand across his stomach to the right with a broad sweeping motion.

"You can use a motion like this to feel more balanced," Michael said. "I often do this—moving my hand from left to right—in the beginning of a ritual or during it, to help balance the energy. It evens out the polarities and gives you more energy." He moved his hand back and forth a few more times. "Just keep doing it from left to right until your energy feels even. It's good for a quick energy fix."

Then bending down, Michael commented, "You can also raise more energy as well as balance it." He moved his hand from his feet up along his body and stood up gradually as he did. "This is a good technique to give you more energy in a ritual. It's like you are sweeping up energy from the earth into and through yourself. At the same time, be sure to call on the forces you need to either assist you in working with power or protect you from any negative power you don't want."

Michael explained how he used the pentagrams and guardians he invoked in the ritual to do this. "As you've seen. I generally start off the ritual by drawing a clockwise circle in the ground around me with my knife, though you can use anything to draw with, even your hand. Then I draw a series of clockwise pentagrams in each of the four directions and give each one a charge with my knife. Sometimes for extra measure, I'll draw one above me and one on the ground. Mainly I use them to set up an energy barrier for protection. and use my own energy to call on the spirits I want to assist. However, you can use these pentagrams to help you invoke or call on the beings you want to assist. And that can be especially useful if you're having problems getting the elements to respond. You can invoke any spirits or beings that have a meaning for you. Then, be sure to end the ritual by banishing anything you called forth."

When Serge asked "What's the best way of banishing things?" Michael described his own method, but stressed the approach was up to us.

"I make a counterclockwise pentagram and really thrust hard with my knife. The motion has a certain resonance. But you can use other motions, like holding out your staff and saying 'be gone.' Or just concentrate on willing something away. The key is your intention, and your motion just supplements or reinforces that. So sometimes I do a backwards motion to clear things out, much like doing a pentagram in reverse or making a reverse circle. Or I might simply wave my hand like I'm clearing out smoke. Use the banishing technique that feels most comfortable for you in a particular situation. But be sure to do something to get rid of what you created when you're done. You want to be tidy. You don't want to leave the spiritual energies you've brought with you hanging around."

Michael didn't do that when he was first training with the ODF in L.A. and the results were nearly disastrous. He had been out on a solo, and when he finished his ritual, he simply walked away from the circle he had created.

"But the problem with doing that," Michael said, "is the energy you've left there doesn't immediately dissipate. It hangs around. Thus, when I turned around, I saw a misty bluish wall of energy which I had left behind, and then I saw a predatory shadow going in and out of my energy. And suddenly I realized what was happening. These shadowy beings were taking pieces out of my energy each time they moved in and left; they were eating my energy. And for a moment I had a real sick queasy feeling, for I suddenly realized these were like piranhas eating me up. Thus, I went back and quickly banished them and cleaned up my energy. And since then, I've never left anything behind."

Teri had one last question. "Why do you have to draw pentagrams or use tools to do magic? If magic is created by your thought and intention, why do you need anything?"

"You don't," Michael said. "Not theoretically. I only use drawing the pentagrams and the circle as an aid. They give me a good feeling, and I've become used to them. Also, their symbolism ties in with some of my other beliefs. But you can use anything—a cross, a Star of David, whatever has meaning for you. What you're really doing is setting up a focus inside yourself

"Similarly, any tools you use, help to get you into a certain level of awareness. They help to set the mood, and the symbols are reminders of what you're doing and what you believe. But again, the particular symbols and tools don't matter, and you can't invoke anything regardless of your equipment or magical language unless you're together yourself. After all, the key to any success with magic is your intent, and you should focus on getting clear about that. Then, you can use the symbols and tools to help you express the finer nuances of what you're trying to do."

Once the questions were over, it was time to learn how to contact our own allies. To demonstrate, Michael asked Serge to lie comfortably on the floor, so he could guide him to the meeting with his allie. Later, we could use the same technique to make our own contact.

Serge settled down on his back on the rug, and Michael dimmed the lights. He sat down in a chair facing Serge, and speaking in a low steady voice, he asked Serge to use the electrical switch technique to turn off and calm his body. When Serge announced he now felt fully relaxed and calm, Michael told him, "Now see yourself in a modern elevator, facing the controls. . . . " Michael paused to give Serge time to visualize this. Then, speaking in a slow, soft monotone to help Serge further relax, Michael continued, "Now ask yourself which floor to press to meet your allie."

When Serge nodded, showing he had received an answer, Michael told him, "Press it."

"The eleventh floor," Serge said.

"Good. Tell me when you've arrived."

Serge nodded again, and Michael continued, "Now step out of the elevator and tell me what you see."

"A hallway, with several doors and windows looking out."

"What's outside the window?"

"There's a light coming through, and there are tree branches swaying in the wind."

"Are there any exit doors?"

"Yes."

"Do these lead outside?"

"Eventually."

Michael paused, deciding which way to guide Serge to meet his allie— outside and the unknown or through the more familiar hallway doors, which Serge had entered before in a past-life experience. To reinforce his hunch that Serge would stick to the tried and true and would prefer the safety of the familiar, Michael asked Serge one more question.

"Now, with the exit doors included, which is the proper door to contact your allie?"

"The three doors opposite the elevator," Serge said, confirming Michael's hunch. Serge would opt for the familiar.

"And what are these doors like?" Michael probed.

"There are three doors there; two plain white ones, and the third has the number 1100 in front. That's the door."

"Go up to it," Michael urged. "Then operate whatever is necessasry to open the door, and tell me what's on the other side when you open it."

Serge hesitated for a few moments before replying and then continued, "The room is all white. The curtains . . . the rugs . . . they're all white, too."

"Now look more closely. What else do you see? Describe the room in even greater detail." Michael probed to get more information and to make Serge's experience of the room more real and intense.

"It's plain and modern," Serge replied. "It's like an executive's office, with a table and desk, a chair, a two-person couch. Very square and blocky-looking, like a business."

Michael pressed further. "Any other doors or passages?"

"To the left of the desk, there's a white door. It's partially open."

Feeling this door was a symbol that the allie was close at hand, Michael pushed on with his questions.

"Good. Now step into that room and if there's an additional door there, go through it to get to your allie."

Michael and Serge fell silent now for a few minutes. The rest of us listened wordlessly.

Finally, Serge's thin soft voice came through, slowly, faintly: "Her name is Noora."

"Can you describe her?"

"She looks like an Arab woman. She's beautiful, almost in a bright transparent way, and she's wearing a veil across her face."

Michael continued his questions to help Serge discover more about his guide and find out how she could help when he needed support or advice.

"Have you met before?" Michael asked.

"Yes. She's a healing guide, here to help me with that."

"Can she be a teaching guide?"

"She has that ability, but that's not her role."

"Who does this then? Is there anyone else you turn to?"

"My nameless companion."

"Can Noora help guide you to an experience with this companion?"

"Noora's here, since I asked for contact with my guides, but my companion is in the next room. In my dreams, I have felt his presence, but I don't know his name."

"Do you feel comfortable meeting this being, though he has no name?"

"I feel fine," Serge replied. "It'll be like seeing an old friend."

Still, Michael wanted to ease into the contact to be sure Serge felt safe and comfortable. Then, too, he felt Serge should proceed cautiously, since the ODFers found their allies had varied personalities. While some were fairly predictable kindly guides, others were somewhat unpredictable, sometimes playful, mischievous beings.

With this concern in mind, Michael continued, "Okay. Now, I'd like to find a way for you to view this being clearly, but it's not advisable to get close yet. Is there any way you can see this person in a veil or in an enclosed space with some protection? Or perhaps your guide can help."

"There's a curtain in the room he could stand behind," Serge said.

"Good. Then I'd like you to see this being behind the curtain. You'll feel more comfortable conversing that way."

"I could go in the other room, and he'll stand behind the curtain," Serge replied.

"Fine," said Michael. "Tell me when everything is in position."

When Serge nodded to indicate he was ready, Michael went on.

"Is there anything you want to say to or ask this being?"

"I want to link up with him and make contact."

"Ask him what would happen if you do that."

Serge was silent for perhaps a minute and then replied with his allie's answer, "I have to be aware of the load on my circuits, since he's a powerful being. So with my lack of experience in bonding with him, I can only contact him for a short time to avoid overloading my circuits."

"What does Noora say about this? What's her role?"

"She'll watch out for me, since her role is in healing. She'll lead me away from the conversation if it gets too intense. She'll also listen and remain aware of my body condition."

"Fine," said Michael.

He felt the dialogue had set the ground rules for Serge's first meeting with his allie, so now he was ready to guide Serge on to this meeting.

"Now can you communicate together, yet maintain communication with me here?" Michael asked.

"Yes. So we can communicate, he'll embrace me and remain bonded with me more directly than usual for a short time. Then, our communication will be more direct, since he will be part of me."

"Okay," said Michael, "if you feel up to it, go ahead. And I'd appreciate it if one or both of you can tell me when your communication is complete."

Serge nodded. "Yes. I feel ready to both listen and respond. Noora told me that when my allie embraces me, I should relax and allow him to do this, so I can speak to him and allow him to respond through me."

"Good. Then go ahead."

Silently Serge concentrated on feeling his allie's presence for about a minute. Then, speaking again, he reported, "I feel his approach now behind the curtain. It feels warm, yet gentle."

"Ask him whatever you want," said Michael. "For example, ask him, 'What advice would you give Serge at this stage on his path?' "

Serge asked the question mentally, and when he replied after another pause, it was in a thin, faraway voice, for he was now speaking in the persona of his allie, "Serge sees the path clearly, and he feels a little hesitant out of a fear he may fail to progress. He fears this may happen because of his uncertainty about trusting others. And he feels he may listen to the past too much."

"Is he afraid of some loss?" Michael probed.

"Yes, he is."

"Of what?"

"Of painful lessons."

"So what should he do?"

"He should learn to cope with what he has."

Serge shifted around several times on the floor, as if he felt uncomfortable. Michael immediately noticed and sought to respond quickly, so Serge wouldn't become too aware of his external environment and thus wake up.

"Is Serge experiencing some problem now in his body?" Michael asked.

"Yes," said Serge still speaking as his allie. "His body is experiencing a rapid build-up of heat. The flow of energy needs to be released, and he can't continue this much longer."

"Then, I would suggest he vent this energy outward along his arms and calves to block off the heat."

Serge shifted around several more times, then settled back on the floor.

"That was helpful," Serge as the allie continued. "So he can go on a little longer. However, his circuitry doesn't have an adequate capacity yet for lengthy conversations. Though he can continue a little longer now without harm."

Michael nodded. "Fine. Let me know when we need to stop."

Serge continued in a slow, spacy monotone. "He needs to have the experience of trust fulfilled. He is very sensitive to betrayal. One of his reasons for being on this path is because of his strong feelings of bonding with others, and these bonds must be maintained through unquestioning trust. Due to recent events, he feels great trust for you and others in the group. Still, it would be good to reinforce this feeling from time to time, so this close bond will continue and propel him along the path with you."

Michael replied with a few recommendations to help Serge feel more secure in his trust. "Yes, this reinforcement will happen. The group will be worthy of his trust. But he needs to armor plate himself now against betrayal in the outside world. He needs to better withstand emotional shocks."

Silently Serge considered how to do this for a few moments. Then, softly, still speaking as his allie, he replied, "Yes, this is true. Serge should do this. The departure of loved ones in the past has been very difficult, and that has been his painful lesson of which I spoke of earlier. But he will work on getting tougher. He'll try to protect himself, so he doesn't experience these departures so severely in the future."

"Good," Michael said. "Then, you will help him."

"Yes."

"Now, my question is, while he knows you well, can you provide him any name?" Michael asked because he felt a name would help Serge feel a clearer sense of his allie's identity after the experience was over. Then, Serge could better feel connected with a spiritual being who could help him.

In reply, Serge's allie said, "He may use the voice sound that resonates with me as his own magical name. I gave it to him when he was working with the wind for his Third Degree, though he may not have been aware of it then. He may call me that and use it as his own name, since we are bonded. But it doesn't matter how he envisions me. Noora likes to maintain her physical appearance in front of others. But that's not important to me. I'm not in a physical form, so my appearance is not relevant. Yet, if Serge feels more connected with me by regarding me as a male, that's fine."

Michael had a few last questions, so the allie would leave Serge with some specific suggestions on what to do next on the path.

"Are there any specific endeavors which would be helpful for Serge to do now? How can he best move forward?"

The allie had several recommendations. "Seeing is difficult for him. His physical vision was diminished early in this lifetime when he was a child, and these limits contribute to his difficulty with psychic seeing. He has a fear of failure, and that's tied to a fear of seeing what might be there. Thus, it would profit for him to practice and gain success from seeing. He will be able to see well but not right now."

Serge moved restlessly on the floor, and Michael viewed this as a sign Serge had enough for now.

"I thank you for your long visit," Michael said to his allie.

"Yes," Serge, as his allie replied. "It has been a fruitful encounter. Serge has learned quickly to control some of his fears which accompanied our bonding, and he has learned to stay out of my way during this. I will now return to my usual connection with him, though he will subsequently be more aware of my presence and more able to communicate with me on a regular basis. But now I will break our intense bond."

As the allie left, Serge trembled slightly and lay back quietly on the floor.

"How are you doing?" Michael asked.

"Okay," Serge nodded, replying softly, but with his normal deep voice.

"Now, you want to come back into your body and engage your biological circuits. So start at your feet and switch it all on. When you're ready, slowly sit up."

As instructed, Serge gradually returned to normal consciousness and sat up. Then, Michael began the questions about Serge's experience.

"How did it feel?" he asked

"I had intense warm, tingly feelings," Serge described. "Also, I had the feeling of a very strong presence inside me."

"Yes, allies usually are very strong. What else?"

"I was aware of a lot of thoughts going on as he talked. I had a clear concept of him, too, but I can't express it in words. It was just a strong sense of him being there and speaking for me."

"It's often like that," Michael said. "And your feeling about your allie is important, though it's not in words. As you continue to work together and pay attention to your experiences, you'll find you can better translate each other. Your allie will have a better sense of what you need and want; and you'll be more aware of how you and your allie relate together. Yet you'll still be separate and apart."

Michael probed still deeper. "What else did you feel? What were you aware of when you spoke?"

"A sense of readiness in advance. Like I had a feeling before he spoke of what my allie would say. Or maybe it was a feeling of confirmation after we spoke. It's hard to define the experience in words, but it's the same feeling I've had when I'm going to do a dive. You wait there, you get ready, you respond. But you don't have words to describe the process. Yet you know what you're doing, and you can see yourself going through the process before you actually do it in your mind. I found communicating with my allie like that."

"Exactly so," said Michael. "A lot of times we have to act and don't have all the facts; we can't explain what we're doing, though we do it. We rely on feelings. However, if someone else says something that makes us aware of the process, we can relate to that. Suddenly, our awareness opens up and we know what we've been thinking and doing, and that opens up the door to sensing where an inner part of us is headed in the future.

"However," Michael warned, "you must temper this new awareness with caution. You can't know or attempt to know everything your allie knows just yet. That's because your allie is nameless. Therefore, he still wants to keep some distance from you, and you want that distance too. Thus, you have to be careful to avoid observing him directly and keep that protective veil. It's much like in the old shamanic tradition. The shamans warn against observing something you shouldn't and say the penalty if you do can be very severe. The knowledge can double back on you when you use it incorrectly, and sometimes you may even open the door on your own death."

Serge shook his head. "No, I looked away before my allie came around the curtain to embrace me."

"That's good. You must take each step into the unknown slowly. Go one step at a time."

"What about the contact process?" Teri asked. "What's the best place to meet your allie? For instance, why did you take Serge to one of the doors in the hallway? Why didn't you take him to meet his allie outside when he mentioned the window and door leading out?"

Michael replied, "When Serge first mentioned the window and trees, I thought it might be more interesting to send him out there. But I didn't because it would be more intense, since that's an outside environment rather than a building for a meeting. And one problem with meeting your allie in the wilderness is there's always the risk of tapping into madness. Inside, you have a constructed, more controlled world."

"I know, I felt that," Serge said. "I sense that the window was an opening into a whole different world, and I wasn't quite ready to deal with it. I felt it wasn't a normal forest out there. There was a strange light from the trees; it was too dark to be daylight; too dark to be starlight; it was like the light was coming from another source through the night."

"That's why you have to be careful in contacting the allie," Michael explained. "Especially at first, because otherwise things can get out of hand. You should do it in a safe, pleasant space, where you feel comfortable and sure of yourself. You don't want to start opening up doors into settings which you may not be able to handle. I sensed that when I took Serge to the window, and that's why I led him back.

"Also," Michael advised, "in working with these beings, be careful to have a sense of your purpose in advance. Then, you can direct your conversation to that goal, and your allie will be better able to help you with what you want. You'll have more control, too, so when possible, speed up your communication and get to the point more quickly."

"I don't think I did that," Serge said. "I didn't feel I had much control. Basically, I just let my allie in and afterwards let him out."

"You'll learn more control in time. Everybody does. This was only your first contact."

"I was also surprised my allie seemed so big when he was inside me. I felt him pushing outward, a definite heavy sensation."

"That's your image," Michael observed. "What you experience is based on what you construct about your allie, which is fine. The main thing is to use your feelings and sensations to help you get to a deeper level, so you can experience and communicate with your allie more fully. Along the way you may travel to strange places to get where you're going, and you may scoop up different kinds of energy to use as fuel to get there."

"I don't understand," Serge said.

"Well, you have different ways of going to meet your allie, and the way you get there can affect the nature of your communication, since you are bringing different energies to the event, depending on how you go. For example, if you fly in to meet your allie, that's a different experience than walking in. In flying, you tend to get there faster and feel less control. If you walk, you make your connection more gradually, more leisurely, and you're more in charge.

"Then, too, you can move in without your body, which is what usually happens, and in that case, you experience infinite speed. It's like you think your allie is present with you, and all of a sudden, he or she is right there. Still, you might prefer the symbolism of actually travelling to a meeting, especially if you fly in with wings. Or you may find that choosing a unique way of making contact makes you feel more involved, so you get more out of the meeting."

"What's the best time to have such a meeting?" asked Teri. "I mean, say I've got this inner helper or guide. When shoiuld I think about making the contact, and when should I simply do whatever it is I'm going to do myself? After all, I do like to be on my own when I can."

"Well, a good time to make contact is when you want some extra help with something or want some advice. For example, suppose you're out in the field on a dark, spooky night, want to do a healing, and thus need to gradually change the energy in a positive direction. This might be a time to call on your allie to help you meet the energy half-way by feeling where it is right now, so you can come in on the same level. Then you gradually project positive energy out of yourself to change the situation."

"Can't you do that on your own?" Teri asked.

"Sure. You can theoretically do anything by looking within yourself. But by calling on your allie when things seem tough, you've got extra help. It's like having a coach or another fighter in your corner. You've got someone to smooth the way for you or up your odds.

"For your allie acts like a leader taking a group into the field. When you go there, one of the leader's jobs is to help prepare the energy for the rest of the group, which can involve pushing negative things away, getting things to calm down, or making the energy feel smooth. In effect, the leader is creating an environment that works for others; he's producing another reality space where people can feel comfortable working. Well, your allie can do much the same thing for you. He or she can help you contact and work with the spiritual energy."

"But what about when you're not in the field? How can your allie help you with what happens everyday?" asked Serge.

"Much as in the field," said Michael, "by making you more aware, more insightful; helping you make the right choices. For example, we've talked about full moments. You should be especially alert then, for it's a time when a moment is compressed. Say you have a deja'vu experience when you encounter a spot which has had meaning for you in the past. You feel a certain emotional focus there; you have a feeling of presence and purpose, like you've happened into a point of destiny or a knot in time.

"Well, your allie can give you information about why you feel that way. Or he or she can help you recognize you are in such a spot. Then, once you recognize where you are, you can use this ripple in time to take some action to direct or modify the future. In other words, in a full moment you have come to an instant when you can shoot your intentions and experiences into a corridor or channel of time, and you'll find the results manifested a year or two later. And these results will occur, because you've taken a certain act."

"So how does your allie affect these moments?" Serge wondered. "Like I'm coming close to thinking about a career transition. Maybe a change from where I'm working to help people in another context. Could my allie help there?"

"Of course," said Michael. "Your allie can give you very important guidance, because these are very powerful moments. You have to be very careful in the choices and decisions you make. It's like knocking over dominoes. One push, and they all fall down. But you have the choice of what direction to push. If you consult with your allie, he or she can help you decide when and where and how to push.

"Then, too, you can create a full moment in time and space yourself, just by talking about it, and you can call on your allie to help you create this space. This is something you can do anywhere—in a coffee shop, while drinking beer. You merely need to focus to see that space opening up for yourself, and it will. In a sense, you're creating a conducive, receptive time space, where you can focus and direct your energy, so you can influence future time for yourself, for others, maybe for the environment around you. It depends on the intensity of your effort; on your level of understanding, focus and will.

"In short, we've all got tremendous powers we can develop, and your allie is one more tool, one more resource person to help you explore and expand your magical side, so you can increase your influence in both the spiritual and the everyday world."

CHAPTER TWENTY-ONE

Going for the Third Degree

The weekend after Serge met his allie was to be the culmination of our training—Teri and I would be going for the Third Degree. Michael met us at Teri's apartment in San Francisco, since Teri wanted to do a ritual with water for her Third and lived near the ocean. Her apartment reflected her explorations of other religious traditions for she had statues of ancient Egyptian gods and goddesses, African ceremonial masks, American Indian gods-eyes, and miscellaneous crystals and talismans displayed here and there in the living room and hall.

She was preparing a plate of fruits and vegetables associated with water, when Michael and I arrived. As she sliced vegetables and arranged them in neat little wedges, Michael tilted on a chair across from her and reviewed the requirements for the Third Degree.

"Your goal is to produce some phenomena. Typically, the way most people do this is by invoking an earth or air elemental and getting it to appear. But if you prefer to work with another element, that's fine.

"In any case, you might encounter some initial resistance, since the elemental might not want to respond to you willingly. But you want to persist and get it to approach anyway. For example, when Serge did his Third, an earth elemental appeared at the top of the hill and started moving down, but then it stopped and turned back. So Serge had to work on getting it to come back to him. And he did succeed in doing that, and he got it to stay there for a brief time, too, which is required for the Third Degree. You must not only be able to get an element to respond, but you must be able to hold it there or briefly direct it to do something to show you are in control of it."

"What did Serge do to keep the earth elemental from resisting?" I asked.

"I can't put it into words," Michael said. "For you have to operate intuitively as you send out energy to call up the being. You use your will and power to get it to respond."

"Are there any differences in the response to expect from the different elements?" Teri asked. "Like I've always felt attuned to water. That's why I chose this place near the ocean and moved to San Francisco in the first place. Water gives me a feeling of freedom. It's open and I don't feel closed in like I did living inland."

"Yes, very definitely, you can expect the different elements to respond differently, in the same way that you have your own affinities to different elements. With the stable elements, like earth and still water, you should be able to get a being to materialize and respond to your control by moving forward and backward. However, with the active elements, like the ocean, wind or a moving fire, the main thing is to get the elements to make some response—like increasing their activity or reducing it, in response to your command."

As Teri arranged the celery, watercress, and slices of watermelon in a wheel pattern on the plate, Michael suddenly turned very somber and reminded us, "Remember, if you pass the Third Degree, you should be prepared for a week or two of challenges that usually occur after people pass this grade. We're not exactly certain why these things happen, but there's usually a week or two after people pass the Third when they have to cope with some difficult experiences. For example, after Serge passed, he experienced some especially intense problems in his relationship with a close friend, and when I took the degree several years ago, I had a variety of things suddenly go wrong in my life.

"We think these experiences may happen as a kind of a test to prove that you really are ready to use your new power and are sincerely ready to make a commitment to this path. It's as if since you've passed the grade, the universe notices you and throws you something difficult to deal with to be sure you can handle it. Then, too, this challenge may occur because you're now more aware of your own power, so you are more aware of power issues generally.

"In any case, we've learned to expect that some sort of challenge may occur, and we know this is a time when some people drop out of the group, because they can't handle their new power. Thus, although a person passing the Third can now take the oath of membership in the ODF, we don't allow anyone to do this until they have worked with this degree for at least two weeks. That way, we know the person has mastered the challenge and is ready to make a commitment to our path."

Teri made a few final preparations for the ritual. She placed four statues along the walls of the living room to act as "watchers" or protectors during the ritual—an Egyptian goddess in the North to represent earth; a Hindu sculpture of two lovers in the South for fire; a statue of a strong cowboy in leather chaps in the East for air; and a wood carving of the Greek sea god, Poseidon, in the West to represent water. She also placed a bowl of water from the goldfish tank of her apartment building lobby in the center of the ritual area.

"Now I'm ready to start the ritual," she announced, and Michael and I sat down on one side of the bowl of water. Nearby was a small altar, covered with a white cloth. On it she had placed several candles, a handful of flowers, a brazier, and a few books of poetry. She brought in the tray of water fruits and vegetables and placed it on the altar. Then she sat down on the floor across from the bowl of water.

"Everything in the ritual is associated with water," she explained. "So it's designed to prepare the way for me to work with the water elements at the ocean later tonight."

Then, as Michael and I remained seated, Teri walked around us in a circle several times to cast the circle. After this, she stood in front of each watcher in turn, asking them to assist in the ritual, and next, circling around, she chanted the words she learned from a magical group she sometimes worked with, "This circle is cast in earth and water, this circle is cast in fire and air."

Then, picking up her book from the altar, she joined us around the fish bowl, leafed through her book of poems, and read several poems about water. These suggested the spirit of water was within all of us, so we could easily bend and flow with this spirit.

When Teri finished reciting, she snapped the book shut and picked up several metal bowls from the altar. Giving one to Michael and one to me, she suggested, "Tap on them, hear the different sounds they make." We did, singly at first, listening to the thin pinging sounds alone, and then we tapped together quickly, blending the gentle pings together into a medley of sound.

After this Michael suggested we try chanting to feel the sounds associated with different elements. We began humming the familiar "Om."

"It's an earth sign," Michael said, "so it has more of an earth vibration. It feels more solid, heavier." Then, we tried "An," a fire chant, with a more ringing sound and feel; and next Michael led us in chanting "Am," representing water. "Notice how it feels more fluid," Michael said.

Finally, Teri concluded the ritual by handing us each a cup and taking a large chalice of water from the altar. "Hold the cup," she asked, and after pouring some water into these cups, we raised them and drank together. Next she passed around a cup of wine, which we poured into our own cups and drank. Lastly, she passed around the vegetables and fruits associated with water. We ate for several minutes, and afterwards she walked around the circle in reverse order undoing it and releasing the gods and spirits she had invoked. Finally, she pronounced the traditional closing words, "Merry meet, merry part. Merry meet again. The circle is now broken," declaring that the ritual was now over.

As she sat down on the floor with us, Michael praised her for the ritual, saying, "That was certainly very creative. And I liked the way everything tied into water. That's a good way to set the tone for what's coming next."

Then, Michael told me it was time to do my working with fire and reviewed what I should persuade the fire to do. "Concentrate on getting it to move to the left or the right. Or make it move forward and backward and up and down. You also might work on making the fire follow you. You'll find that the fire is very hard to control and may often fight against you. So we won't expect you to do it 100 percent of the time. But if you can get it to respond to you, say 70 percent of the time, that'll do."

Michael removed the fishbowl and placed the brazier from the altar in the center of our group. A small metal cup with alcohol was inside, and Michael lit a match to ignite it. In moments, the flames burst up and flashed around the room.

"I thought I would be working with something small, like a candle flame," I told Michael. "This seems so large."

"Don't worry about the size," he reassured me. "It's better to work with a stronger concentration of elements. That way any effects you have on the element will be more apparent."

Michael also suggested I use a few words of Fermese, the ODF magical language, to help me control the fire elementals. They sounded like "Arafey, corey, cudahey." However, after I stumbled over the pronounciation several times, I gave up and said "I'd rather do the working without the words."

"Fine. Do what feels most comfortable for you," Michael said.

I meditated briefly to relax and get in the mood. Then, I picked up my staff, which was by my side pointed it at the flames, and extended my left hand which I would use to motion to them. I watched the fire for a minute or two, concentrating on sending my energy through my staff as Michael had taught us. Soon I sensed the flames' movement and where they might go next. So now I tried to follow the flow of the flames, and I moved my hand up, down, left, and right to follow where I sensed they would go. Then, after about a minute, I felt my hand was moving to some extent with the flames, and I began to concentrate on trying to direct the movement of the flames myself. I moved my hand with sweeping gestures towards my left and focused on the flames going there; I moved my hand to the right and did the same. Similarly, I concentrated on moving the flame upwards or downwards by moving my hand in that direction.

I wasn't sure whether, or how much I was actually moving the flame, but Michael seemed convinced I was, for from time to time, he made encouraging comments, "Good," "Nice work," "Keep on going."

However, at other times he felt the flame was acting contrary to my motions, and he admonished me when this happened. For instance, one time, he cautioned, "It's playing with you. It's doing the opposite of what you're trying to do. Don't let it. Get with it, control it." And another time he suggested, "Give it some more power. Focus. Concentrate more."

After several minutes of this he suggested, "Now try to get the flame to follow you around. Just walk around and concentrate on it following you."

I began by extending my staff and walking briskly around the circle. But Michael stopped me, "You're moving too quickly. Slow down. The fire can't follow you that fast."

Then, as I moved more slowly, Michael said, "Now change direction. Move back and forth. That way you get the flame to break its pattern. You show you're in control."

Again, I did as instructed, concentrating on the flame moving towards me, and from time to time, I noticed that the flame seemed to lean slightly in my direction. Or did I just perceive it that way, because I was moving around? But while I wasn't sure, Michael and Teri, sitting across from me and watching, intently, seemed convinced it moved with me.

"You're doing fine," Michael said. When I paused for a moment and let my staff drop, because I was feeling tired, Michael cut in with "Okay, that's fine. You've done enough. You need to work on perfecting your connection with fire and developing additional control. But the fire was obviously responding. And that's the test of the Third Degree."

Michael congratulated me and unpinned the double corporal bars on my shirt collar and put the single gold bar of the lieutenant in their place.

Then, Teri said she wanted to work with the flames, too. She stood up, walked around the circle, and spoke to the flames asking them to follow her. She changed her direction now several times, darting back and forth several times, almost as if she was teasing the flames by her sudden reverses.

After a few minutes, she stopped, and looked plaintively at Michael, "I don't feel like I have a helluva lot of control over the fire," she said.

Michael agreed. "You showed a little control, but it's something you need to work on." As he explained, "Some elements come easier for different people. You can start with anything, though fire and water are usually the most difficult elements. Since I did my first with the earth elementals, many people in my groups have gone for this on their Third. However, it's best to do your Third with the element you feel most akin to first, and then work with the others."

"That's why I chose water," Teri said. "I guess I never did feel that fiery. It's so active and contrary to me. Like a little kid that always tries to misbehave it you let it. But water's more calm, more placid, and I like that."

Since we were talking about water again, Michael suggested this was a good time to go to the ocean, so Teri could try for her Third. Soon, we were on our way in my station wagon. About two miles from the city, we found an isolated strip of beach, and parked at the side of the road near two battered cars. Then, we walked down a high embankment onto the beach.

The night was clear and crisp, with a full moon that lit up the waves. Teri ran out ahead of us towards the water, and she stood at the edge of the tide line, watching the water rush in and swirl around a few inches from her feet.

When we caught up to her, Michael had some suggestions on what she could do to increase her chances of doing the Third Degree successfully.

"You should concentrate on seeing beings near the horizon, rather than looking directly into the water. They're more likely to appear there, and you can see them better there, too. If you can manifest some beings, that's great. But even if nothing shows up, you still can pass. With active flowing water like the ocean, the test of the Third Degree is getting the water to react to your presence. So a response in the way it moves is sufficient. With still water, since it's not moving, you have to manifest something. So the requirement is to produce a being."

"What kind of response in movement are you looking for?" Teri asked.

"We want to see some indication that you have affected the movements of the water. For example, an unusual swell in the waves, the tide coming up much higher than usual or maybe a sudden stillness would all qualify."

Michael and I moved back about 30 feet to give Teri plenty of space to work, and she turned towards the water. At first, she tried to project her energy out to it, imagining a light beam of energy cascading outward from her. As she later explained, she wanted to begin by relying on her own resources.

Then, she walked a few feet forward, since the tide had receded slightly, and bent down to touch the water with her hand to "get a better feel for it," as she later put it. After a few minutes of feeling it, she stood up and projected her energy outward again.

We watched her work for several minutes. As she did, it seemed to get a little warmer, and Michael went over to tell her there had been some response.

When he returned he told me, "The rise in temperature shows she's putting out some energy."

"Why should it get warmer?" I asked, since Michael had previously told us to view drops in temperature as a sign some spiritual effects were occurring.

Michael explained, "Different people have different styles of working. With some people, like myself, it gets much colder around us when we work. But Teri has a warmer, lighter vibration; she's more on the light side magically, so she produces a warmer current."

Then, suddenly, as we spoke, the tide surged higher on the beach, and Teri jumped back and ran towards us to get away from it. "Notice, that's another response," Michael said.

Once the water retreated, Teri turned back to the ocean and continued to concentrate on projecting her energy. After a few minutes, she came over to us. "I'm concerned I haven't observed any beings," she said. "So I was wondering how I'm doing."

"You're doing fine, so continue," Michael told her. "The main thing is you've gotten some response, since the tide is coming in faster now in the few minutes you've been out there."

Teri walked back to the edge of the water and stood there quietly for several minutes. Soon both Michael and I observed a whitish blob of energy projecting out in front of her, which was larger and more intense than the fuzzy white aura I usually saw about people when they worked in the darkness. But later, Teri had an explanation for why we probably saw what we did. She had, she explained, decided to draw on more energy than she had herself by calling on the moon to send down its lunar energy. So perhaps what we saw was this projection.

After we watched for several more minutes, we noticed that the waves seemed to move even higher up on the beach than before.

"Also notice some movements of energy slightly to her right," Michael told me. He pointed towards a dark gray shadowy concentration on the horizon.

After perhaps ten more minutes, Teri returned to us, still feeling insecure. "I'm still not sure if I was actually doing anything," she said.

But Michael reassured her. "It's a good beginning. See that dark mass in the distance." He pointed to the horizon. "That's a response from a water elemental. Now see if you can get this energy to form into a being and come forward."

Teri went back to the water and tried again. This time, the waves quieted down and the tide receded. After a few minutes, she came back again, complaining that her energy was burned out and she couldn't do anymore.

But Michael was pleased with what she had done. "That's fine. You've done enough. Now I have a few questions to see if you passed. Were you aware of the presence of several beings on the horizon?"

"A little," Teri nodded slightly.

"How many did you see?"

"Well, what I saw was really vague, but I guess it would be less than five," she stated tentatively.

But Michael was satisfied. "Good. That's enough. The elements responded, and you have indicated you had at least some awareness of the energy forms out there. So you passed the test. Now your task is to work with the water more so you can better manifest the forms."

"What should I do to improve my ability with water?" Teri asked.

"You might try going down to the ocean to practice on your own, and it's better to do this at night, since if it's too bright, you can't see the beings very well, because of all the outside distractions."

Then, Michael gave Teri her Third Degree gold lieutenant bars to pin on her shirt.

Before we left, I tried invoking some elementals from the water, much like Teri had experimented with fire after my Third Degree. I walked to the water, held out my knife, made a pentagram of protection, and held out my staff. Then, as I imagined a beam of light projecting from it like a searchlight, I scanned the horizon and concentrated on projecting my energy outward. Here and there I saw concentrations of darkness, and I focused on trying to visualize a humanlike form. Occasionally, I saw some glimmers of shapes emerge, and I noticed that the waves seemed unusually still now, whereas they had churned about so much more when Teri was doing her Third.

However, when I returned to Teri and Michael, Michael felt this wasn't enough. "This is a form of elemental you need to work on more. I saw a few sparkles of energy, but that was all."

As we drove back, Michael talked about what we could expect after passing the Third Degree and where we could go in the ODF from here.

"Be prepared for whatever crisis or difficult situation might occur in the next week or so," he began. "Then, after two weeks, you can consider whether to take the oath to become a formal ODF member. Also, work on perfecting the Third. Work with the element you have controlled tonight some more until you have mastered it, and learn to work with the other three elements so you can go for the Fourth, which involves doing the same thing you have tonight with each of the other elements."

Michael described other ODF possibilities. We could now join him and other ODFers, like Gene and Paul, in experimenting with magical practices, such as shape shifting, geoteleportation, or communicating with several allies at once. Additionally, he mentioned the Courier program, which involves exploring things that haven't been done before.

"Like what?" Teri asked.

"Like investigating other worlds and realities," Michael said. "You could try going someplace no one has been, and afterwards let us know about it. For instance, maybe you could spend a few days by yourself on the desert exploring altered states of consciousness. The idea is to push against known limits, whatever you do.

"In short, you can go in many directions at this point. You've gotten the basics, and now the possibility of full membership and many other options for magical growth are open to you. In the ODF, we only insist on some basics and otherwise encourage you to develop your own magical style. These basics include using the power objects, developing your seeing, having a good intention when you work with the elements, and having a moral obligation and commitment to others in the group. We require these so people share some basic understandings of magical reality with other members.

"In turn, our degree system is important, because it shows where a person has gotten to magically. This way, regardless of the other areas you explore, there's a basis for knowing where you're at. And that can be especially important in a situation where someone has to take charge, such as on a field trip. Then, you know to follow the person with the most advanced degree. It's important for the leader to get some feedback from the group to be sure he's doing something the members can go along with. But then, the leader has to be strong and make the decisions.

"However, this organized structure only applies in certain situations when we do things as a group or you work on your degrees. Otherwise we want you to experiment and find your own magical style. The structure helps keep the group together through some basic understandings. But then, we encourage you, go your own way, form your own group, or become a teacher yourself using your own personal style. Serge is going to be doing that.

"I'm training him now to lead his own group and like other Third Degrees you're invited to do the same. But, of course, first you must decide if you want to continue along this path."

Did we? That was the big questoin now that the ODF basic training program was over. Now Michael encouraged us to decide what other realities we wanted to explore.

As he concluded: "Of course, I hope you each will decide to remain on the path. But there are no guarantees. Each person, each student, maps out his or her own path. The way can be hard at times; it may be a struggle. But if you keep at it, you'll continue to grow magically, and you'll discover new things about yourself and the other worlds that become open to you. You've passed the first series of tests; you've shown you are worthy of the magical path. So now it's up to you to decide what you want to do and where you want to go. You can go as far and as fast as you choose. That's the choice anyone has."

About the Author

Gini Graham Scott, Ph.D. is a nationally known writer, consultant, speaker, and seminar/workshop leader, specializing in business and work relationships, professional and personal development, and popular culture and lifestyles. She is the founder of *Changemakers* and *Creative Communications and Research*, and has published over 40 books on diverse subjects. Recent books include *Fantasy Worlds*, *The Creative Traveler*, *The Truth About Lying*, *Resolving Conflict*, *Mind Power: Picture Your Way to Success*, and *The Empowered Mind: How to Harness the Creative Force Within You*. Scott has received national media exposure for her books including appearances on *Good Morning America*, *Oprah*, *Montel Williams*, and *CNN*. Her Web site is www.ginigrahamscott.com.

978-0-595-43378-0
0-595-43378-2

2038488R00128

Printed in Great Britain
by Amazon.co.uk, Ltd.,
Marston Gate.